THE THREE TEMPTATIONS:
MEDIEVAL MAN
IN SEARCH OF THE WORLD

THE THREE TEMPTATIONS

MEDIEVAL MAN
IN SEARCH OF THE WORLD

BY DONALD R. HOWARD

PRINCETON, NEW JERSEY

PRINCETON UNIVERSITY PRESS

1966

Publication of this book has been aided
by the Whitney Darrow Publication Reserve Fund
of Princeton University Press.

The initials at the beginning of each chapter
are adaptations from *Feder und Stichel*
by Zapf and Rosenberger.

Printed in the United States of America by
Princeton University Press

FOR

ROBERT M. ESTRICH

ACKNOWLEDGMENTS

I should like to express my gratitude to Professors Morton W. Bloomfield and Francis Lee Utley, my former colleagues at The Ohio State University, for their advice and encouragement from the time when this book was only a subject for conversation. Both read and criticized chapters in various stages of completion, and then the manuscript in a more final form; their suggestions saved me from many blunders. Professors Robert F. Gleckner and Robert L. Peters, my colleagues at the University of California, also read the manuscript, and there is hardly a page which does not reflect their close attention to matters of logic, clarity, and style. Professor R. E. Kaske, another reader, brought to it the scholarship and critical intelligence which has characterized all his work. Many others have read individual chapters and have talked with me about particular problems; I am grateful to each for performing what must be the most delicate as well as valuable office of a friend —that of revealing one's faults so that the knowledge of them pleases. Of my teachers I want especially to thank Professors Van L. Johnson, Alfred L. Kellogg, and R. H. Bowers, who aroused my interest in various phases of medieval literature. In dedicating the volume to the best of my unofficial teachers I acknowledge more lessons, of more kinds, than I have yet been able to learn.

Some of the material, notably in Chapter Two, was gathered during a Fulbright Research Fellowship to Italy, where I studied medieval and Renaissance works treating "contempt of the world." This material will be the subject of a future book, but I should like now to express thanks for what use I have made of it here. I wish also to thank The Ohio State University and the University of California for financial assistance. I am indebted to the officials and staff of the Vatican Library, the British Museum, the New York Public Library, The Ohio State University Library, and the libraries of the University of California at Berkeley and Riverside, to Mr. Christian Zacher for his help in preparing the proofs, and to Mr. Carl Markgraf for his help in preparing the index. Finally I am grateful to the Mediaeval Academy of America, publisher of *Speculum*, and the University of Chicago Press, publisher of *Modern Philology*, for permitting me to borrow some paragraphs from articles of my own which appeared in these journals.

D.R.H.

Riverside, California
April 1965

CONTENTS

Contents

ABBREVIATIONS

AHR = *American Historical Review*
AJS = *American Journal of Sociology*
AM = *Annuale Mediaevale*
AR = *Antioch Review*
CE = *College English*
CSSH = *Comparative Studies in Society and History*
CUAPS = Catholic University of America Patristic Studies
CUSECL = Columbia University Studies in English and Comparative Literature
CUSHEPL = Columbia University Studies in History, Economics and Public Law
EC = *Essays in Criticism*
EETS = Early English Text Society
E&S = *Essays and Studies*
ELH = *Journal of English Literary History*
ES = *English Studies*
FranS = *Franciscan Studies*
HSCL = Harvard Studies in Comparative Literature
HSCP = *Harvard Studies in Classical Philology*
HSNPL = Harvard Studies and Notes in Philology and Literature
JAF = *Journal of American Folklore*
JEGP = *Journal of English and Germanic Philology*
KR = *Kenyon Review*
LMS = *London Mediaeval Studies*
MA = *Medium Aevum*
MHP = *Miscellanea Historiae Pontificiae*
MLQ = *Modern Language Quarterly*
MLN = *Modern Language Notes*

MLR = *Modern Language Review*
MP = *Modern Philology*
MS = *Mediaeval Studies*
N&Q = *Notes and Queries*
NDPMS = Notre Dame Publications in Mediaeval Studies
PBA = *Proceedings of the British Academy*
PG = Migne, *Patrologia graeca*
PL = Migne, *Patrologia latina*
PMLA = *Publications of the Modern Language Association*
PR = *Partisan Review*
RES = *Review of English Studies*
RP = *Review of Politics*
RR = *Romanic Review*
SAQ = *South Atlantic Quarterly*
SP = *Studies in Philology*
SR = *Studies in the Renaissance*
TRSC = *Transactions of the Royal Society of Canada*
WSLL = *University of Wisconsin Studies in Language and Literature*
YSE = Yale Studies in English

THE THREE TEMPTATIONS:

MEDIEVAL MAN

IN SEARCH OF THE WORLD

. . . now thou hast aveng'd
Supplanted *Adam*, and by vanquishing
Temptation, hast regain'd lost Paradise,
And frustrated the conquest fraudulent.
—*Paradise Regain'd*, IV, 606-609

INTRODUCTION

IN PROCLAIMING the historic significance of Christ's triumph at the end of *Paradise Regain'd*, Milton made the last great statement of a medieval idea that equated the three temptations of Adam and Eve with the three temptations of Christ, identifying them with the three "lusts" of 1 John 2:16, "the lust of the flesh, the lust of the eyes, and the pride of life." That idea explored, as the greatest events of human history, the Fall of Man and his Redemption by Christ. Milton himself, of course, chose those two events as the subjects of his two greatest poems.

"Vanquishing temptation," the means by which Milton says Christ regained Paradise, had been the central theme of Christian writers since St. Paul. Central to the great drama of Christian history in the Fall and the Redemption, it was central also to the moral and ethical system of the Augustinian Christianity that dominated the Middle Ages. When the Fathers wrote of the Three Temptations, they made use of a psychological theory to describe the occurrence of sin within the individual soul. Temptation began as a "suggestion" only, proceeding then to interest or delight the victim, but it became sin only when the sinner had gone beyond the dangerous stage of "delectation" and given to the object of his temptation a free and rational consent. And since the process had been experienced by Adam and withstood by Christ, the lives of men were seen in some sense to recapitulate the Fall and the Redemption, in rather the same way as, in modern biological or psychoanalytic theories, the development of the individual is said to recapitulate that of the race. The mental process through which Satan had lured Adam and Eve was something all Christians had to guard against. To follow God's commands, in humility, and thus to live in charity, enabled man to resist temptation; to follow one's own impulses, in pride, was to yield to temptation and live in cupidity and sin. Human life was a perpetual psychomachy in which men had to fight against the temptations of the world, the flesh, and the devil. Human history was therefore most compellingly understood as a constant repetition of this process in the lives of individual men, ending for some in virtue and ultimate salvation, for others in sin and ultimate damnation. On the social side as well, the formation of a Kingdom of Christ in this world was understood to end with its redemption in the world beyond—not as a mere conglomeration of saved souls but as a unified "body." Hence the central meaning of history, individual and social, was objectified and dramatized for medieval man in the story of the Fall and the Redemption.

The Fall and the Redemption were of course understood to be historic events; the Three Temptations was an idea *about* those events, an attempt to show not merely how the events of the Fall prefigured those of the Redemption, but how the nature of temptation itself, in its psychological aspect, lay at the heart of human experience. As an "idea" it was the property of intellectuals, and its *locus operandi* was sermons and the written page. The two events, as recorded in Scripture, remained the same; they entered into medieval thought, took part in the life of medieval culture, only as men responded to them and interpreted them. Of the several possible ways of getting at these medieval responses and attitudes—among them the study of popular literature, folklore, and sermons—I should like to suggest that the most useful source is the work of the literary artist. My reasons would be that his creative genius places the ideas of his age in their cultural context; that his critical sensitivity sees in them their moral import; and that his subtlety of linguistic expression succeeds in portraying them in their full complexity. This is to say that the historian of culture comes as close as he can to direct observation by studying style. By "style" I do not mean, of course, mere verbal elegancies, but the whole range of forms and qualities which characterize a work. I use the word in a general sense, as when one says "a style of life" or "a style of civilization"; such styles of thought and behavior, immanent in a culture, are reflected in a literary style.[1] The problem of literary criticism, as I conceive it, is to discover through historical exegesis the authentic responses to a work in relation, on the one hand, to styles in this sense and, on the other, to the

---

[1] On the meaning of "style," see Roy Harvey Pearce, *The Continuity of American Poetry* (Princeton, 1961), pp. 12-15. Pearce quotes Meyer Schapiro's definition: "By style is meant the constant form—and sometimes the constant elements, qualities, and expression —in the art of an individual or a group. The term is also applied to the whole activity of an individual or society, as in speaking of a 'life-style' or the 'style of a civilization.' . . . Style is, above all, a system of forms with a quality and a meaningful expression through which the personality of the artist and the broad outlook of a group are visible. It is also a vehicle of expression within the group, communicating and fixing certain values of religious, social, and moral life through the emotional suggestiveness of forms. It is, besides, a common ground against which innovations and the individuality of particular works may be measured." ("Style," *Anthropology Today*, ed. A. L. Kroeber [Chicago, 1953], p. 287.)

fundamental experience of humanity. "It is," R. P. Blackmur has said, "one of the possibilities of history, taken as an art, to remind us in images of permanent horror and permanent glory, that although we live because of the long view, because of some leap or at least some overlap of minds, the conditions of life are anterior and posterior to any long view whatsoever. . . . The conditions of life are immitigable; its significance always to be created, again."[2]

I shall deal in the first chapter with a theoretical problem of historical criticism—the relationship of theology and hermeneutics to medieval poetry. In the second chapter I shall attempt to trace in detail the idea which I call the Three Temptations; it is this complex of ideas which I believe defined "the world" for medieval men. The three chapters that follow will deal one by one with the three temptations as each is shown, in a particular poem, to conflict with a phase of medieval culture. In Chaucer's *Troilus* the problem is the conflict between courtly love and the lust of the flesh; in *Piers Plowman*, between medieval political ideals and the lust of the eyes; in *Sir Gawain and the Green Knight*, between the chivalric ethos and pride of life. In the style of these works I hope to discover some of the means by which the later Middle Ages attempted to resolve conflicts immanent in its thought and culture. It is my hope that in speaking of the style of these works I can say something of the style of medieval life itself. Hence I should like to regard the study in some measure as an experiment in critical method; the closing chapter will contain some reflections on that experiment.

Each of the three central chapters ends with a discussion of the "world" of the poem studied. By "world"

[2] *The Lion and the Honeycomb* (New York, 1955), p. 35.

Introduction

I mean the sense of setting, environment, atmosphere, and mood which a poem creates in a reader through description, imagery, tone, and the like. The world of a poem is the poet's representation of the world itself, his experience of the common sphere of activity and made objects which stands between man and nature. I shall, then, be using "world" in two senses. One is this technical sense which it has in literary criticism. The other is its medieval sense, as in phrases like "contempt of the world" or "love not the world," where it translates *mundus* or *saeculum*. I have as far as possible followed the practice of capitalizing "World" when I use it in its medieval sense. I do not mean this double usage for a bad pun: in the worlds of the three poems we do find a changing concept of "the World." The received idea of the World, as propagated for the most part by medieval monastic writers, came to be altered and finally opposed not through any a priori change in the ideology of the Middle Ages but through the thoughts and feelings of men as they experienced the world itself. Ideology and felt experience were inseparable; the ideology was shaped and altered by men's experience, while at the same time men's experience was shaped and colored by ideology. My thesis is that each of these three fourteenth-century poets is in search of some means to resolve the conflict between worldly interests and otherworldly strictures; that each finds in medieval institutions and ideas, including the idea of the World, a way of counterbalancing worldly and secular concerns with otherworldly and Christian ideals; that these contrarieties are themselves immanent in medieval life and thought; and that they are a phase of the cultural change in western European history which marks the break between "medieval" and "modern."

7

The three poems, though written within a period of less than twenty years, are very different from one another in genre, style, and content; yet they all explore the conflict between the ascetic spirit of medieval Christianity and the claims which the World makes upon men. They all deal therefore with the psychology of temptation and with the relative imperfection of worldly creatures. Naturally I do not propose that the three authors collaborated unwittingly on a three-part extravaganza illustrating the Three Temptations. I take it as a coincidence—a happy one, for my part—that the *Troilus* is concerned with fleshly love, *Piers Plowman* with problems about supplying and possessing temporal goods, and *Sir Gawain* with the matter of preserving one's life. I hasten to grant that the three poems are also "about" many other things as well. Each poem does, however, deal from a particular vantage point with the conflict between religious and secular thought, a fundamental *ideological* problem of the period which few of its literary works fail to touch upon. The Three Temptations was surely one of the clearest and most ubiquitous medieval *ideas* about the World; I believe, and will try to show, that each of the three poems is concerned with this ideological problem and influenced by this idea. In attempting to construct what would be called a normative study I have selected the three poems as a matter of convenience, for the sake of exploring what the "World" meant to medieval man; or, one might say with equal validity, I have selected this idea for the sake of exploring the three poems.

That these ideas are still current in western thought—that they are part of our heritage, transmitted from the past as a part of our education—does not mean that we grasp them with the same understanding or feeling, or even with the same frame of reference as a man of the fourteenth century would have done. To recognize precisely their uniqueness and pastness requires very special efforts of scholarship and concentration. It is the kind of effort with which, when we listen to Bach, we realize that we are not hearing him as he intended to be heard—we play him on different instruments, with different tonal colorings and a different kind of dynamics. And even if we make an effort to restore the instruments of his time and recapture its musical spirit, we shall never *listen* as his contemporaries did—we shall never quite be able to erase Brahms and Bartók from our minds, to forget the sound of a hundred-piece orchestra, to know what music was like in a world without the phonograph. The problem of the past has to be granted; and because of its variousness and subtlety the experience of a work of art, taken as a unique event, is especially difficult to recapture. We would, no doubt, learn more about Chaucer in one day than from all our researches if we could only talk with a member of his audience, watch the glint in his eye, see where his attention flagged, hear where he laughed. But even if we could do this, our informant could not always *tell* us exactly how he felt or *why* he laughed. And we would not understand much of his behavior—it would not have the meaning that a glance or grimace conveys among those who live at the same time in the same culture. Nor could we be sure that our informant was typical, for a literary work does not mean the same thing to all members of its audience: imagine critics of the future seeking out the true contemporary response to *Waiting for Godot*!

Yet it is the very subtlety and complexity of a work of art that gives it its special value for the study of the past. Even with those works in which we find an unchanging human value, we shall finally understand a wider truth, have a broader knowledge of life and the world, if we can establish, in spite of the difficulties, the authentic responses to a work in its total relationship to its cultural milieu. Of course a work which has been read continually for six centuries has a milieu going far beyond its own time and place. In the end we shall understand the *Troilus* best, get closest to its "existential," or at least its human, meaning, if we know how it was read not only in its own age but in the sixteenth or eighteenth century, not only in England but in France and Italy—and if we know how it is variously read in our own time. Part of the value of knowing this, and it can hardly be overemphasized, is that it enables us to differentiate a work's initial meaning from later ones. This initial meaning is important not because it uncovers the author's "intention," but because the author's own milieu gave his work its first hearing and therefore gave it its first being. It conferred upon the author the occasion to touch men's thoughts and feelings and hence permitted his work to be not a design merely, or a text, but an *action*. To know what a poet wrote for his contemporaries is our first means of knowing what essential truth he sought for himself and for posterity.

CHAPTER ONE

MEDIEVAL LITERATURE
AND THE
HISTORY OF IDEAS

"Our judgments of value are dependent not only on our own experience, but also on the conception we are able to formulate of the experience of humanity."

—D. W. Robertson, Jr.,
"Historical Criticism."[1]

"The literary work, properly read, would be our means again to affirm that rule which our own culture, in its fear of difference, variation, and the like, trembles to affirm: value-charged then; *therefore* value-charged now."

—Roy Harvey Pearce,
"Historicism Once More."[2]

I. ALLEGORICAL INTERPRETATION

EDIEVAL POETRY, until recent years, was traditionally disposed into the categories "religious" or "secular," "secular" meaning any work which did not specifically treat a Christian subject. This secular literature was thought to be indebted very little, if at all, to the prevailing religious climate of the Middle Ages. Chaucer's *Troilus* was read as a romance, a story of courtly love, to which the author had appended a conventional Christian palinode; one student of the poem went so far as to say that Chaucer at the end of the work "suddenly denies and contradicts everything that has gone before," so that the ending illustrates the "complete separation of the pure artist from the religious man."[3] *Sir Gawain and the Green Knight* was normally read as a chivalric romance composed of Arthurian legend and folkloristic elements like the "green man" and the "beheading game," its religious implications little recognized except insofar as Christianity influenced the chivalric core.[4] Even *Piers Plowman*, an explicitly Christian poem, was often read for its detailed vignettes of contemporary social life.

In the last thirty years students of the period have tended more and more to see medieval poems, even "secular" ones like the *Troilus* and *Sir Gawain*, as being influenced in large measure by the predominantly Chris-

[1] *English Institute Essays, 1950*, ed. Alan S. Downer (New York, 1951), p. 31.

[2] *KR*, xx (1958), 584.

[3] Walter Clyde Curry, *Chaucer and the Mediaeval Sciences* (New York, 1926), pp. 294, 298.

[4] For the influence of religion on romance, see A. B. Taylor, *An Introduction to Medieval Romance* (London, 1930), pp. 166-189.

13

tian ideology of the Middle Ages. The epilogue of *Troilus and Criseyde* is now felt to be an integral part of the poem, prepared for by the Boethian and ironic elements in the body of the work. Sir Gawain's flaw is understood as a violation of a Christian ideal. Even the *Canterbury Tales* has come to be seen more and more as the product of a culture dominated by Christian ideas: the work as a whole has been viewed as an "allegory" on the pilgrimage of human life itself,[5] and its most secular tales—the Miller's Tale and the Merchant's Tale, for example—have been read as treatments of Christian morality and doctrine.[6] This increasingly religious view of late medieval literature can perhaps be explained by the change in our feeling about Christianity itself. Until quite recently Christianity was still a part of most people's habitual thoughts. For this reason the Christian element in medieval poetry was more easily taken for granted, or brushed aside. With the progressive dechristianization of the modern world, Christian references now strike us more and more as something exotic, like the myths of antiquity, for which we must make a special effort of comprehension (and about which we may nurture nostalgic feelings). This is an important development and will perhaps be an enlightening one, though it will mean taking a small gain for a large loss. As Christian ideals and conventions become stranger and quainter, we shall become more conscious

[5] Ralph Baldwin, *The Unity of the Canterbury Tales* (Copenhagen, 1955), pp. 24-29, 47-52.

[6] R. E. Kaske, "The *Canticum Canticorum* in the Miller's Tale," *SP*, LIX (1962), 479-500; D. W. Robertson, Jr., "The Doctrine of Charity in Medieval Literary Gardens: A Topical Approach through Symbolism and Allegory," *Speculum*, XXVI (1951), 43-45, and *A Preface to Chaucer: Studies in Medieval Perspectives* (Princeton, 1962), esp. pp. 382-386, 468-469.

of them; but in the same degree we shall lose any real and spontaneous feeling for them. They will come to be like artifacts excavated from a former civilization, and we shall need to be on our guard against overestimating the importance of what we unearth from the buried past or mistaking its meaning.

The problem applies especially to the tradition of biblical exegesis which has lately been the subject of much historical and literary study. That tradition provided medieval men with a vast body of Christian images and symbols: is it possible that much of what we take as "secular" is, through the use of these images and symbols, actually Christian?

Since the Bible was the revealed word of God, theological writings during the Middle Ages took the form of commentaries on Scripture. Medieval studies are unique in having such a body of stated belief; its consistency, for which there is perhaps no parallel in the entire history of the West—none at least of comparable volume—is owing to the centrality and authority of Scripture and to the power of the Church itself as a worldly agency for organizing and directing ideas. It is as if one could gather up de Tocqueville, Max Weber, Veblen, and the scores of other writers concerned with democracy and discover that, despite divergencies and controversies, all were commenting on a single book from a relatively consistent point of view. Even in the later Middle Ages, when a rational Aristotelian philosophy dominated theological study, the revealed word of God retained its initial place; the Protestant Reformation itself was urged as a proper interpretation of Holy Writ. And because many works of secular literature contain references to the ideas and iconography of this scriptural tradition, the body of exegetical writings, furnishing what one scholar has called "a sort of massive index to the traditional meanings and associations of most medieval Christian imagery,"[7] has become a kind of torch, or Aladdin's lamp, to critics of medieval literature.

There were various theories about interpreting Scripture. One was, of course, that the reader could take literally or "historically" what he read: that Christ died on the Cross, on a Friday, at Golgotha, was an historic fact recorded in the conventions of language, and elsewhere in Scripture one could find comments on its significance.[8] But what to do with passages which were obscure, or which, like the Song of Songs, seemed to have no relevancy to doctrine? In such cases other methods of interpretation, as for example number symbolism, could be used.[9] Etymology, that particularly imaginative activity of the medieval mind, could be applied to words, especially to proper names, in order to bring an otherwise unaccountable passage within the sphere of Christian speculation.[10] It is unlikely that such methods would have been developed had all of Scripture been amenable to Christian interpretation on the literal level. But once developed, they were used even on passages which had a manifest Christian significance.

The most common method of scriptural interpretation was the so-called allegorical or symbolic method.[11] It

[7] R. E. Kaske, "Patristic Exegesis: The Defense," *Critical Approaches to Medieval Literature*, English Institute, 1958-1959 (New York and London, 1960), p. 28.

[8] On the ambiguity of the term "literal" and the views taken toward the *sensus litteralis*, see Anthony Nemetz, "Literalness and the *Sensus Litteralis*," *Speculum*, XXXIV (1959), 76-89.

[9] See Vincent F. Hopper, *Medieval Number Symbolism*, CUSECL, 132 (New York, 1958); and Ernst Robert Curtius, *European Literature and the Latin Middle Ages*, trans. Willard R. Trask, Bollingen Series XXXVI (New York, 1953), pp. 510-514.

[10] See Curtius, pp. 495-500.

[11] For general treatments of allegorical interpretation, see C.

dealt neither with numbers nor with words, but with what I shall call "symbols"—i.e., with actual physical things which were thought to have special significance, as when a rose signified martyrdom. Since "things" were, after all, represented in the Bible by words, the theory was literary in the sense that it was applied to a written text. But it was not conceived of as literary criticism—it was a method of theology to be applied to the Bible. A symbol might signify a great many things. Its value depended chiefly on similarity in selected (and sometimes imagined) properties: the rose signified martyrdom because its color was that of blood. Other physical properties of the rose would allow it to signify other things as well. Thus a symbol could signify two opposing concepts, one good and one bad: a lion might stand either for Christ or Satan, depending upon context. Symbols, as D. W. Robertson, Jr., argues, were not ambivalent in the fashionable modern sense, and did not function through emotional appeal; they were means by which one could rationally perceive a higher truth, though of course they could in particular contexts create emotional effects. Moreover, a symbol might signify three different concepts on three "levels" beyond the literal one. The "allegorical" or doctrinal level made it possible to show how passages in the Old Testament prefigured the events described in the New Testament. The "tropological" level made it possible to derive

---

Spicq, *Esquisse d'une histoire de l'exégèse latine au moyen age*, Bibliothèque Thomiste, XXVI (Paris, 1944); Beryl Smalley, *The Study of the Bible in the Middle Ages* (Oxford, 1952); and Henri de Lubac, *Exégèse médiévale: Les quatre sens de l'écriture* (2 vols., Paris, 1959-1964). On the background of biblical study in the monastic milieu, see Jean Leclercq, *The Love of Learning and the Desire for God: A Study of Monastic Culture*, trans. Catharine Misrahi (New York, 1961), pp. 87-109.

moral principles and truths. The "anagogical" level applied to eschatology. Thus the author of a Middle English treatise on the Marriage at Cana[12] tells us that according to the allegorical sense, "Our Lord cam to þe bridale whan bi þe gret misterie of his incarnacioun he couplid to hym þe trewe Cristen puple þᵗ ben clepid Holi Chirch and his spouse; of þese bridalis wern þe apostles brouȝt forþ, and also alle þei þᵗ bi hem bileueden in Crist." According to the tropological sense, he goes on, "such bridalis shulden be doon vertuosli ech dai among Cristen puple, for þanne Crist wold turne þe werisch watir of oure inward felyng and oure worchyng in to sauery wyn of perceyuyng of his wisdom and of trewe lyuyng þer aftir." According to the anagogical sense, the wedding signifies the Resurrection, "whan oure kyng Ihesu shal make Cristen folk þᵗ ben his spouse to be fillid wᵗ endeless blisse." Not every exegete was so explicit in identifying the level on which he was interpreting a passage, for his purpose was sometimes to "connect his private theory with established truth,"[13] or, more often, to use the established truth of Scripture to teach the established doctrines of the Church.

Only recently has anyone suggested that this theory of biblical exegesis was adapted during the Middle Ages to the problem of interpreting "secular" literature, that is, to poems like *Beowulf* or *The Wanderer* or to prose works like the *De amore* of Andreas Capellanus. This is the opinion of Mr. Robertson. Because that opinion and those opinions which have accrued to it are so controversial, we shall have to examine not just his funda-

---

[12] R. H. Bowers, "A Middle English Treatise on Hermeneutics: Harley MS. 2276, 32ᵛ–35ᵛ," *PMLA*, LXV (1950), 590-600.

[13] E. K. Rand, "Mediaeval Gloom and Mediaeval Uniformity," *Speculum*, I (1926), 267.

mental notions but the bases on which he defends them.[14]

The Bible was thought to have a "cortex" of literal meaning which covered a "nucleus" of truth, and the allegorical method was a way of getting at this nucleus. In English the words "fruit" and "chaff" were used, or "kernel" and "shell." The image is that of removing a useless cover to get at a palatable core within. This nucleus might be on any of the higher levels of interpretation. Such truths were in Scripture because it was inspired by the Holy Ghost. Pagan literature was of course not inspired by the Holy Ghost; but it could be read with profit by Christians if through allegory, number symbolism, or techniques like etymology—or in some cases, as with Seneca's *De ira*, literally—they could find in it Christian truth, not intended by the author but understandable from the text.[15] In interpreting secular literature one could draw an analogy between poetic techniques and scriptural techniques,[16] and so find in poetry something *like* the nucleus of revealed truth which existed in Scripture. In a poem by a Christian author one might find biblical symbols, not inspired by the Holy Ghost, which the author had, as it were, borrowed from Scripture. These, and other objects not normally combined in nature, might be brought together in a Christian poem through a process called *conjunctura*, in order to form a *pictura*. An examination of such a

[14] See especially Robertson, *A Preface to Chaucer*. There is further material in Bernard F. Huppé and D. W. Robertson, Jr., *Fruyt and Chaf: Studies in Chaucer's Allegories* (Princeton, 1963), and *Piers Plowman and Scriptural Tradition* (Princeton, 1951). Robertson's earlier articles will be referred to in the footnotes which follow.

[15] On the interpretation of pagan literature, see Robertson, *A Preface to Chaucer*, pp. 337-365. On the study of pagan authors in monasteries, see Leclercq, pp. 139-184.

[16] Robertson refers to Scotus, *Super Ierusalem coelestem*, PL 122: 146, and Petrarch, *Familiari*, x, 4.

pictura would reveal a nucleus of Christian truth within the poem. That examination could be performed by a process analogous to hermeneutics: one began with the *littera* (grammar and the like) in order to establish the *sensus* or meaning, and from there one proceeded to establish the doctrinal significance or *sententia* of that meaning.[17]

That such a theory of literary criticism existed during the Middle Ages there is no doubt. That some writers bore it in mind as they wrote, and expected their poems to be interpreted in the light of it, there is a degree of evidence. Mr. Robertson, however, claims that all did so, and that therefore every "serious" medieval poem by a Christian author has a Christian *sententia*. This *sententia*, he tells us, was always the same: it was the doctrine of charity. Charity means loving God and one's neighbor; cupidity, its opposite, means loving only one's self. In charity one fears God; in cupidity one fears, through pride and self-love, an earthly misfortune.[18] Charity is, then, the whole moral expression of the Christian life; it is both individual and social. It is so broad a concept, amenable to so much variation, that it did not limit the medieval artist.[19] But however broad, it is specifically Christian, is indeed the very core of Christian doctrine; and it is the set theme of all "serious" medieval poetry. On this point Mr. Robertson is very clear. "Medieval Christian poetry," he tells us, "and by Christian poetry I mean all serious poetry written by Christian authors, even that usually called 'secular,' is always allegorical when the message of charity or some corollary of

[17] Robertson, "Historical Criticism," pp. 9-16; "Some Medieval Literary Terminology, with Special Reference to Chrétien de Troyes," *SP*, XLVIII (1951), 669-692; and *A Preface to Chaucer*, esp. pp. 286-317.

[18] "Historical Criticism," pp. 4-7.

[19] "Some Medieval Literary Terminology," p. 689.

it is not evident on the surface."[20] Elsewhere he remarks, "If it is clear on the surface but does not conduce to Charity on the level of *sensus*, then the poem is allegorical and it is necessary to determine the *sententia*. Whatever 'poetic license' a poet may have had in the Middle Ages, the fact of his being a poet did not give him any license for heresy. . . . In the category of 'serious' poetry, however, we should not include occasional poems written either for political purposes or for the expression of personal feeling."[21]

One may seem to see in this concept of "seriousness" a certain back alley of escape: confronted with a poem which does not yield up a lesson of charity, one could dismiss it for its lack of seriousness. But it deserves to be said that neither Robertson nor, so far as I know, any of his adherents has ever stolen away from the main avenue of their position. They have not shrunk from accepting the Merchant's Tale or the Nun's Priest's Tale as serious poems and finding in them the doctrine of charity.[22] While they would not deny, I think, the possibility here and there of a medieval poet without religious motives, the burden of their work has been to show that poems not normally considered religious are in fact allegorical and do evince the doctrine of charity.

Moreover, they regard the presence of the doctrine of charity as intentional on the part of the artist. True, the theory is a *critical* theory, dealing with the problem of reading and interpreting a poem. The medieval literary theorist, like some modern ones, might well have argued

[20] "Historical Criticism," pp. 14 f. He quotes John of Salisbury that nothing is worth reading unless it promotes charity.

[21] "Some Medieval Literary Terminology," p. 687.

[22] See Mortimer J. Donovan, "The *Moralite* of the Nun's Priest's Sermon," *JEGP*, LII (1953), 498-508; Charles Dahlberg, "Chaucer's Cock and Fox," *JEGP*, LIII (1954), 277-290; Robertson, "The Doctrine of Charity in Medieval Literary Gardens," pp. 43-46.

that the critic can see in a poem possibilities which were not consciously intentional with the poet; but such an argument seems never to have been advanced. Rather, Mr. Robertson asserts, the medieval Christian poet *knew* what he was doing. For one thing, "medieval literature was produced in a world dominated intellectually by the church,"[23] so that one could not very well write a poem without its reflecting and indeed teaching Christian doctrine. And the way to write a poem which was still a poem and not a tract was the allegorical method. Works like the *Ovide Moralisé*, Robertson says, "show the principles of medieval poetic theory in operation and are good indications of the kind of interpretation a medieval poet might expect his own work to be subjected to."[24]

*

One can hardly deny that Christianity, being important to medieval life, was important to medieval litera-

[23] "Historical Criticism," p. 4.

[24] *Ibid.*, p. 16. Cf.: "There is no evidence of pagan ideals or superstitions in the picture of Grendel's mere, no evidence of any seriously maintained system of 'courtly love' in Andreas' description of Amoenitas, no sentimental naturalism in the gardens of the *Roman de la Rose*, and no 'humanism' of the kind which exalts human flesh above God, except as an object of satire, in the garden of the Merchant's Tale. On the contrary, all of these works either condemn or satirize cupidity and hold forth Charity as an ideal either directly or by implication. This is exactly what we should expect of Christian authors. Moreover, the assumption that the authors had in mind a series of higher meanings seen in the light of wisdom tends to resolve apparent inconsistencies and contradictions in their works. . . . The persistence of the higher meanings involved in poetic allegory gives to the thousand years of the mediaeval tradition a surprising unity and continuity. And this continuity is enforced by the attitude that Christ's New Law is the ultimate expression of truth and the only source of any real beauty." ("The Doctrine of Charity in Medieval Literary Gardens," p. 46.)

ture; and it is true that much of that literature, even
when it is not "religious," contains references to the
exegetical tradition. When old January in the Merchant's Tale sings ludicrously "The turtles voys is herd,
my dowve sweete," we know that Chaucer is putting
into his mouth a passage of the Song of Songs which
was glossed as an allegory of the marriage between
Christ and His Church. It was one of the commonplaces
of exegesis and would, unlike more recondite references,
have been known by his audience.[25] Moreover, any
writer, if he was to draw a moral, would almost certainly have done so in the light of Christianity, because
it was to all intents the only system of thought available
to him. We cannot, then, read a medieval poem without
some historical grasp of the dominantly Christian conditions under which the medieval poet wrote. And
among these there was a particular method, patterned
on the theory of biblical exegesis, for finding the universal and general, the *sententia*, in the concrete and
specific.[26] But it was a method of reading, not of writing.
It describes indeed a perfectly natural process of reading,
in which one begins with the literal sense and draws
from it more general and universal applications. Some
writers no doubt had this method in mind as something
which their readers would apply to their works. Dante
did, assuming the letter to Can Grande is authentic.[27]
And Mr. Robertson has found in Chrétien terms like
conjointure, *sens*, and *matière* which suggest that Chré-

[25] See Charles Sears Baldwin, *Medieval Rhetoric and Poetic to
1400, Interpreted from Representative Works* (New York, 1928),
pp. 241-244; and Leclercq, pp. 106-109.

[26] With these remarks, cf. Morton W. Bloomfield, "Symbolism in
Medieval Literature," *MP*, LVI (1958), 73-81.

[27] See Charles S. Singleton, "Dante's Allegory," *Speculum*, XXV
(1950), 78-86.

tien was conscious of the theory.[28] But that theory was certainly applied in a very loose way. Even with Dante, in the teeth of whatever claims he may have made, scholars have never succeeded in delineating any consistent four-level allegory.[29] Indeed Mr. Robertson, in interpreting medieval literature, rarely attempts to distinguish among levels or interpret on more than one level. And why should he? the theory was simply not applied that rigorously. A Christian and moral *sententia* beyond the literal level was as much as any poet intended. Had it been more complicated than this, we would have a far greater body of medieval commentaries on medieval secular works than the few we actually have.

The poet's intention was therefore central to the medieval *littera-sensus-sententia* theory quite as much as it is to the "organic" theories of modern criticism. To be sure, in the interpretation of pagan authors like Vergil and Ovid, as in modern Freudian or mythographic criticism, one attempted to find basic truths which existed in the work but of which the author was unaware. The "higher meaning" was in the work because it was in the world of objective reality with which the work dealt, and was thus available to human reason. But with the Christian author the case was different. The *conjunctura* by which he created his *pictura* was made up of symbols consciously chosen: he needed to know the Bible, Christian doctrine, and the exegetical tradition, and he had

[28] "Some Medieval Literary Terminology," esp. pp. 669-671, 684-692.

[29] See Bloomfield, "Symbolism in Medieval Literature," p. 79. Bloomfield has also remarked, at the MLA of 1961, that the anagogical level would be impossible in Dante since the poem deals with eschatology at the literal level. Cf. Charles G. Osgood, *Boccaccio on Poetry*, Library of Liberal Arts ed. (2nd ed., New York, 1956), p. xviii.

to *intend* a Christian *sententia*. It was, in short, up to the poet whether he should choose to have a Christian *sententia* or not. No one ever claimed that any Christian who set pen to paper would express the doctrine of charity in some dark way against his will. On the contrary, moralists told Christian poets they were expected to write this way and were in the wrong if they did not. When John of Salisbury argues that writings which verge from the doctrine of charity deserve the wrath of God,[30] his assumption is that there *were* such writings. And the fact that poets like Boccaccio and Chaucer retracted their secular works hardly indicates that they expected them to be read as Christian allegories.

With those poems which do use the exegetical tradition the problem is at what point and in what way do *references* to the tradition make a poem Christian in its "teaching." And this raises a further problem: when is a detail a reference and when is it not? R. E. Kaske argues that the line about the Summoner, "Wel loved he garleek, oynons, and eek lekes" (*Canterbury Tales*, I, 634), is a patristic reference signifying the Summoner's cupidity.[31] The notion is wholly possible, just as is Curry's suggestion that this diet aggravated the alopecia of which he shows symptoms.[32] In its context the line, read literally, carries out in a clear and artistic way the description of the Summoner as physically repulsive and antisocial; does it not then also mean that he liked garlic, onions, and leeks? The allusion to exegetical lore, or the one to medical lore, is surely not the cornerstone of the whole passage; and the physical and moral diseases thus suggested do, after all, illustrate the loath-

---

[30] *Polycraticus*, VII, 11.

[31] R. E. Kaske, "The Summoner's Garleek, Oynons, and eek Lekes," *MLN*, LXXIV (1959), 481-484. The exegesis is based on Num. 11:5.

[32] See Curry, pp. 37-47.

someness of the Summoner which is apparent from the literal sense of the text. But even given a bit of tropology for garlic, onions, and leeks, where are we to go from there? Certainly the thing is not made any easier by the fact that the identification of symbols depended solely on tradition; if there were various meanings for almost anything animal, mineral, or (as with the Summoner) vegetable, how are we to choose among those meanings?[33] and how avoid coincidences? If every noun were not what it seems, reading medieval literature would become a mechanical problem of cryptology.

Obviously, to find the intention in all the particulars of the poem itself is the control which one must exercise in the use of such a theory. I should be surprised if Mr. Kaske did not agree with this, since he exercises that control, and favors doing so. The alternative is to assume that poets were didactic whether they seem so or not, or that medieval readers were indifferent to the literal sense of what they read. The centrality of the doctrine of charity in medieval literature is not a very cogent consideration unless one attempts to demonstrate in what ways it was central, in what manner it was treated by poets or accepted by readers. For, however universal his theme, the poet's intention is nonetheless historically determined. To suppose that every medieval poem taught charity is to say that medieval poetry and medieval literary theory were isolated from the swarming diversity of the world which produced them. Such an attitude has indeed been characteristic of intellectual historians, who tend to regard "ideas" as having a life of their own,

[33] Cf. Bloomfield, "Symbolism in Medieval Literature," p. 80. To cite an extreme example, see, on various meanings of garlic, Petrus Berchorius, *Reductorium morale* (ed. Venice, 1589), XII, 10 (pp. 507-508); on onions, XII, 40-41 (p. 518); on leeks, XII, 129 (p. 556).

in an unbroken continuity, quite apart from the culture which sustained them.[34] The attitude derives from the narrower philological estimate of the literature of the past—that it is a "body" of texts having a "tradition" of its own. This scholarly reductionism easily becomes conflated with the nostalgic view that medieval Europe was an "integrated" culture—as Carlyle conceived it, a kind of gigantic Benedictine monastery—in which a certain hard core of believers were able, in T. S. Eliot's phrase, "collectively to form the conscious mind and the conscience of the nation."[35] But we will never know the intentions of the medieval poet, never see their significance, unless we look at the *particular* poet, writing a particular poem at a particular moment in history, in a culture whose extraordinary "integrity" existed nonetheless in diverse, contradictory, particular elements.

This possibility of a pluralistic approach has been granted by the allegorists with one hand and taken away with the other. Some allegorists appear to speak of their method as being only one of many things which may contribute to a polysemous interpretation of a poem.[36] In this one seems to glimpse a pleasant nucleus of common sense. Mr. Robertson, in *A Preface to Chaucer*, has recently come up with an estimate of medieval culture which, at first blush, appears to justify this pluralism. Medieval man, he argues, thought in terms of hierarchies, whereas modern man thinks in terms of oppositions and polarities. This tendency in modern thought—

[34] Cf. Hannah Arendt, "History and Immortality," *PR* (Winter 1957), pp. 16-17.

[35] T. S. Eliot, *The Idea of a Christian Society* (London, 1939), p. 42.

[36] See, for example, D. W. Robertson, Jr., "Chaucerian Tragedy," *ELH*, XIX (1952), 11-13; and Hans Schnyder, *Sir Gawain and the Green Knight: An Essay in Interpretation*, Cooper Monographs, 6 (Bern, 1961), p. 74.

which he lays at Hegel's door—has been projected upon medieval culture by "modern scholarship," with the result that we mistakenly observe an "antithesis" of secular feeling creating a later "synthesis." Robertson finds it characteristic of medieval style that secular and even very earthy details are permitted in art with the understanding that they are an inferior part of a hierarchical order. Medieval man felt no "tensions" or conflicts when reading works like the Merchant's Tale or viewing works of religious art in which earthy sexual acts were displayed—all was understood "in terms of symmetrical patterns, characteristically arranged with reference to an abstract hierarchy."[37]

This emphasis on the hierarchical nature of medieval thought is, to me at least, exceedingly appealing. In it Robertson has put his finger on something central to the medieval mind, not merely an attitude or an idea but the very cast, the *feel* of medieval thinking. In much of what follows I shall, in speaking of the idea of perfection, be reiterating this same principle. That is why it seems to me so grave that Robertson draws from this true insight so many false implications. He feels, for one thing, that because medieval men thought in hierarchical patterns they could therefore live without intellectual or emotional conflicts. They did not think in *terms* of polarities; ergo, we must not find polarities or contrarieties in their thought and culture. As Kaske has remarked, all of the fundamental ideas of medieval thought, though they *are* hierarchies showing the better over the worse, are still great oppositions—as heaven and hell, salvation and damnation, good and evil.[38] Moreover, because he wishes to remove conflict and opposition from medieval

[37] *A Preface to Chaucer*, p. 6.
[38] See R. E. Kaske, "Chaucer and Medieval Allegory," *ELH*, xxx (1963), 187-188.

culture, Robertson takes a puzzling view of the secular element in medieval thought. On the one hand he believes that the hierarchical cast of medieval thought was not "puritanical," that the flesh and even the obscene were worked into the normal order of things, and that medieval writers did not hesitate to name and depict them.[39] On the other hand he believes that every mention of the flesh and every use of the obscene in medieval literature is really an allegory intended to discredit sensuality and preach charity. Whatever is normally cited as a secular and mundane tendency in medieval life itself Robertson dismisses as nonexistent. Chaucer had "never heard of" the conventions of courtly love because courtly love did not exist;[40] the love affair between Abelard and Heloise (it is hinted) never took place;[41] Petrarch's ascent of Mt. Ventoux was an allegory[42] and so was Laura.[43] (Even if these *were* all fictions made for allegorical reasons, which I do not grant, do they not still reveal a marked fascination with worldly things?) Finally, because a literature so starkly and unilaterally Christian seems to deprive poetry of much of its excitement, he creates for it an audience which did not respond to literature "dramatically" or vicariously in the ugly modern fashion, felt no "tensions" in literature, felt emotion only over the wrongness of vice and the rightness of virtue;[44] it read and heard works with a sweet reasonableness, not to say a vast knowledge of

[39] *A Preface to Chaucer*, pp. 20-23.

[40] *A Preface to Chaucer*, pp. 110, 391-503.

[41] *A Preface to Chaucer*, p. 11.

[42] *A Preface to Chaucer*, p. 241. Probably the ascent of Mt. Ventoux *was* a late invention; see Giuseppe Billanovich, *Petrarca letterato*, Vol. I (Rome, 1947), pp. 193-198.

[43] *Fruyt and Chaf*, p. 25.

[44] *A Preface to Chaucer*, pp. 31-33, 37-51.

iconography. This audience which he depicts is Chaucer's audience—John of Gaunt's circle and the court of Richard II, with all their quarrels and private interests, their mistresses, their intrigues. These turbulent nobles, we are told, understood Chaucer's poems as doctrinal allegories, enjoying with donnish merriment the frosty irony with which poets condemned sin.

Having removed conflict from medieval thought and emotion from medieval readers, Robertson is able to build up a picture of late medieval life as a world of "quiet hierarchies," a world "without dynamically inter- acting polarities." Courtly love is nothing but "reason- able love for a woman based on a love of virtue."[45] Any view other than this is written off as "romantic" and "sentimental"—a projection of nineteenth-century atti- tudes. Hence the modern age is to blame not just for misunderstanding the Middle Ages so badly but for changing and destroying the ideal world which Robert- son imagines the Middle Ages to have been. For in spite of his hostility to the romantic, the sentimental, and the emotive, Robertson himself presents a wholly romanti- cized view of the period as one of universal serenity in which men felt no emotional conflicts. In doing so, though in his nostalgic view of the past he expresses everywhere a contempt for the present, he has fallen into a mode of criticism which itself illustrates the most distressing tendency of modern man, that of dehuman- izing and mechanizing the works of the human mind and spirit. For the conditions of human life are prior to any system of beliefs. Without beliefs we do not cease to exist, it is only harder. Medieval writers wrote of their experience: the system of beliefs by which they inter- preted their existence was an important part of their

[45] *A Preface to Chaucer*, pp. 51, 457.

experience, but it can hardly be used to explain *every* facet of their behavior. The fact that what they wrote has ultimate meaning—*sententia*—and that this meaning is usually consistent with Christian doctrine can hardly surprise us. It is in the nature of literature and indeed of understanding to be symbolic, to find the general in the particular, the universal in the concrete. But in the criticism of literature one does not grasp only, with a kind of metaphysical leap, at the general and the universal; one attempts to experience the poet's wrangle with the particular and the concrete, to live with him the *vita activa* of his art.

2. THE CONCERNS OF CHRISTIAN LITERATURE

One may argue for a "symbolic" meaning in a literary work on the grounds that it is consistent with the author's intended development of his theme; or, on the grounds of some historic, mythic, or psychological theory, one may argue that a symbolic meaning was intended *un*consciously by an author, was an unconscious expression of the beliefs or myths of his own age, or of universal archetypal forms. To designate this latter kind of "intention," as it may be found in a literary work quite apart from the author's consciousness of it, I am going to use the word "concern." "Concern" is by no means a new word in literary criticism, and my specific and technical use of it is based on its usage in the common parlance of critical writing. It is something that *happens* in the relationship between the poet, his culture, and his work. Unlike "intention," it does not suggest an understood purpose; unlike "theme," it does not suggest a single, expressible idea; unlike "import," it does not suggest an effect on readers. The poet's consciousness of this con-

31

cern is a matter of degree: he may be oblivious to it or wholly conscious of it, or he may be unaware of the psychological and ideological forces working upon him which bring him toward awareness of it. But in the work itself the concern—complex, paradoxical, often unresolved—is central in the formal structure as it is central in the poet's creative imagination. The concern of the poem is the informing dialectical force; it is historically and culturally determined. Without it, "theme" is impossible. It is the area of struggle, of "tension" or "paradox," in which particular cultural elements converge within a formal structure and become a whole. The term, as I am using it, can be compared with the word "battle," which, though seemingly abstract, describes an historic action or event which has no reality apart from the struggle of its component elements, and whose significance is in its outcome, its final human import. As with "battle," the concern or concerns of a poem are concentric: as a war may contain a number of battles, a poem may have a number of concerns. There may be one central concern, as there may be one single battle, which trips off all the others. Yet we often speak of a "battle" even though it was in reality composed of a number of component battles. And in the same way the multiple, concentrically related concerns of a poem, conscious or unconscious, constitute its dominant concern. Whatever (for example) may be the "theme" of *Hamlet*, whatever it may be "about," its concerns are those of a youthful prince unhappily caught up in court affairs, a political murder revealed by a ghost, a state indefinably rotten, a situation which must be set right but for which the means to do so are not clearly at hand. And all of this seems centered in that concern which most troubled the Elizabethans, whether a just Providence could be discerned in men's just and unjust actions, whether revenge and sudden death showed God's hand, whether in the corrupted currents of this World a divine plan could be found.

The fallacy of "allegorism" is that it takes a literary theory as the essence of literature itself, without determining the way in which that theory came to be part of the concern of poems. It mistakes what moralists said poets ought to do for what poets themselves did. The difficulty of reading oneself back into a former age is something more than to uncover a dominant notion; it is rather to confront the area of struggle, to reconstruct the correspondences and oppositions among which an idea or institution existed and among which poets wrote.

Let me draw a modern parallel. The historian of the future may well be puzzled by the fact that in the twentieth century, when unprecedented hopes are put in science and technology, men constantly doubt that they have the capacity to improve their state. While the conquest of space is regarded as a goal of immense importance which can be reached only by human ingenuity, we discover that even in science fiction, the subject of which is almost by definition the "conquest" of space, there is a notable tendency to look to aliens from the outer world as the only ones who in the end can solve human problems.[46] In this anti-utopianism one sees faith in technology baffled by fear of it: though technology holds out the hope at last of attaining the "other" world, it has at the same time produced the means of destroying this one. What seems like the old religious dichotomy of worldliness and otherworldliness comes to take a new form, centered in technology, producing a new emotional tension between futility and hope. Such a tension, seen in a literary work as a contextual relationship, an "irony,"

[46] See Walter Hirsch, "The Image of the Scientist in Science Fiction: A Content Analysis," *AJS*, LXIII (1958), 506-512.

at base reflects anxieties and conflicts of the age itself.[47] So the historian of the future, reading a work like Tennessee Williams' *A Streetcar Named Desire*, might well be puzzled to find that the central character is made almost to speak of eschatology: "In this dark march toward whatever it is we're approaching. . . . Don't— Don't hang back with the brutes!" And at the climactic moment of the play, while an old woman outside murmurs like a figure in a Dance of Death *"Flores para los muertos . . . ,"* the tortured heroine cries out that desire is the opposite of death, and ends screaming "Fire! Fire! Fire!" It would be possible to say that the concern, at least in part, is for survival and progress in a world where destruction and failure everywhere threaten— certainly a central concern of the twentieth century. Yet, ironically, survival is seen to be easiest for those who hang back with the brutes; and at the end the agonized heroine is given over to a science (psychiatry) with no suggestion at all that it will help. But the historian of the future would never understand the play, let alone the age which produced it, if he explained its evocation of the horror and pity of life as being occasioned simply by the twentieth-century invention of Eros and the death instinct—or of nuclear fission. Nor would he understand it if he pointed to the emphasis of contemporary critics on paradox and irony and said that this critical concept "shows the principles of twentieth-century poetic theory in operation and is a good indication of the kind of interpretation a twentieth-century poet might expect his own work to be subjected to."

To uncover the essential concern of a literary work is to reconstruct the thought of its age and especially to relive, through a creative act of the historical imagination, the feelings which it would have evoked. The dif-

[47] See Pearce, "Historicism Once More," pp. 582-583.

ferences among artistic representations of human experience are not solely in the experience represented, but neither are they solely in the stylistic and historical terms with which experience is understood and expressed. Hence any analysis of a work's content of ideas will find a certain twilight zone where history shades into the general experience of humanity. In the excellent studies of Erwin Panofsky, for example, we find a carefully worked-out system of symbols, or icons, which gives to the art of the high Renaissance a dimension of historic meaning unavailable to us without the benefits of historic scholarship. There can be little question that the man of the Renaissance would have responded, say, to the elder Brueghel's "The Harvesters" in a manner very different from the way we do. The fruit trees would suggest the Garden of Eden, the weary reapers would suggest Time; the moment itself might recall the long winter of the World, the harsh punishment of worldly toil and trouble which was to follow that first fatal harvest in the primeval garden. And yet, confronted with "The Harvesters," we find that, even prior to our accounting for its iconographic motifs, the painting gives us the strongest sense of weariness, even in sight of the world's ripeness. We see laborers, like laborers of all times, worn by their toil, cheerless without being discontent, at rest in the fields—the harvest not yet reaped, the season of ripeness passing. Robert Frost creates the same effect in "After Apple-Picking"; so might such an actual scene anywhere, on any autumn afternoon.

Erich Fromm has used the terms "existential" and "historical dichotomies" to distinguish those incongruities and conflicts which rise out of the basic conditions of human life from those which may be changed over periods of time.[48] Men resolve, he says, the existential dichotomies by rationalization, the historical ones by ideologies. Now the presence in a literary work of these emotionally charged dichotomies, existential and historical, is what makes it difficult to speak of a "Christian" poem, except to mean a poem containing Christian ideas. The flat premise that the Middle Ages was dominated intellectually by the Church, and its literature by the doctrine of charity, underestimates the complexity of the period itself. While the historian of ideas can easily discover a dominant intellectual system and find it reverberating from all sides in an unbroken sequence well into the seventeenth century, it is still impossible to neglect the undeniable rise of secular thought and feeling beginning about the twelfth century. From the viewpoint of the history of ideas, it is possible to see the seeds of this secularization much earlier in medieval thought, at the heart of Christian doctrine in its earliest development.[49] If the Middle Ages had truly been a monolithic culture in which nothing diverged from orthodoxy, it would be hard to account for the ultimate secularization of European thought—for the distinct changes which we call a Renaissance and a Reformation and for the radically different nature of the modern world; those changes rose out of the resolution of earlier historical dichotomies.

With this in mind, we shall have to think twice about the notion that under the surface of their literal meaning all medieval poems conceal a nucleus of Christian truth. The notion was advocated by the Fathers in order to bring certain non-Christian works within the

[48] *Man for Himself: An Inquiry into the Psychology of Ethics* (New York, 1947), pp. 38-50.

[49] See, for example, Étienne Gilson, *The Spirit of Mediaeval Philosophy*, trans. A. H. C. Downes (New York, 1936), pp. 26-28.

sphere of Christian speculation. The emphasis was therefore upon Christian ideas discoverable in non-Christian works through symbolic interpretation (though literal reading was not ruled out); the purpose was, in St. Augustine's words, to use non-Christian works like those of pagan philosophers "for the just use of teaching the gospel." Augustine employed the figure of the Israelites fleeing the Egyptian idols but taking with them vases, ornaments of gold and silver, and clothing in order to put them to better use. So, he says, pagan writings contain "liberal disciplines more suited to the uses of truth, and some most useful precepts concerning morals."[50] This is not far from the argument of Renaissance humanists that truth, by whomever spoken, comes from God; St. Paul himself had allowed that "whatsoever things were written aforetime were written for our learning" (Rom. 15:4). The difference is one of degree. To St. Augustine secular learning is an aid to theology and preaching; to the Renaissance humanists it was good for its own sake just so long as one was a Christian. While the Renaissance humanists often argued, with Paul and Augustine, that secular writings aided the propagation of the faith, in actuality they felt secular letters worthwhile per se and often made the profession of Christianity a perfunctory requirement only.[51]

A *sententia* acceptable to Christians in the pagan or secular work, then, posits a value in such works and provides a reason for preserving, studying, and writing them. If such works had not appealed to the tastes of

[50] *On Christian Doctrine*, II, 40, trans. D. W. Robertson, Jr., Library of Liberal Arts ed. (New York, 1958), p. 75.

[51] For a good summary of the Renaissance controversy, see the introduction to *Iohannis Dominici Lucula noctis*, ed. Edmund Hunt, NDPMS, 4 (Notre Dame, Indiana, 1940), pp. vii-xx. See also Osgood, *Boccaccio on Poetry*, pp. xxix-xlix.

medieval men, it is unlikely that they would have been at such pains to accommodate them in the Christian scheme. Hence there is little reason to suppose that medieval "secular" poets like Chaucer, even when they were conscious of a Christian nucleus, would have been indifferent to the cortex of particular detail—had they been so, they could scarcely have treated it so well. Would Chaucer have taken so much trouble with Book III of the *Troilus* if the literal dimension of the story were not very important to him? Would *Sir Gawain and the Green Knight* be quite so rich in descriptive detail, would it have quite the wit or the comic spirit which it has, if its author were indifferent to secular life and secular ideals? It is not too much to say that the tension between cortex and nucleus is of the very essence of medieval literature—that one cannot have Christian grain without human chaff. For it was the uneasy fascination with cortex that created the rationale of nucleus. The notion rises directly out of conflict between the secular and the Christian, the actual and the ideal. It illustrates the diversity of medieval thought precisely as it attempts to resolve it.

The struggle of ideas which is everywhere bound up in history expresses itself in traditional forms. What the allegorists call cortex in early writings on courtly love, like the *De amore* of Andreas, came in the later writings of the courtly tradition—for example, the sonnet sequence—to be in effect the nucleus. The large amount of Christian imagery in the *De amore* recommends, we are told, the doctrine of charity. But Christian images continue to appear in the sonnets of Petrarch and Petrarchism when something other than charity is clearly the writer's concern. No one, I think, would argue that the entire sonnet tradition was one massive allegory on charity. Where, then, is the line of demarcation, unless we say that it runs horizontally throughout the tradition between the poles of an ideological conflict? It is the same with the drama: it began in liturgy, but it would never have become drama at all without the enticement of cortex. Later, when the drama of Shakespeare's time is secularized and worldly in its concerns, we can still see the receding nucleus, the medieval heritage. In its early development the drama took its very form from the tension between Church and market place, between rite and representation.[52]

At the heart of everything, Christianity—through its emphasis on the afterlife and the divine, through its negation of the secular—drew attention to the World and the individual. Its hierarchical view of perfection brought into the life of every Christian an inescapable tension: it demanded of him more than he could be expected to do.[53] It asked sainthood from men who, according to its own most fundamental doctrines, were corrupted since the Fall by ignorance, concupiscence, and death. The notion of adjusting the ideal to the capacity of the performer was as foreign to the Middle Ages as the strident idealism of medieval Christianity is to us. The result was that to take seriously the responsibilities of the Christian life was to submit oneself to an unending

[52] On the religious heritage of Elizabethan drama, see Willard Farnham, *The Medieval Heritage of Elizabethan Tragedy* (Berkeley, 1936); James V. Cunningham, *Woe or Wonder: The Emotional Effect of Shakespearean Tragedy* (Denver, 1951); Franklin M. Dickey, *Not Wisely but Too Well: Shakespeare's Love Tragedies* (San Marino, California, 1957); Bernard Spivack, *Shakespeare and the Allegory of Evil* (New York, 1958). See also D. R. Howard, "Hamlet and the Contempt of the World," *SAQ*, LVIII (Winter 1959), 167-175.

[53] On the medieval concept of perfection, see Morton W. Bloomfield, "Some Reflections on the Medieval Ideal of Perfection," *FranS*, XVII (1957), esp. 229-232.

struggle, a lifelong psychomachia between *cupiditas* and *caritas*, between pride and humility, between temptation and virtue, between this World and the next. It was this element of struggle in the Christian life that informed all of medieval thought. The literature of monasticism amply bears testimony to the struggle which existed in the souls of medieval writers between their desire to follow Christ's command, "Be ye therefore perfect" (Matt. 5:48), and their recognition of the fact of human weakness, the inherent difficulty of human perfection in this life. That difficulty, which is perhaps the central preoccupation of medieval Christianity, was formulated in the idea of temptation, the unavoidable suggestions and the state of delight which precede espousal of the World.

CHAPTER TWO

THE THREE
TEMPTATIONS

Love not the world, neither the things that are in the world. If any man love the world, the love of the Father is not in him. For all that is in the world, the lust of the flesh, and the lust of the eyes, and the pride of life, is not of the Father, but is of the world.

—1 John 2:15-16

I T IS everywhere apparent that medieval man, laboring under the punishments of original sin, was obligated to shun the forces which lured him toward damnation. From the moment he was born he was besieged by the lures of the World, the suggestions of his appetites, the snares of Satan—by "the World, the flesh, and the devil." These temptations, according to 1 John 2:16, were the lust of the flesh, the lust of the eyes, and pride of life. Scourged by them daily as he was, the medieval Christian found the same snares looming up at two overwhelmingly important moments in Christian history, the Fall and the Redemption. Man's adversary Satan had assaulted Adam in the garden and Christ in the wilderness with the same three temptations which plagued individual men throughout their lives.[1]

This list of three sins or "lusts" implies also a psychological process by which sin occurs. Gluttony, the lust of the flesh, had been the initial *suggestion* of the tempting serpent. Avarice, the lust of the eyes, had appealed to Eve and caused *delectation*. And vainglory, the pride of life, had brought in Adam a free and rational *consent*. In this double role as a list of sins and a process of sinning, the notion is like its more popular counterpart, the Seven Deadly Sins—a schema used in sermons and handbooks and as an aid to recollection in the confessional, which also described the progress of evil in the individual soul.[2] The three temptations were, in the

[1] As original sin was transmitted through the physical unity of all men with Adam, so all men experienced Adam's temptations. See Odon Lottin, *Psychologie et morale aux XIIe et XIIIe siècles* (6 vols. in 8, Louvain and Gembloux, 1942-1960), Vol. IV, pp. 271-280.

[2] See Morton W. Bloomfield, *The Seven Deadly Sins: An Introduction to the History of a Religious Concept, with Special Reference*

same way, a description of the psychological process of temptation, the process *anterior* to sin, which begins as a suggestion and proceeds through delectation to consent.

In describing this tradition, I shall be reviewing matters which others have already described.[3] Though I have organized details differently and used some new sources, I do not claim any important "originality"; I shall in the main draw together background information as a convenient alternative to sending the reader off for an afternoon in the library. In the last section of the chapter, however, I shall raise a point which has not been raised before and which is essential to my argument: that the medieval idea of the "World," traditionally the object of "contempt" and renunciation, was defined by the idea of the three temptations and understood in terms of it. What this means is that everything we read about the temptations of Adam and Christ, or about the process of suggestion, delectation, and consent, was a part of what men understood by the "World." The word always meant—as it did among the ancients and does among us—the terrestrial globe; but to medieval Christians it was, like everything, moralized. It meant a realm of human activity which lured the righteous and from which one needed to withdraw in "contempt."

I. LUST OF THE FLESH, LUST OF THE EYES, AND PRIDE OF LIFE

In the late sixth century, St. Gregory the Great described the Fall of man in one of his homilies:

---

to Medieval English Literature (East Lansing, Michigan, 1952), pp. 43, 49 (and n. 42), 70-74.

[3] Elizabeth Marie Pope, *Paradise Regained: The Tradition and the Poem* (Baltimore, 1947), pp. 51-55; and D. W. Robertson, Jr., *A Preface to Chaucer: Studies in Medieval Perspectives* (Princeton, 1962), pp. 72-75, 383-384.

The ancient enemy rose up against the first man, our common parent, with three temptations, gluttony, vainglory, and avarice. . . . He tempted him with gluttony when he showed him the forbidden food of the tree and persuaded him to eat. He tempted him then with vainglory when he said, "Ye shall be as gods." He tempted him by avarice when he said, "knowing good and evil." For avarice is a desire not only for money but for high position; it is rightly called avarice when sublimity is sought beyond measure. For if snatching at honor does not pertain to avarice, then did Paul say in vain of the only begotten Son that he "thought it not robbery to be equal with God" [Phil. 2:6]. And it was in this that the devil drew our first parent to pride, exciting him to avarice of high position.[4]

Elsewhere, dealing with the same passage of Scripture, Gregory calls the three categories cupidity, avarice, and pride;[5] he says nothing of seeking worldly knowledge, but subsequent authors sometimes followed St. Augustine in identifying it with avarice.

In a long passage of the *Confessions* inspired by 1 John 2:16, Augustine grouped things to be "held in contempt" under three headings. Lust of the flesh (x, 30-34) comprises a range of excesses—gluttony, greed, self-indulgence, drunkenness, sexual pleasure—and includes even the love of shapes, colors, art objects, clothes, or vessels. Lust of the eyes (35) includes a part of these, since it is

[4] Gregory, *XL Homiliarum in evangelia libri duo*, I, xvi (*PL* 76:1136). (Translations mine except where noted.)

[5] *Homiliarum in Ezechielem prophetam libri duo*, II, Hom. VII, 18-19 (*PL* 76:1024-1025). The passage in Gregory is commented on in Paterius, *Liber de expositione Veteris ac Novi Testamenti, de diversis libris S. Gregorii Magni libris concinnatus*, PL 79:1101; and in Alulfus, *De expositione Novi Testamenti*, PL 79:1392.

"gaining personal experience through the flesh"—the craving to know. "From this craving," Augustine explains, "comes the tendency to examine closely the hidden things of nature outside of us; although knowledge of them is of no value, men crave for nothing but to know them."[6] Pride of life (36-40) is envy and the pursuit of riches, vainglory, praise, and honor.

The origin of this notion is obscure. It was formulated, presumably, in the early Christian era, against the background of oriental mystery religions—Mithraism, say, or Gnosticism—and under the influence of Hellenistic philosophy. Writers of the period were fond of making conventionalized lists of vices and virtues[7] and were devoted to the threefold form.[8] Probably the idea itself was related to the notion of the tripartite soul: the chief philosophers of the ancient world had made the soul the source of good and evil desires, had divided the soul

[6] Trans. Vernon J. Bourke, *Fathers of the Church*, Vol. 21 (New York, 1953), pp. 311-312.

[7] The threefold list may have originated in ancient philosophy, for example in Stoicism, and the passage in 1 John 2:16 may itself be indebted to such a source. But the question falls outside the scope of the present study. On such lists of vices and virtues, see Bloomfield, pp. 37-41. Boethius (*Consolation*, III) lists the world's vanities as riches, high place, kingdom, glory and fame, noble birth, and lusts of the flesh, so that it would have been possible to cast such a list into a threefold form simply by making all except the first and last synonymous, as in some sense they are. Lactantius, *Institutes*, VII, 1 (*PL* 6:733-739), referring to the "world," speaks a warning to those who are inflamed with avarice, lusts, and ambition, this without reference to 1 John 2:16.

[8] That man was made in the image of a triune God, see St. Augustine, *De civ. Dei*, XI, 26, and *De Trinitate*, X, 11-12 (*PL* 42: 982-984). On the mystical significance of the number three, see Vincent F. Hopper, *Medieval Number Symbolism*, CUSECL, 132 (New York, 1938), pp. 70, 83 *passim*; and Petrus Bungus, *Numerorum mysteria* . . . (Bergomi, 1591), pp. 95-191. There was also a threefold division of the terrestrial world; see Edmundo O'Gorman, *The Invention of America* (Bloomington, 1961), esp. pp. 136-137.

into three parts, and had named three unworthy kinds
of life which corresponded to them.[9] Following their
example, certain early Christian writers, in East and
West, named the three parts of the soul as a basis for
classifying sins.[10] Moreover, gluttony, avarice, and vainglory were arranged in a hierarchical order beginning
with the flesh and concluding with the rational faculty, a
parallel to the ancient division of the soul.

The three sins were related elsewhere to the three
"lusts" of 1 John and to the temptations of Adam and

[9] In Plato the division of the soul into three parts (rational,
spirited, and desiring) underlies the concept of the four cardinal
virtues. Prudence is the virtue of the rational faculty, courage of
the spirited faculty, temperance of the desiring faculty; temperance
and justice are the harmony of all (*Republic*, IV, 441-443). In Book
VIII of the *Republic* (544-556) Plato traces the decline of a state
and of the souls in it: intemperance, avarice, cowardice, and im-
prudence are the sins mentioned, and the chief objects of sin are
wealth, honors, and the indulgence of appetites, but there is no stated
correspondence between the soul's properties and its virtues or vices.
See Irl Goldwin Whitchurch, *The Philosophical Bases of Asceticism
in the Platonic Writings and in Pre-Platonic Tradition* (New York,
1923), pp. 96-102. Aristotle mentioned the tripartite soul (*De anima*,
III, 9 [432b]), but only as one of a number of possible divisions
and without placing any emphasis upon it. On the other hand, in the
sum of Aristotle's thought, the soul has three principal functions,
which may be described as nutritive, sensitive, and rational. See W. D.
Ross, *Aristotle* (5th ed., rev., London, 1949), pp. 129-130. In the
Nicomachean Ethics (1, 5 [1095b12–1096a10]) Aristotle describes
three kinds of life which one may mistakenly think good—pleasure,
honor, and riches.

[10] See Gregory of Nyssa, *Epistola canonica ad S. Letoium Melitines
Episcopum*, PG 45:221-236; John of Damascus, *De virtute et vitio*,
PG 95:85-98; John Cassian, *Collatio*, XXIV (PL 49:1279-1328, esp.
1306-1307); Alcuin, *De animae ratione*, PL 101:639-650; the
anonymous *Liber de spiritu et anima*, PL 40:784; Isaac of Stella,
Epistola . . . de anima, PL 194:1875-1890. On the classification of
virtues among twelfth and thirteenth century theologians and their
relation to the soul, see Lottin, Vol. III, pp. 99-252.

Christ. In Genesis 3 the early Greek Fathers saw the beginning and pattern of all temptation. By eating the fruit, Adam and Eve were guilty of pride and disobedience—they desired what the devil suggested, that "in the day ye eat thereof, then your eyes shall be opened, and ye shall be as gods, knowing good and evil" (Gen. 3:5). And, because Eve saw "that it was pleasant to the eyes," they committed a sin of inordinate desire—what was later to be "avarice," the desire to *have* things. There was also a clear suggestion of fallen sexuality in their shame at their nakedness (Gen. 3:7).[11] Augustine, speaking of the promise to be like Gods, says Eve had "a certain proud presumption about herself" (*quaedam de se superba praesumptio, qua per illam tentationem fuerat convincenda et humilianda*). That "the eyes of them both were opened" and that they felt shame (Gen. 3:7) was the result of an "audacious curiosity"—they offended by their "proud love of their own power" and were punished by concupiscence.[12] In Ecclesiasticus

[11] St. John Chrysostom mentions all but the last of these in *Homiliae in Genesim*, PG 53:127-129. Gregory of Nyssa mentions the knowledge of good and evil, the pleasant appearance of the fruit, and the desire to taste it; he introduces the idea of avarice, but does not associate it directly with the fruit (*De hominis opificio*, PG 44:195-199). Anastasius Sinaita makes a protracted comparison between the temptation of Adam and Eve in the garden and the temptation of Christ in the wilderness; both were tempted by food, worldly objects, and glory, and both temptations were carried on in a series of questions and answers (*Anagogicarum contemplationum in hexaemeron ad Theophilum libri duodecim*, PG 89:1005-1024).

[12] *De genesi ad litteram*, XI (PL 34:445-447). The passage is adopted by Eucherius, *Commentarii in Genesim in tres libros distributi*, PL 50:911, who mentions the sin of curiosity (912). It was in this same work, *De Genesi ad litteram*, that Augustine had made the love of one's own power the opposite of the love of God and had based his concept of the two cities on these two loves, promising a future work, *De civ. Dei*, with this as its theme (PL 34:436-437).

10:15 he found authority for the idea that pride is the basis of sin, but 1 Timothy 6:10 named avarice its basis; Augustine reconciled the contradiction by making a most true observation—that men desire money because they think it will give them power. Hence, though it is not his central point, St. Augustine associates avarice, fleshly sin, and pride with man's Fall.

There were two orders into which the three sins could be cast—one following 1 John 2:16, the other Genesis 3.[13] In Genesis the fruit obviously suggested "gluttony"; the wish to be like gods was "vainglory"; and the knowledge of good and evil, plus the visual appeal of the luscious fruit, was "avarice," "curiosity," or "lust of the eyes." But the order of temptations is different in Genesis and 1 John. Then, too, because Adam's temptation in Eden prefigured Christ's in the wilderness, there was a further problem: the two gospel accounts (Matt. 4:1–11 and Luke 4:1–13) arranged Christ's temptations in different orders. Both gospels agree on the command to make bread out of stone; since Christ had been fasting this temptation was universally accepted as gluttony. In Matthew, however, the temptation of the tower (where Satan invites Christ to show his power by jumping from it) is second; in Luke it is last. (This temptation was the hardest to define: it could be curiosity for corporal abilities and thus avarice, or it could be vainglory or pride.) The third temptation in Matthew was that of the mount, where Satan showed Christ "all the kingdoms of the world and the glory of them." Luke, who puts this second, says he showed the kingdoms to Him "in a moment of time"—which Raban Maur took as evidence of their vanity.[14] The word "glory" in the Matthew ac-

[13] Cf. Pope, pp. 53 f.
[14] *Commentaria in Matthaeum, PL* 107:784.

count suggested vainglory, but some writers preferred to call it avarice.

One treatment makes the temptations of Christ conform to the order of Genesis. This disposition seems to spring from the passage in Gregory the Great quoted above; and Gregory's language is followed closely in the *Sententiae* of Peter Lombard, the standard theological text of the late Middle Ages.[15] Dealing with Genesis, Gregory connects gluttony with the temptation of the fruit, vainglory with the flattery of being like gods, and avarice with the promise of knowing good and evil. He associates the temptations of Christ, using the account in Matthew:

> But by the same means that he overcame the first man, he was himself overcome upon tempting the second man. Through gluttony he tempted Him when he said "Command that these stones be made bread." Through vainglory he tempted Him when he said "If thou be the Son of God, cast thyself down." Through avarice of high place he tempted Him when he showed Him all the kingdoms of the world, saying "All these things will I give thee, if thou wilt fall down and worship me." He was conquered by the second man through the same means by which he prided himself on having conquered the first man; so that being captured, he went out of our hearts by the same way that, gaining entrance, he once held us.[16]

[15] *Sententiae*, II, v (*PL* 192:1048-1049).

[16] Gregory, *PL* 76:1136; Haymo of Auxerre (possibly Haymo of Halberstadt) remarked that while Luke accorded with the literal facts, Matthew made the sins conform with Genesis and so preserved the correspondence between the temptations of Adam and Christ (*Homiliae de tempore*, XXVIII [*PL* 118:200]). Gregory's sentiment that avarice is not only for money but for high place suggests that he had read Augustine, *De Genesi ad litteram*, *PL* 34:436-437,

The Three Temptations

A second and more widespread treatment, however, conformed to 1 John 2:16. Apparently, since it placed the sins in a hierarchy with the worst and most inclusive, pride, at the end, this arrangement was better suited to the medieval temper. At any rate, Anselm of Laon, in the twelfth century, took the trouble to explain his preference for St. Luke's account. His reasons may now seem quaint: Luke's order (which agreed with 1 John) followed history, he said, because "nature required that the devil tempt first by concupiscence of the flesh, then by concupiscence of exterior things, and last by pride of life." Making the sins conform to Genesis was unneces-

---

on the point. Gregory is quoted in Raban Maur, *Commentariorum in Matthaeum libri octo*, PL 107:784-785, and *Commentaria in Genesim*, PL 107:488-489, and is followed by Peter Lombard (see n. 15). Angelom of Luxeuil, *Commentarius in Genesin*, PL 115:137, mentions only the temptations of Christ without giving the parallel in full. Hugo of St. Victor, *Adnotationes elucidatoriae in Pentateuchon*, PL 175:41, mentions pride, avarice, and gluttony. St. Peter Damian, *Testimonia Novi Testamenti*, PL 145:903-904, mentions the three, equating them with 1 John 2:16, referring the fruit itself to the flesh, *et pulchrum oculis aspectuque delectabile* to the eyes, and *eritis sicut dii scientes bonum et malum* to pride of life. Other writers used *scientes bonum et malum* for curiosity, *eritis sicut dii* for vainglory or pride. As it happened, either association gave the same order of sins in the Genesis passage. Cf. *Hugh of Saint Victor on the Sacraments of the Christian Faith* (*De sacramentis*), trans. Roy J. Deferrari (Cambridge, Mass., 1951), I, vii, 1-8 (pp. 121-124) and esp. sec. 6 (pp. 122-123). Haymo seems to follow Bede; see *In Matthaei evangelium expositio*, PL 92:20. For other treatments, see Rupert of Deutz, *In opus de gloria et honore Filii hominis super Matthaeum*, PL 168:1374-1375, who adds an association with 1 John 2:16; and pseudo-Jerome, *Expositio quatuor evangeliorum*, PL 30:559. St. Thomas Aquinas, *Summa theologica*, III, q. 41, art. 4, follows the Gregorian order, but quotes St. Augustine, *De consensu evangelistarum libri quatuor*, II, xvi (*PL* 34:1093-1094), that the order is unimportant. For a treatment in Middle English verse, see *A Stanzaic Life of Christ*, ed. Frances A. Foster, EETS, o.s. 166 (London, 1926), pp. 176 ff.

sary, and for this he gave an equally ingenious reason:
Adam would not have felt concupiscence before the Fall,
so there was no need of a "natural" order.[17] This second
tradition had appeared in rudimentary form as early as
St. Hilary of Poitiers.[18] One could, of course, use it with
Matthew as easily as with Luke by calling the temptation of the tower avarice and that of the mount vainglory. St. Augustine himself used the Matthew order
in this way, calling the temptations "fleshly desire,"
"curiosity," and "kingdoms," and equating them with
I John 2:16.[19] With inevitable variations other writers
followed suit,[20] but I shall omit this wearying tale and
summarize the main stream of the tradition in a table:

[17] Anselm of Laon, *Enarrationes in evangelium Matthaei, PL* 162:
1272-1273. Cf. *Glossa ordinaria, PL* 114:85, 254.

[18] In dealing with Matthew 4, St. Hilary speaks of Adam and
mentions temptations of food, glory in human power, and worldly
ambition. See *In evangelium Matthaei commentarius, PL* 9:930-931.
Cf. Ambrose, *Expositio evangelii secundum Lucam, PL* 15:1697-
1709.

[19] St. Augustine, *In epistolam Joannis ad Parthos tractatus decem,
PL* 35:1995-1997. Augustine does not mention the Genesis passage
here.

[20] The Venerable Bede makes the Genesis passage conform to
I John 2:16, then associates with that the temptations of Christ in
the Matthew order, calling them gluttony, curiosity, and vain boasting; see *Expositio in primam epistolam S. Joannis, PL* 93:92-93, and
cf. *In Lucae evangelium expositio, PL* 92:370. The *Glossa ordinaria,
PL* 114:254, quotes Bede, using the terms gluttony, avarice, and
pride and vainglory. Radulphus Ardens, *In epistolas et evangelia
dominicalia homiliae, PL* 155:1794, makes the Luke order accord
with I John 2:16. See also Hugo of St. Victor, *Miscellanea,* v, lxiii
(*PL* 177:790-792); Werner, Abt. of St. Blase, *Deflorationes SS.
Patrum, PL* 157:863-872; Isaac of Stella, *Sermones,* XXXII (*PL*
194:1793-1797); St. Martin of Leon, *Expositio epistolae I B. Joannis, PL* 209:262-263; Pope Innocent III, *Sermones de tempore,* XIII
(*PL* 217:371-376); *Twelfth Century Homilies in MS. Bodley 343,*
ed. A. O. Belfour, EETS, o.s. 137 (London, 1909), pp. 96-107.

	1 John 2:16	Genesis 3	Matthew 4	Luke 4
gluttony	lust of the flesh	fruit	stones	stones
avarice[21]	lust of the eyes	knowledge of good and evil	tower	mount tower
vainglory	pride of life	be like gods	mount	

There are, of course, some peripheral bits and scraps in this ragbag of associations. St. Ambrose compared the temptations of Moses in Egypt,[22] and in one source the three lusts of 1 John 2:16 are contrasted with faith, hope, and charity.[23] Some writers compare the Parable of the Supper (Luke 14:16-24), where the excuses of the invited guests were identified with the three sins (in Bede, the man who took a wife stood for gluttony or lust of the flesh, the one who bought ground stood for avarice or pride of life, and the one who bought oxen stood for "curiosity of corporal things").[24] Some writers made formulas of the remedies for the three sins. Bede makes fasting the remedy for gluttony, almsgiving for avarice, prayers for vainglory; Haymo names abstinence, largess, and humility.[25] Some put special emphasis on the temptation of gluttony: because concupiscence of the flesh begins with overeating—it did at least in Eden—the faithful should combat that sin with fasting.[26]

[21] On the use of the term "curiosity" (desiring to know forbidden things) see Rupert of Deutz, *De Trinitate et operibus ejus, in IV evangelistas, PL* 167:1547-1548; and Isaac of Stella, *Sermones,* xxxii (*PL* 194:1795).

[22] St. Ambrose, *Expositio evangelii secundum Lucam, PL* 15:1700-1701.

[23] Lottin, Vol. v, p. 250 (No. 314).

[24] Bede, *In Lucae evangelium expositio, PL* 92:370; see Pope, p. 53. Cf. Haymo, *Hom.* xxviii (*PL* 118:201); and Werner, *Deflorationes, PL* 157:866.

[25] Bede, *PL* 92:371; Haymo, *PL* 118:201. Cf. Werner, *PL* 157:866. John of Damascus had given poverty, continence, and humility; see *PG* 95:95. Cf. Hugo of St. Victor, *PL* 177:790-792.

[26] See Anselm of Laon: "Concupiscentia vero carnis solet incipere

What defines the three sins most clearly, however, is the specific, tangible things of this World which were said to be their objects. (Pope Innocent III names these objects as a triplicity separate from other sets of terms: he speaks of "pleasures, riches, and honors,"[27] equating the three terms with those of I John 2:16.) The lust of the flesh was clearest: it was gluttony or fleshly desire, and sometimes fornication, lechery, and pleasure. Its objects were food and drink, sexual pleasure, excessive sleep, and other fleshly indulgences. The lust of the eyes was avarice or curiosity but, not always distinguished from pride of life, was also called vainglory or boasting. Its objects were money, gold, silver, gems, and other worldly attractions such as honor, high position, glory, and rich garments—Augustine mentions spectacles, theaters, sacraments of the devil, magic arts, and misdeeds in general as the objects of curiosity, and Bede adds seeking out and carping on the vices of neighbors. The pride of life, not everywhere distinct from the concupiscence of the eyes, was called worldly ambition, pride, or vainglory, and occasionally boasting. The objects of this *superbia vitae* were kingdoms, power, worldly honor, and dignity, but it was also associated with riches, human praise, large households, pomp, false doctrines, and knowledge. These varying designations were fairly traditional; the only evident historical development is a tendency later to neglect curiosity and

---

a gula, quia satur venter luxuriam appetit, et caeteras voluptates. Et ideo debet fidelis prius gulam domare, quae est porta et initium caeterarum voluptatum; et quia contra gulam primitus insurgit a jejunio, quod est fraenum gulae, incipit." (*PL* 162:1270-1271) Cf. Rupert, *PL* 168:1375; and Radulphus, *PL* 155:1793-1797. For other references, see Pope, p. 55, n. 13.

[27] Pope Innocent III, *Sermones,* XIII (*PL* 217:371).

pride in knowledge, perhaps a reflection of the increased stature of learning after the twelfth century. Chaucer, in the Parson's Tale (x, 185 ff.), speaks of "three maneres of defautes, agayn three thynges that folk of this world han in this present lyf, that is to seyn, honours, delices, and richesses."[28]

No one, to my knowledge, has ever noticed the correspondence between this tradition and the three-part monastic rule—poverty, chastity, and obedience. And no one has suggested that the tradition may, as I believe, have influenced the formation of the rule. It is not hard to see that poverty is opposed to the desire for riches (lust of the eyes), chastity to the desire for pleasure (lust of the flesh), and obedience to the desire for power and importance (pride of life). In fact John of Damascus, in *De virtute et vitio*, collectively opposed humility (ταπεινοφροσύνη), continence (ἐγκράτεια), and poverty (ἀκτημοσύνη) to the pleasure of the flesh, vainglory, and the desire for riches,[29] observing a three-fold division of both. And St. Peter Damian, in his *Apologeticum de contemptu saeculi*,[30] a work about laxness in monastic discipline, begins by deploring the fact that monks revert to the things they had renounced in their vows; he gives many examples, arranged under the desire for possessions, pride and vainglory, and the desire for pleasure. The formation of monastic vows into the familiar triplicity occurred late, and its origin is obscure. In the

---

[28] *The Works of Geoffrey Chaucer*, ed. F. N. Robinson (2nd ed., Boston, 1957), p. 232. The passage does not seem to appear in the known sources; see Kate Oelzner Petersen, *The Sources of the Parson's Tale* (Radcliffe College Monographs, 12, Boston, 1901), p. 13 and n. 2. Cf. *Melibee*, VII, 1410.

[29] *PG* 95:96.

[30] Secs. 3-28 (*PL* 145:251-292).

West monastic practices themselves seem to have recommended the later formulation of the rule in three set terms, probably under the influence of St. Benedict.[31] In the East the monastic vows do not appear to be crystallized in set terminology even today. Perhaps among western writers the three temptations and the tripartite monastic rule were parallel developments, both rooted in some fundamental schema like the terms of 1 John 2:16. But it seems likelier that ubiquitous treatments of the three temptations influenced the shaping of the triplex monastic vows: it was the World which monks renounced, and the World was defined in the passage from 1 John.

2. SUGGESTION, DELECTATION, AND CONSENT

With this exegetical tradition the Fathers associated a psychological description of sin as it occurs within the soul. The earliest full delineation was probably in St. Augustine's *De sermone Domini in monte secundum Matthaeum*.[32] Here Augustine named three steps which go to make up sin—suggestion, delectation, and consent.

---

[31] On the early origin of the monastic rule, see Otto Zöckler, *Askese und Mönchtum* (Frankfort, 1897), pp. 151-165; on earlier rules, see pp. 174-192. See also Herbert B. Workman, *The Evolution of the Monastic Ideal* . . . (London, 1913), pp. 54-74; and Matthäus Rothenhäusler, "Die Anfänge der klösterlichen Profess," *Benediktinische Monatschrift zur Pflege religiösen und geistigen Lebens*, IV (1922), 21-28. For terms used in Greek, see St. Nilus, *De voluntaria paupertate*, PG 79:967-1060, and *Epistolarum liber I*, 307 (*PG* 79:193). See also W. K. Lowther Clarke, *St. Basil the Great: A Study in Monasticism* (Cambridge, England, 1913), pp. 107-108. The most comprehensive study of the objects of monastic vows is in the article by P. Séjourné, *Dictionnaire de théologie catholique* (Paris, 1950), XV, 3247-3266.

[32] I, xii (*PL* 34:1246).

Suggestion, he says, comes either from memory or from sense, and is followed by delectation and then consent. What he describes is the process by which sin occurs, by which a wrong choice is made. He likens it to the temptation in Genesis: the serpent made the suggestion, delectation occurred in Eve's carnal appetite, and consent occurred in Adam's reason.

What has this formula to do with the three sins or "lusts" of 1 John 2:16? As we have seen, the devil tempted both Adam and Christ with the three sins, arranged in a hierarchy which put pride, the deadliest, last. What took place in the souls of Adam and Eve, and in the souls of all men, was a suggestion from without (or from "the flesh"), delectation within, and at length a full consent of the rational faculty. Both concepts, then, were associated with the temptation of Adam. Hence both often appear together in a single context, notably in the *Sententiae* of Peter Lombard. But there is also a parallel between them in their hierarchical arrangement. Suggestion is the first hint of sin, delectation the wavering of will, and consent the ultimate rational determination; so the lust of the flesh involves the sins of the body, the lust of the eyes involves longings for money and power, and the pride of life is the deadliest and most fundamental evil, that of putting one's self in place of God.

Perhaps both originate in, or are at least shaped by, the notion of the tripartite soul. The tripartite soul is a hierarchy in which reason should govern will and will should govern passion. The suggestion-delectation-consent formula depicts sin as beginning with passion, which influences will and finally captivates reason. Thus the distinction between moral good and moral evil depends on whether sense or reason rules the soul. Such a view is made clear by Augustine in *De genesi ad litteram*.[33] The cause of fleshly lust, he tells us, is not only in the flesh but in the soul. His text is Galatians 5:17—"For the flesh lusteth against the Spirit, and the Spirit against the flesh." There is an interdependence and interaction between man's good and evil desires; it is the nature of the flesh to lust, as it is of the eye to see or of the ear to hear, and in each case the function is really that of the soul working by means of flesh, eye, or ear. The problem is whether the spirit or the flesh will gain the upper hand. The spirit desires to love God, the flesh to love its own power; and these two loves, in the development of Augustine's thought, become the moral basis of the two cities in *The City of God*.[34]

For the concept of suggestion-delectation-consent, Augustine may have owed a debt to St. Ambrose. In *De paradiso*, Ambrose, speaking of the temptation of Adam and Eve, explains that the serpent is the type of "corporal delectation," Eve of *sensus*, Adam of *mens*. Delectation conquers sense, he tells us, and sense conquers mind:

> For the serpent deceived the woman, and the woman led the man into prevarication. Corporal delectation takes the type of the serpent: the woman is a symbol of our sense, the man of mind. So delectation moves sense, and sense passes on to the mind whatever passion it receives. Therefore delectation is the first origin of sin, whence it is clear why the serpent was condemned first in God's judgment, the woman second, and man third. The order of damnation followed the order of error. For delectation captivates sense, and then sense captivates the mind.[35]

But where St. Ambrose made delectation influence sense,

[33] *PL* 34:416-417.   [34] *PL* 34:436-437.   [35] *PL* 14:329.

St. Augustine made it the mediating function of choice, not influencing sense but influenced by it. To make this clear he added the term "suggestion" prior to delectation, the resulting "consent" after it.[36] And, significantly, he related the whole to the temptation of Adam and Eve, the serpent representing suggestion, Eve delectation, Adam consent.[37] Gregory the Great, in the important passage on the three temptations, begins with an explanation of the suggestion-delectation-consent formula: "But we must know that temptation is brought about in three ways, by suggestion, delectation, and consent, because we are born of the sin of the flesh. . . . Christ was able to be tempted, therefore, through suggestion, but delectation of sin did not take hold upon His mind."[38] In the *Moralia* Gregory follows Augustine in relating suggestion to the serpent, delectation to Eve, and consent to Adam. The Venerable Bede, and Peter Lombard in the influential *Sententiae*, both make the same equation, and both say that consent springs from reason and results in sin.[39] In addition to the temptations

[36] Cf. *Commentarii in Genesim in tres libros distributi*, attributed to Eucherius, a younger contemporary of Augustine and Ambrose, *PL* 50:911-912: ". . . non potest ratio nostra seduci ad peccandum, nisi praecedente delectatione in carnalis infirmitatis affectu, qui magis debet obtemperare rationi, tamquam viro dominanti. . . . et quia omnino carnalia persuadent, quasi ad carnalium oculorum adapertionem conantur adducere, ut interiores oculos obscurent."

[37] *De sermone Domini in monte secundum Matthaeum*, I, xii (*PL* 34:1246).

[38] *XL Homiliarum in evangelia*, I, xvi (*PL* 76:1135).

[39] Gregory, *Moralia*, IV, 27 (*PL* 75:661); Bede, *In Pentateuchum commentarii*, *PL* 91:214; Peter Lombard, *Sententiae*, II, xxiv, 5-11 (*PL* 192:701-706). Gregory is quoted in Raban Maur, *Commentarius in Matthaeum*, I, iv (*PL* 107:781), and *Commentarius in Genesim*, I, xv (*PL* 107:491). The latter passage is found in Angelom of Luxeuil, *Commentarius in Genesin*, *PL* 115:140. Gregory's language is echoed in St. Paschasius Radbertus, *Expositio in*

or lusts of 1 John 2:16, then, we have these associations:

tripartite division of the soul:	nutritive (sense and experience)	irascible (desire, leading to choice)	rational
growth of sin in the soul:	suggestion	delectation	consent
temptation of Adam and Eve:	serpent's suggestion	Eve's delectation	Adam's consent

Presented in this manner, as a series of influences tumbling across the centuries, or as a table of correspondences, such a notion seems dreadfully abstract and intellectual. Taken in context, however, one sees that it must have been passed down from one writer to the next because it was pointed, clear, appealing—because the associations built up a vivid, natural picture and because that picture was meaningful and important. The idea, for all its abstractness, *was* dramatic: it was the familiar story of Adam and Eve, specific, historical, yet having reverberations which touched all the sons of Adam. Even the most unlettered layman must therefore have listened with curiosity when the very nature of the great event was explained—for all of this, he knew, was in him. This immediacy and clarity of the idea itself is reflected in the style of most treatments, and is illustrated very well, for speakers of English, by Chaucer's:

> And when that they knewe that they were naked, they sowed of fige leves a maner of breches to hiden hire membres. There may ye seen that deedly synne hath, first, suggestion of the feend, as sheweth heere by the

evangelium Matthaei, III, iv (PL 120:191), and in Werner, *Deflorationes*, PL 157:864.

naddre; and afterward, the delit of the flessh, as sheweth heere by Eve; and after that, the consentynge of
resoun, as sheweth heere by Adam. For trust wel,
though so were that the feend tempted Eve, that is to
seyn, the flessh, and the flessh hadde delit in the beau-
tee of the fruyt defended, yet certes, til that resoun,
that is to seyn, Adam, consented to the etynge of the
fruyt, yet stood he in th' estaat of innocence. Of thilke
Adam tooke we thilke synne original; for of hym
flesshly descended be we alle, and engendred of vile
and corrupt mateere. And whan the soule is put in
oure body, right anon is contract original synne; and
that that was erst but oonly peyne of concupiscence, is
afterward bothe peyne and synne. And therfore be we
alle born sones of wratthe and of dampnacioun per-
durable, if it nere baptesme that we receyven, which
bynymeth us the culpe. But for sothe, the peyne
dwelleth with us, as to temptacioun, which peyne
highte concupiscence. And this concupiscence, whan it
is wrongfully disposed or ordeyned in man, it maketh
hym coveite, by coveitise of flessh, flesshly synne, by
sighte of his eyen as to erthely thynges, and eek
coveitise of hynesse by pride of herte.[40]

The familiar phrase "the world, the flesh, and the
devil" is cousin to this idea: it names the sources of suggestion. The devil made the first suggestion to Adam
and Eve; Gregory, in the *Moralia*, develops this by
saying that "suggestion is made by the Adversary, delectation by the flesh, consent by the spirit."[41] In Hugo of

---

[40] *Parson's Tale*, X, 329-335 (Robinson ed., p. 237); and see
Petersen, p. 34. For other texts treating the suggestion-delectation-
consent formula, many of them indebted to Gregory the Great, see
Lottin, V, Nos. 85, 218, 312, 450, 452, 453, 523.

[41] *Moralia*, IV, 27 (*PL* 75:661). Cf. Lottin, V, No. 218.

St. Victor the World is associated with the lust for prosperity and the fear of adversity: "We conquer the devil when we resist his suggestions; we conquer the world when we neither lust after prosperity nor fear adversity; we conquer the flesh when we neither extinguish its desires in necessary things nor relax them toward things allowed."[42] A passage in the *Meditationes piissimae de cognitione humanae conditionis*, attributed to Bernard of Clairvaux, associated the World with sense, the flesh with delectation and consent, and the devil with the resulting sin.[43] Elsewhere "the World, the flesh, and the devil" were associated with the temptations of Christ as well as those of Adam, and with the three sins of "gluttony, cupidity, and vainglory."[44] We find the formula used without reference to other elements of the tradition in the *De miseria humane conditionis* of Pope Innocent III,[45] in *Piers Plowman*,[46] and in Chaucer.[47] It occurs frequently in Old French literature;[48] in the *moralitates* of the *Gesta Romanorum* it is often joined with "the lust of the flesh, the lust of the eyes, and the pride of life"; and it is encountered in the liturgy.[49]

[42] *PL* 177:585. [43] *PL* 184:503.

[44] See Radulphus Ardens, *PL* 155:1794.

[45] Ed. Michele Maccarrone (Lucani, 1955), I, xviiii (pp. 27 f.).

[46] A-text I, 37-38, and IX, 38. See also Carleton Brown, ed., *Religious Lyrics of the XVth Century* (Oxford, 1939), No. 145.

[47] *Melibee* (VII, 1420) and *Parson's Tale* (X, 349-356).

[48] See Paul Meyer, "Le Roman des Trois Ennemis de l'Homme," *Romania*, XVI (1887), esp. 2-5 for a number of references to Old French literature. See also *Le miroir de mariage* in *Oeuvres complètes de Eustache Deschamps*, Vol. IX, ed. Gaston Raynaud (Paris, 1894), lines 7337-7365. For appearances of the concept in legends of the Inquisition, see Henry Charles Lea, *A History of the Inquisition of the Middle Ages* (3 vols., New York, 1900-1901), Vol. I, pp. 245, 304.

[49] Similar formularies are found in Gallican rites of the late seventh or early eighth century, but clearly the baptismal service is

The Three Temptations

"The World, the flesh, and the devil" are easy tags, but behind them were subtle philosophical problems, lying in wait for the schools. Odon Lottin, in his imposing study of psychology and morality in late medieval thought, shows how in technical discussions these vague formulas were clarified. In the first place, suggestion was understood to come both from without and within, so that the devil and the World, as well as the sensual appetites of the flesh, should properly have been connected with suggestion alone.[50] Now suggestion was itself blameless unless somehow responded to; consent, on the other hand, was a rational intention and determination to sin. The ambiguous point at which temptation became sin was therefore centered in the notion of delectation: Was it sin to be "delighted" with a suggestion if one did not give to it a full and rational consent? The formula seems still less adequate when we compare St. Thomas Aquinas, whose elaborate analysis of the nature of an act includes *voluntas, intentio, consilium, iudicium, electio,* and *consensus,* plus *imperium, usus,* and *fruitio.*[51] Rational consent, given this analysis, be-

---

not the source of the expression. L. Duchesne, *Christian Worship: Its Origin and Evolution,* trans. M. L. McClure (4th ed., rev., London, 1912), p. 324 n. 4, quotes the *Missale gallicanum,* "Abrenuntias Satanae, pompis saeculi et voluptatibus ejus?" St. Cyprian mentions the flesh, the world, and the devil, though not precisely as a formula; he does not mention suggestion, delectation, and consent, but he does go on to speak of avarice, lust, and ambition. See *Thasci Caecili Cypriani de Mortalitate: A Commentary, with an Introduction and Translation,* ed. Mary Louise Hannan, CUAPS, 36 (Washington, 1933), pp. 22-24.

[50] "Suggestio est alia extrinseca, alia intrinseca. Extrinseca que fit diabolo suggerente, intrinseca que est naturalis. Suggestio est quando homo de re aliqua cogitat et non delectatur inde; et hec non est peccatum." Lottin, Vol. V, p. 138 (No. 218).

[51] See Lottin, Vol. I, pp. 393-424.

comes more than a pat decision of reason. St. Thomas distinguishes among the superior reason, the inferior reason, the practical reason, and conscience.[52] Free will, he says, is a faculty whose proper act is choice; it is in its formal concept identical with will, but is "impregnated" with reason.[53] In the same way consent, being an act of choice (or one following upon it), is informed by the practical reason. Yet of course the practical reason, thus involved with will, had lost its sway over sensitive appetite as a result of original sin, so that the movements of sense were undeliberate.[54] To what extent, then, were the first movements of sense blameless? And at precisely what point did the suggestions of sensitive appetite and the delectation of a weakened practical reason assume the voluntary and intentional character of sin?

The discussion centered on the degree of sin involved in each function. The sensual appetites, for example, could only be blamed for sins of negligence. As to reason, the guilt in consenting to the *thought* of the forbidden fruit was less than the guilt of determining to act on that thought: the sin of the inferior reason was therefore less serious than that of the superior reason, though both would require penitence.[55] Beyond this, many theologians agreed that the undeliberate movements of sense were not imputable, that sin existed only in consent. St. Thomas, however, argued that the involuntary movements of sense were imputable at least insofar as reason failed to exert over them the habitual vigilance and control which was the source of moral rectitude, allowing them sway in the area where reason could, and therefore must, be ruler.[56] Suggestion was everywhere, both in the

[52] Lottin, Vol. I, p. 514; Vol. II, pp. 349 *et passim*.
[53] Lottin, Vol. I, p. 216.
[54] See Lottin, Vol. I, pp. 220-221; II, p. 493.
[55] Lottin, Vol. II, pp. 493-496.   [56] Lottin, Vol. II, pp. 588-589.

64

World without and the appetites within, and man had
to be actively on guard. This was one more reason why
poets and moralists used the knight, with his armor and
weapons, to symbolize the Christian life. In *Piers Plowman* Christ himself is presented in the figure, already
traditional, of a knight jousting at a tourney. In *Troilus
and Criseyde*, though it is set in a pagan world before the
time of Christ, Troilus dies nobly as a knight and, from
the eighth sphere, sees as if with Christian wisdom the
vanity of his human errors. Even in *Sir Gawain and the
Green Knight*, for all its wit and with all its attention to
aristocratic ideals, the hero, "perfect" in a religious sense,
is tempted three times; and his one flaw, really a breach
of the chivalric ethos, is presented as a sin.

3. THE WORLD

Of itself the World was a thing indifferent: it was not
intrinsically evil, but it *was* a source of suggestion because
the lusts of the flesh and the lures of the devil led men
into undue worldly loves. Hence man's evil will comes
to be projected upon it. In 1 John 2:16 the "World"
(*mundus*) was actually equated with lust of the flesh,
lust of the eyes, and pride of life. In the exegetical tradition, these three lusts, associated with the temptations
of Adam and Christ, were what led men to accept the
suggestions of World, flesh, and devil. The monastic
rule appears to correspond to the three divisions; and
upon vowing chastity, poverty, and obedience, the monk
was said to have "died to the World."[57] Indeed, from
early times the World was named in the baptismal rite
among those things which all Christians must renounce.

The Latin words used in this spiritual context, *mundus*
and *saeculum*, continued to be used in their literal senses,

[57] The phrase is probably based on Col. 3:3. Cf. Rom. 6:2, 8, and
Gal. 2:19.

so that the contrast with the literal sense gave dimension to the figurative one. *Mundus* was at base a geographical term, referring to the earth and the planets, and later to the sublunary realm which existed in time, both terrestrial and celestial, as opposed to heaven. It included earth, sky, and sea, and the creatures in them. It was made from unformed matter, which was in turn made out of nothing, and was said to be in constant motion.[58] But in the early Christian era *mundus* came to be used, especially among the Fathers, in a pejorative sense, referring to those aspects of the terrestrial order which were corrupt, evil, and transitory, as in scriptural phrases like "the prince of this World."[59] To monastic writers *mundus* signified whatever was outside the cloister, but here too the literal sense receded into the background. The monk was said to renounce and be dead to the World because he had sequestered himself from it, that is, he had left family and society for an unworldly existence, comparable to paradise, in which he would imitate the life of the angels. Hence the monastery itself was not "of the World," but a kind of earthly paradise modeled on the kingdom of heaven.[60] As such it was a state or condition of life, distinct from the World not so

[58] See Isidore, *Sententiae*, I, vii (*PL* 83:549-552), and *Etymologiarum*, XIII, 1 (*PL* 82:471-472); for an expansion of the latter passage, see Raban Maur, *De universo*, IX, prol. (*PL* 111:257-261). See also Honorius Augustodunensis, *De imagine mundi*, PL 172:121, and O'Gorman, esp. pp. 61-69.

[59] See *Totius latinitatis lexicon* . . . , IV (Prati, 1868), 197, and DuCange, *Glossarium mediae et infimae latinitatis* (Niort, 1883-1887), V, 547, and VII, 264.

[60] On the elaborate parallel between the monastic life and the life of the angels, see Jean Leclercq, *La vie parfaite: Points de vue sur l'essence de l'état religieux* (Turnhout and Paris, 1948), pp. 19-56; on the parallel between the cloister and paradise, pp. 164-169. On the monastery as an earthly paradise, see Morton W. Bloomfield, *"Piers Plowman* and the Three Grades of Chastity," *Anglia*, LXXVI (1958), 229 n. 1.

much in its physical sequestration as in its higher spiritual quality.

Saeculum also came to be used in a figurative sense, though less often in a pejorative one. Here it was the dimension of time, rather than of place, which receded. Originally referring to the period of a man's life, a "generation," it came to refer even in classical Latin to "the age" or "the times," to a period of a hundred years, or to an indefinitely long period, and by metonymy to the men living during such a period. It corresponds closely to the Greek αἰών, which translated Hebrew *olam* in the Septuagint. The Fathers, influenced no doubt by the Hebrew and Greek, used *saeculum* to suggest that sphere of human activity which would pass away, that is, the life of the individual man and the collective state of earthly life from the Fall to the Last Judgment. Germanic *world* (*wera- plus *aldi-, "age of man") thus originally corresponded to *saeculum* rather than *mundus*. That period of earthly life, in contrast to eternity, was a duration in which individuals were constantly being tempted to love the transitory "things" of the World. Hence the *saeculum*, seen from this moral point of view, was a state of life to be renounced. As such, especially among monastic writers, it was synonymous with *mundus*.

But if the World, this realm of time and place, was not to be loved, was it then to be despised? To this Augustine had answered that worldly things, being the creations of an immutably good God, were good; but, being lesser than God in their goodness, they were "mutable." In effect he adopted the position of the Stoics, that the World is a thing indifferent, good or bad only insofar as it is used by men.[61] Hence neither

[61] See Joseph Ward Swain, *The Hellenic Origins of Christian*

matter nor the World was the source of evil, but only the evil will. In the *Confessions*, Augustine wrote that the things of the World—listing them under the three divisions of 1 John 2:16—were to be held in *contempt*. This phrase *contemptus mundi* is used by St. Jerome in the early fifth century to describe the attitude of indifference by which one kept the will from loving actively the things of the World.[62] Later it becomes the name of a vast body of writings, and I shall describe them briefly, as far at least as they touch on the idea of the World.[63]

"Contempt of the World" did not become a set theme for treatises until the twelfth century, when it appeared as a more violent attitude, one of scorn, with overtones of disillusionment. This new frame of mind seems to spring from the rift between church and state which began between 1050 and 1130. Until the eleventh century the *mundus* and the *ecclesia* were regarded as interdependent, often as identical: the Church was to embrace

---

Asceticism (New York, 1916), pp. 121-123; and Willard Farnham, *The Medieval Heritage of Elizabethan Tragedy* (Berkeley, 1936), pp. 1-22.

[62] St. Augustine, *De civ. Dei*, XI, 22; XII, 6; XIV, 4, 11. *Confessiones*, X, 30-40. Jerome, *Biblia Sacra iuxta latinam vulgatam versionem ad codicum fidem . . .* , XI (Rome, 1957), pp. 8-9.

[63] On the contempt of the World, see Donald R. Howard, *The Contempt of the World: A Study in the Ideology of Latin Christendom with Emphasis on Fourteenth-century English Literature* (Univ. of Florida diss., 1954). Here and elsewhere I shall be drawing on private notes and materials, collected since the completion of this dissertation. For the idea of contempt of the World in earlier Christian thought, see Robert Bultot, *Christianisme et Valeurs humaines; La Doctrine du mépris du monde*, IV: *Le XIe siècle*, 2: *Jean de Fécamp, Herman Contract, Roger de Caen, Anselme de Canterbury* (Paris and Louvain, 1964). Dr. Bultot's proposed study of this theme in the intellectual history of medieval Europe will, when completed, cover the period from St. Ambrose to Pope Innocent III.

the World, the two working for common aims. This equilibrium of church and state was upset and permanently altered by the Gregorian reforms of the eleventh century, which attempted to divest kingship of its traditional quasi-sacramental character and urge upon the *mundus* ascetic and eremitic ideals. In the failure of this movement lies the separation between *ecclesia* and *mundus* which was to characterize the coming centuries. The immediate result was a retreat of the ascetic reformers into new orders like the Cistercian, from which they angrily rejected the *mundus*.[64] In this climate of monastic reform, and against this separation between church and World, we begin to find treatises and poems *de contemptu mundi* which urge a "contempt" and rejection of the World in far more violent language than had been used before. And many such treatises survey the *mundus* under the categories of the triple temptation.

These writings begin with the reformers themselves. In the eleventh century St. Peter Damian, dealing with monastic corruption in his *Apologeticum de contemptu saeculi*, categorized sins according to the three points of the monastic rule.[65] Later in the same century, in the hexameter poem *Carmen de contemptu mundi*, attributed to St. Anselm of Canterbury, the poet tells us that the proud should be humble, the lecherous should be chaste, and those who seek property and honors should turn their thoughts to God; when he comes to castigate particular sins he marshals them under the lust of the eyes, the lust of the flesh, and the pride of life.[66] In the

[64] See Norman F. Cantor, "The Crisis of Western Monasticism, 1050-1130," *AHR*, LXVI (1960), 47-67. See also Gerhart B. Ladner, "Aspects of Mediaeval Thought on Church and State," *RP*, IX (1947), 403-422.

[65] *PL* 145:251-279.

[66] *PL* 158:689, 692-700. On the authorship of the *Carmen de*

early twelfth century, the three temptations and the suggestion-delectation-consent formula are mentioned in the conclusion of the *Meditationes piissimae de cognitione humanae conditionis* (often attributed to St. Bernard), whose theme is the necessity of rational choice, self-knowledge, and repentance.[67]

The association of the three "lusts" or sins with the phrase *contemptus mundi*, in works belonging to the genre called by that name,[68] was made in nearly all parts of Europe from the twelfth until the fifteenth century. I hope the reader will indulge my eagerness to provide evidence. For one thing, the text from 1 John 2:16 served as the organizational principle for the second book of the *"De contemptu mundi"* of Pope Innocent III, the great and influential classic of the genre.[69] Perhaps following Innocent's example, many unpublished fourteenth- and fifteenth-century works on the contempt of the World identify the triple division with the World and its snares. The *De fuga seculi* by Joannis de Genzenstein, archbishop of Prague (d. 1413), quotes 1 John 2:16 in the dedicatory epistle as a text for the

---

contemptu mundi, see PL 158:27-28, and B. Hauréau, *Des poèmes Latins attribués à Saint Bernard* (Paris, 1890), pp. 24-25, who suggests Roger of Bec.

[67] The concept is also mentioned in two of a group of three poems attributed to St. Bernard. See PL 184:1307-1318. On the authorship of these poems, see Hauréau, pp. i-v and 1-30; cf. Thomas Wright, ed., *The Latin Poems Commonly Attributed to Walter Mapes* (Camden Soc., London, 1841), pp. 147-170, 208-212; and Hyder E. Rollins, ed., *The Paradise of Dainty Devices 1576-1606* (Cambridge, Mass., 1927), pp. 5-7, 180-182. See also F. J. E. Raby, *A History of Christian-Latin Poetry from the Beginnings to the Close of the Middle Ages* (Oxford, 1927), pp. 288-290.

[68] That it was the name of a genre, see *Lotharii Cardinalis (Innocentii III) De miseria humane conditionis*, ed. Michele Maccarrone (Lucani, 1955), pp. xxxii-xxxv.

[69] *Ibid.*, II, i ff. (p. 39).

entire work.[70] The *Epistola de contemptu mundi* by Heinrich Hembuche von Hassia (d. 1397) deals in three consecutive chapters (5, 6, and 7) with the "three vices of the world"—*voluptas carnalis, superbia mundi,* and *avaritia mundi.*[71] Chapter 4 of the *Speculum saecularium sive mundi hujus amatorum* by Jacobus de Gruytroede, in various manuscripts called *"De contemptu mundi"* and *"De mundo fugiendo et odiendo,"*[72] and the *Tractatus de contemptu huius mundi (*"*Epistola de fuga mundi"*) of Johannis de Scoonhovia (d. 1431)[73] both begin by quoting 1 John 2:16, as do a number of other treatises

[70] Vatican Library, Vat. Lat. 1122, fol. 267ʳ–277ᵛ (s. xiv), *Inc*: Sepe mecum vir nobilis compater. . . . Excerpts ed. K. Höfler, *Geschichtsschreiber der hussitischen Bewegung in Böhmen,* Vol. II (Vienna, 1865), 12-14; Book II ed. I. Sedlák, *M. Ian Hus* (Prague, 1915), pp. 49-67.

[71] See mss Munich: Staatsbibliotek, Clm. 4696, fol. 136ʳ–142ʳ (s. xv) and 3586, fol. 148ᵛ–155ʳ (s. xv), *Inc*: Post mundana celestia, post Marte sollicitudinem Marie requiem. For other mss, see Rainer Rudolf, *Ars Moriendi: Von der Kunst des heilsamen Lebens und Sterbens* (Köln-Graz, 1957), p. 33 n. 46; and R. W. E. Roth, *Zur Bibliographie des Henricus Hembuche de Hassia,* Centralblatt für Bibliothekswesen, II (Leipzig, 1888).

[72] The work is Book IV of *Specula omnis status humanae vitae,* printed in *Doctoris ecstatici D. Dionysii Cartusiani opera omnia . . . ,* Vol. XLII (Monstrolii, 1913), pp. 766-794. On its authorship, see D. A. Mougel, *Dionysius der Karthaeuser, 1402-1471; Sein Leben, sein Werken, Eine Neuausgabe seiner Werke* (Mülheim a. d. Ruhr, 1898), p. 100.

[73] *Inc*: Nolite diligere mundum, neque ea . . . O vita mundi, non vita sed mors. . . . To my knowledge this interesting work has never been printed. mss are at Brussels: Bibl. Royale 1386, fol. 98ʳ–128ʳ (s. xiv); 1503, fol. 128-132 (s. xv); 1618, fol. 245-255; 2165, fol. 3-17ᵛ (s. xv); 2187, fol. 79-82ᵛ (s. xv); 2190, fol. 254-261ᵛ (s. xv); 2205, fol. 80-97 (s. xv); Vatican: Vat. Lat. 10068, fol. 284ᵛ–294ᵛ (s. xv); Belgium: Grand Séminaire de Maline, Cod. 48, fol. 21ʳ–40ʳ; Utrecht: Univ., 161. See J. G. R. Acquoy, *Het Klooster te Windesheim en zijn Invloed,* Vol. II (Utrecht, 1876), pp. 89, 318-319.

and sermons of the period.[74] The *De seculo et religione*
of Coluccio Salutati (ca. 1381), a classic Renaissance
treatment of the theme, quotes 1 John 2:16 in five different chapters, notably in the concluding one, where
the three monastic vows are juxtaposed against lust of
the flesh, lust of the eyes, and pride of life.[75]

The association was made even where the text of

[74] Other works of the period which use the text of 1 John 2:16 are
the following: (1) "Tractatus de contemptu mundanorum et ap-
petitu caelestium metricus cum commentario," attributed to "Johannis
praedicator Viennensis," Prague: Bibl. Universitatis 2041. XI.D.7,
fol. 2^r–20^v (s. xv), *Inc*: Heu heu mortales homines, *Inc. commentary*: Nolite diligere mundum. See Hans Walther, *Initia Carminum*
. . . (Göttingen, 1959), No. 7751; and Hauréau, p. 30. (2) Anon.,
De contemptu mundi, Ravenna: Bibl. Comunale 297, fol. 60^r–61^r
(s. xv), *Inc*: [A]d mundi contemptum non solum Christus inducit
sed multa alia docet . . . ; a short treatise made up mostly of
scriptural texts, the first of which is 1 John 2:16. (3) It is quoted
in St. Bernardino of Siena, *Speculum amatorum mundi*, or *Speculum
peccatorum de contemptu mundi*, *Inc*: Videte quomodo caute ambu-
letis . . . Apostolus Paulus. Conscius consiliorum dei sciens quod
infinite sunt delicias. . . . For some of the MSS, see Rudolf, p. 31 n.
35. (4) It is quoted in a fourteenth-century sermon on vainglory
and worldly excellence, Vatican Library: Vat. Lat. 10964, fol. 53^{r-v},
Inc: Quanta audivimus facta in . . . ; and (5) in the preface to a
fifteenth-century sermon *de contemptu mundi*, Vat. Lat. 11439, fol.
5^{r-v}, *Inc*: Falax grava et vana est pulcritudo mulieris timens deum
ipsa laudabitur. . . . (6) It is the text of a sermon *de viginti peri-
culis mundi* by Giovanni da Capestrano, in Breslau: Royal Library
Cod. IQ 152, fol. 317^r–326^v, *Inc*: Nolite diligere mundum neque
ea. . . . Noticia istorum periculorum dat eciam cautelam . . . ; see
P. Aniceto Chiappini, *La produzione letteraria di S. Giovanni da
Capestrano* (Gubbio, 1927), p. 144, No. 448. (7) It is the text for
each of a group of five anonymous lenten sermons *de contemptu
mundi*, Padova: Bibl. Civica 327, fol. 1^r–79^r (s. xv), *Inc*: Nolite
diligere mundum. . . . Prima visio beati Joannis agit de similitudine
filii hominis quod per angelum S. Johanni apparuit. . . .

[75] B. L. Ullman, ed., *Colucii Salutati de seculo et religione*, Nuova
collezione di testi umanistici inediti o rari, Vol. XII (Florence, 1957),
pp. 19, 45, 70, 104, 161.

1 John 2:16 was *not* mentioned. Since any treatment of moral or social problems was likely to speak of the worldly order, one often finds the three sins mentioned at the beginning of literary works, where the author states his theme. The *Imitatio Christi*, referred to in manuscripts as *"De contemptu mundi*," warns men in its opening chapter to scorn the lusts of the flesh, riches, and honors. In his youth Erasmus wrote a *De contemptu mundi*,[76] dealing in his second, third, and fourth chapters with riches, the pleasure of the flesh, and worldly honors. In the opening canto of Dante's *Inferno* the three allegorical figures which stand in the poet's way—a leopard, a lion, and a she-wolf—are identified by some commentators as worldly pleasure, ambition, and avarice.

Contempt of the World and the temptations associated with it ceased to be a tenable doctrine only when men ceased to regard the natural order as corrupt and transitory, when they came to consider nature good or even, as Spinoza did, identical with God.[77] Still, even in Spinoza, the triple temptation makes its appearance at a crucial point. In the unfinished *Tractatus de intellectus emendatione*, a forerunner of the *Ethics*, Spinoza begins, not unlike Thomas à Kempis, by pointing to the three aspects of life which in men's actions are considered the highest good.[78] These, he tells us, can be classified as

[76] *Desiderii Erasmi Roterdami opera omnia* . . . , Vol. V (Leiden, 1704), cols. 1239-1262. See Albert Hyma, *The Youth of Erasmus* (Ann Arbor, 1930), pp. 167-181.

[77] On the development of a normative concept of nature during the Middle Ages, see Ernst Robert Curtius, *European Literature and the Latin Middle Ages*, trans. Willard R. Trask, Bollingen Series XXXVI (New York, 1953), pp. 106-127.

[78] Spinoza, *Opera*, ed. Carl Gebhardt (Heidelberg, 1925), Vol. II, p. 5: "Nam quae plerumque in vita occurrunt, & apud homines, ut ex eorum operibus colligere licet, tanquam summum bonum aestimantur, ad haec tria rediguntur; divitias scilicet, honorem, atque libi-

riches, fame, and the pleasures of sense. In this he is surprisingly close to the medieval view of the three temptations. He argues that they are a love of transitory things, that this love is unsatisfying, that there is a greater good. He differs from the medieval view in favoring the activity of the mind, the "improvement of the understanding," as a means to the *summum bonum*; and, unlike any medieval thinker, he sees that good in man's union with nature rather than in his hope of scorning and transcending the worldly order. To Spinoza it was through the right use of the World that one could attain the greatest good, not through "contempt" of it.

The contrast is, of course, revealing. It points, for one thing, to the importance of a normative concept of nature, nature no longer seen as corrupted and inferior—an idea with its own medieval background, as for example in Alain de Lille. Given this change of emphasis, it was less pressing for men to analyze the pitfalls of the worldly order, less necessary to point to men's "natural" lusts as inevitably a source of error. Petrarch, in the *Secretum*, easily identified the three lusts with his own private passions: his love for Laura, his love of learning, and his desire for fame. In these senses the lusts refer to activities which, far from being sins, were among the most important enthusiasms of Renaissance men—the notion of courtly or "platonic" love, the new fervor for classical and scientific learning, and the humanistic emphasis on the individual's worldly achievements and reputation.

In the later Middle Ages the three temptations, so central to the medieval notion of the World, came to be

---

dinem. His tribus adeo distrahitur mens, ut minime possit de alio aliquo bono cogitare." Spinoza goes on to discuss the effects of the three sins in some detail. For another preservation of the notion in modern philosophy, see Pascal, *Pensées* (Modern Library ed.) secs. 460-461.

the battlegrounds upon which men fought over the worth of secular things. If perfection was no longer to mean a total renunciation of the World, if ideal conduct could be something other than poverty, chastity, and obedience, men would then need to struggle for some compromise, some justification by which they might find an allowable place for fleshly love, for learning and possessions, for honors, reputation, and fame. Those three temptations, seen "existentially," deal with three important objects of human desire: pleasure, property, and fame or power. In these areas—however impalpable the turning point—lies a major difference between medieval and modern. To the medieval man pleasure, property, and power were (theoretically at least) fruitless "things" in a transitory "World" and deserved to be renounced. To modern man they have been legitimate goals in a world conceived of as the successive stream of human lives;[79] these goals are at the foundations of modern psychological, economic, and political ideas. The remainder of this book will explore some phases of this revolution in human thought.

In the following three chapters, I shall examine each temptation individually. In each case a particular medieval institution offered an ideology to resolve the historical dichotomy, and to these I shall give some attention: courtly love had to reckon with the lust of the flesh, feudalism and medieval economic ideas with lust of the eyes, and the chivalric code with pride of life. In each case I shall examine the stylistic means by which a fourteenth-century English poet attempted to rationalize the underlying historical and existential dichotomies, to carry out the underlying search for legitimate reasons to espouse the World.

[79] Hannah Arendt, "History and Immortality," *PR* (Winter 1957), pp. 11-15, and *Between Past and Future: Six Exercises in Political Thought* (New York, 1961), pp. 41-90.

CHAPTER THREE

COURTLY LOVE AND
THE LUST OF THE FLESH:
TROILUS AND CRISEYDE

TROILUS AND CRISEYDE

Swich fyn hath, lo, this Troilus for love!
Swich fyn hath al his grete worthynesse!
Swich fyn hath his estat real above,
Swich fyn his lust, swich fyn hath his noblesse!
Swych fyn hath false worldes brotelnesse!
And thus bigan his lovyng of Criseyde,
As I have told, and in this wise he deyde.
                    —Chaucer, *Troilus and Criseyde*,
                         v, 1828-1834[1]

HESE LINES from the epilogue of *Troilus and Criseyde* occur after Troilus, transported to the eighth sphere, has looked down upon "This litel spot of erthe, that with the se / Embraced is." From this celestial vantage point, removed from the tragic circumstances of his earthly life, he experiences contempt of the World. Chaucer tells us that he

> . . . fully gan despise
> This wrecched world, and held al vanite
> To respect of the pleyn felicite
> That is in hevene above. (v, 1816-1819)

His removal from the terrestrial globe makes Troilus see the insignificance of human affairs: he sees the *earth*, then begins to despise the *World*. He laughs at the woe of those who weep for his death, and for "al oure werk that foloweth so / The blynde lust, the which that may nat laste" (v, 1823-1824).[2]

Chaucer explicated Troilus' contempt by adding to the material of his sources the three kinds of evil desire traditionally associated with the love of worldly things. The passage is based on a stanza of the *Filostrato* in which Boccaccio emphasizes the "ill-conceived love of Troilus for Criseyde," Troilus' grief, and the "brilliant splendor that he held in store for the royal throne":

> Cotal fine ebbe il mal concetto amore
> Di Troilo in Criseida, e cotale
> Fin' ebbe il miserabile dolore

[1] The text used is *The Works of Geoffrey Chaucer*, ed. F. N. Robinson (2nd ed., Boston, 1957), by permission of Houghton Mifflin Co.

[2] On the meaning of the eighth sphere, see Morton W. Bloomfield, "The Eighth Sphere: A Note on Chaucer's *Troilus and Criseyde*, v, 1809," *MLR*, LIII (1958), 408-410.

Di lui, al qual non fu mai altro eguale;
Cotal fin' ebbe il lucido splendore
Che lui servava al solïo reale;
Cotal fin' ebbe la speranza vana
Di Troilo in Criseida villana.[3]

In this passage Boccaccio himself, as Alfred L. Kellogg
has shown, may have used commentary on Isaiah 40
from the *Somme le roi* of Frère Lorens; and Chaucer,
at the corresponding point in the *Troilus*, may have
been indebted to the same work or to its English version,
the *Book of Vices and Virtues*.[4] There are the following
correspondences:

Chaucer	*Book of Vices and Virtues*
estat real[5]	richesse
worthynesse	honoure
noblesse	noblesse
	fairenesse

Chaucer has no term corresponding to the "fairnesse"
of the *Book of Vices and Virtues*. And while "love" and
"estat real" correspond to terms in Boccaccio, there is

---

[3] *Filostrato*, VIII, 28. *The Filostrato of Giovanni Boccaccio*, trans.
Nathaniel Edward Griffin and Arthur Beckwith Myrick (Philadel-
phia, 1929), p. 496. On the differences between the endings of the
Filostrato and the *Troilus*, cf. Sanford B. Meech, *Design in Chaucer's
Troilus* (Syracuse, 1959), pp. 129-138.

[4] Alfred L. Kellogg, "On the Tradition of Troilus's Vision of the
Little Earth," *MS*, XXII (1960), 204-213. Kellogg mentions contempt of the World, but takes the "little earth" as synonymous with
"world."

[5] "Real" here is *royal* (OF *real* from L. *regalem*; a variant of *rial*,
royal, in MSS ca. 1400). It would be tempting to make it "real" (L.
realis, from *res*, OF *real*, *reel*), as used in law. The *OED* does not,
however, give this usage before 1448. Moreover, Chaucer in all cases
uses the word in the sense of "royal"—see *Troilus and Criseyde*, III,
1534, and *Legend of Good Women*, F. 214, 284, 1605.

nothing which corresponds with Boccaccio's "speranza vana / Di Troilo in Criseida villana." On the other hand, Chaucer has added "lust"—an echo of "the blynde lust" of line 1824, also not found in its source[6]—and the summary phrase "false worldes brotelnesse." "Lo here," he adds later (1851), "thise wrecched worldes appetites." In omitting terms from the sources and adding others, Chaucer has brought the passage more closely in line with the traditional three divisions of worldly vanity.

By adding "the blynde lust" (1824) and "lust" (1831) to his "auctor," Chaucer has also put emphasis on one aspect of worldly vanity which lay at the heart of courtly love. From a churchly point of view, courtly love was objectionable for the sensuality and adultery which it seemed to foster; more important still, love in the courtly sense was sensual love of a worldly object and therefore contrary to the love of God. All this seemed to be acknowledged by courtly writers. In the literature of courtly love, the pattern of temptation and sin described by the suggestion-delectation-consent formula is discernible in the plight of the lover. The lover is aroused by an inward stimulus, in response to a worldly object; he suffers, he struggles; and, the power of Love being unavoidable, he must at length give consent. Yet, while it is clear that he has gone through the classic process of moral choice, it is never clear whether he has chosen well or ill. True, we are told that love is the source of all virtue, that the lady has given him "grace," that he is brought to a state of felicity and blessedness; yet from the soberest Christian point of view we know the lover has committed sin—he has consented to put a worldly object in place of God, which is pride, and he may, given the circumstances which the

[6] The stanza (v, 1821-1827) is based on *Teseida*, XI, 1-24. See Kellogg, pp. 207-208.

courtly system was meant to encourage, commit adultery.

The extent to which, generally in the *Troilus*, Chaucer had in mind the three temptations and the suggestion-delectation-consent formula is a problem to which we shall return. In the body of the poem it is evident that little or no attention is given to riches or honors: it is a poem about love. But we know that in the epilogue Chaucer distinguishes, as Boccaccio does not, between fleshly love and Christian love. He refers twice in the epilogue to "lust" ("enjoyment" or "delight" in modern English), and, in speaking of "love," puts emphasis upon the love of God for man where Boccaccio points only to the fickleness of women:[7]

> O yonge, fresshe folkes, he or she,
> In which that love up groweth with youre age,
> Repeyreth hom fro worldly vanyte,
> And of youre herte up casteth the visage
> To thilke God that after his ymage

[7] The passage in Boccaccio (VIII, 29-30) reads:

> O giovanetti, ne' quai coll' etate
> Surgendo vien l' amoroso disio,
> Per Dio vi prego che voi raffreniate
> I pronti passi all' appetito rio,
> E nell' amor di Troilo vi specchiate,
> Il qual dimostra suso il verso mio,
> Perchè se ben col cuor gli leggerete,
> Non di leggieri a tutte crederete.

> Giovane donna è mobile, e vogliosa
> È negli amanti molti, e sua bellezza
> Estima più ch' allo specchio, e pomposa
> Ha vanagloria di sua giovinezza;
> La qual quanto piacevole e vezzosa
> È più, cotanto più seco l' apprezza;
> Virtù non sente nè conoscimento,
> Volubil sempre come foglia al vento.

Yow made, and thynketh al nys but a faire
This world, that passeth soone as floures faire.

And loveth hym, the which that right for love
Upon a crois, oure soules for to beye,
First starf, and roos, and sit in hevene above;
For he nyl falsen no wight, dar I seye,
That wol his herte al holly on hym leye.
And syn he best to love is, and most meke,
What nedeth feynede loves for to seke?

(v, 1835-1848)

This conflict between Christian love and "courtly" love, which I take to be the concern of the *Troilus*, had already in Chaucer's time a long history. To study the "lust of the flesh" in the *Troilus* we shall therefore have to say something first about the tradition of courtly love. There are, I think, two central problems: How could courtly love, based as it was on purely worldly considerations, be advocated by men who continued to profess themselves Christians? And was courtly love after all anything more than a literary and social convention? To phrase these questions differently, was there anything in the *style* of courtly love, and of its literature, which was consistent with the style of medieval Christianity?

I. LOVE AND PERFECTION

Everyone agrees that courtly love, if taken literally, would be unchristian; the problem is whether or not it *should* be taken literally. What we know is that suddenly in aristocratic circles during the twelfth century there appears a lore and mystique which runs counter to anything that has been said before. Woman, usually regarded in law as chattel and in theology as the inferior of man, becomes elevated to a position like that of sainthood, even deity: on her account the lover suffers, be-

83

comes her servant, beseeches her grace. She is no longer the traditional antifeminist snare leading good men into evil sensuality; she is a prize, the possession of which becomes a goal comparable to God's grace, to salvation. Hence, as C. S. Lewis has pointed out, courtly love appears to be one of the great reversals of human sentiment, a revolution in the emotional life of western culture.[8] But in its earliest forms was it genuinely a cultural change, or was it only a literary convention which *later* came to affect behavior?[9] Do we, that is, misinterpret that literature, read into it the romantic notions of a later time? If, as Mr. Robertson urges, all medieval Christian poetry "is always allegorical when the message of charity or some corollary of it is not evident on the surface," do we not gravely mistake the point in supposing that authors were advocating this heretical love? Were they not rather, by the use of a subtle and highly elaborated irony, warning their public *against* the lusts of the flesh? Speaking of the ambivalent nature of scriptural symbols, Robertson argues that "love" (*amor*) was used as a synonym for both charity and cupidity. This, he remarks, "opened enormous possibilities for literary word-play," and was "responsible for the manifest preoccupation with 'love' in mediaeval literature."[10] For in fact (we are told) the medieval writings of courtly love are really doctrinal;[11] they echo clerical notions of sensuality and their intention is to condemn sensual love.

[8] C. S. Lewis, *The Allegory of Love: A Study in Medieval Tradition* (Galaxy ed., New York, 1958), pp. 1-12.

[9] See Lewis, p. 22.

[10] "The Doctrine of Charity in Medieval Literary Gardens: A Topical Approach through Symbolism and Allegory," *Speculum*, XXVI (1951), 28. For a full statement of Robertson's theory of medieval love, see *A Preface to Chaucer: Studies in Medieval Perspectives* (Princeton, 1962), pp. 391-503.

[11] For example, see "Love Conventions in Marie's *Equitan*," *RR*, XLIV (1953), 241-245.

The opposite view—or extreme, as it should be called—is that courtly writers were seriously advocating a heretical convention which was actually practiced, that the convention itself had an historic origin, and that its tenets were in open conflict with Christian morality. The late Alexander J. Denomy argued that the chief characteristics of courtly love were diametrically opposed to Christian doctrine and indeed heretical. That love is an ennobling force, that the beloved is elevated above the lover, that love is an ever unsatiated and increasing desire—such notions, Denomy argued, were *not* similar to the idea of Christian charity and *not* influenced by twelfth-century mysticism;[12] their fundamental pattern of thought was more like the doctrine of Plotinus, because the relation of the lover to the lady corresponds to the relation in Neoplatonism of the Soul to the One. Such Neoplatonic and gnostic beliefs were picked up in the ninth century by Arab mysticism; they are present to a considerable extent in Arabic poetry and are discernible in the philosophy of Avicenna; and they provide a framework of thought, centering in the doctrine that the soul of man is divine, on which notions of courtly love could have been formed.[13] Even that side of courtly poetry which favored "ideal" or "pure" love, however

[12] Cf. Eduard Wechssler, *Das Kulturproblem des Minnesangs* (Halle, 1909). Wechssler's thesis was disputed also by Étienne Gilson, *La théologie mystique de Saint Bernard*, Études de philosophie médiévale, xx (Paris, 1934), pp. 193-215.

[13] Alexander J. Denomy, "An Inquiry into the Origins of Courtly Love," *MS*, vi (1944), 175-260. On the Arabic origin of courtly love, see A. R. Nykl, *Hispano-Arabic Poetry and Its Relations with the Old Provençal Troubadours* (Baltimore, 1946). Denomy argued elsewhere that direct contact with Arabic culture was possible through the crusades, through Cluny monks, and through the pilgrimage to St. James of Compostella. In architecture there *was* Moorish influence in the south of France during the eleventh century. In particular, Avicenna's *Treatise on Love* offers an elaborate parallel with courtly

much it excluded intercourse and opposed lechery, allowed of a "mixed" love in which desire and the things which incite desire may be a means to a higher end, a method of attaining growth in virtue. In presenting such a concept poets used Christian language, but that did not make it a Christian doctrine; for the Church specifically forbade evil thoughts and the incitement of desire whether they ended in intercourse or not.[14]

But how could such non-Christian ideas have been held by poets who continued to profess themselves Christians—who in many cases also wrote Christian poems? Such a conflict of beliefs, Denomy suggests, can itself be explained by another Arabic heresy, the doctrine of the "double truth." This doctrine, proposed by Averroës in his *Philosophy and Theology* (1179), which appeared only later in Latin, held that there was a separation of truth between nature and grace, between reason and faith, between philosophy and theology; and that these separate truths, derived by different means, did not need to harmonize. Averroës' work was of course too late to influence the twelfth-century courtly writers, even Andreas (whose *De amore* was written between 1184 and 1186), but there is a possibility of a common origin in preexisting Arabic sources. We do know that the one theoretical work on courtly love, the *De amore*, was condemned as heretical in 1277 by Stephen Tempier,

---

doctrines; it is this work which Denomy offers as the origin of courtly love. See "Concerning the Accessibility of Arabic Influences to the Earliest Provençal Troubadours," *MS*, xv (1953), 147-158, but cf. Theodore Silverstein, "Andreas, Plato, and the Arabs," *MP*, XLVII (1949-1950), 117-126, in which it is shown that not all the ideas of courtly love are in Avicenna.

[14] Alexander J. Denomy, *"Fin' Amors*: the Pure Love of the Troubadours, Its Amorality, and Possible Source," *MS*, VII (1945), 139-207.

Bishop of Paris, and, along with it, several works on the doctrine of the double truth.[15]

The heart of the problem, then, is the relationship between Christian morality and the non-Christian tenets of courtly love. The conflict between them is apparent in courtly writings themselves, notably in the *De amore*, the *Roman de la rose*, and the *Troilus*. But no amount of close reading is going to explain this conflict until our knowledge of the cultural background permits us to decide what is ironic and what is not. The presence of Christian language in courtly writings is undeniable; but one can take it, with Denomy, as an open and heretical perversion of doctrine or, with Robertson, as an ironic play meant to discredit sensuality. So, too, when we find, as in the *De amore*, a final Christian utterance following a protracted treatment of love, we cannot be certain whether that final statement was added as lip service or was intended to deny and discredit what had gone before. And yet we need only look ahead several centuries to know that courtly love did make an impression on western culture and leave behind a body of literary and behavioral conventions. Whatever we say about its earlier stages, the fact stands before us that it was, in C. S. Lewis's phrase, a "real change in human sentiment," a new complex of ideas and emotions which at length imposed a nearly impenetrable barrier between the modern world and the classical and Christian past.[16] At the same time, courtly love never altered or weakened Christi-

---

[15] Alexander J. Denomy, "The *De amore* of Andreas Capellanus and the Condemnation of 1277," *MS*, VIII (1946), 107-149. See also *The Heresy of Courtly Love* (New York, 1947) for a summary of Denomy's position. On Stephen Tempier there is some interesting material in E. J. Dijksterhuis, *The Mechanization of the World Picture*, trans. C. Dikshoorn (Oxford, 1961), p. 161.

[16] Lewis, p. 11.

anity—at least no more than anything else. As one element in a climate of increasing secularity, it may have done its share. But courtly writers and courtly lovers continued to be Christians: from Andreas, through Petrarch, and as far at least as Andrew Marvell, it was a *parti pris* that the love of a lady was not incompatible with the worship of God. And the poetry of love reveals fully this complexity.

On this account there does indeed seem to be a "double truth" at the heart of courtly love. What I wish to suggest, however, is that this duality came not from an Arabic heresy smuggled in *sub rosa*, but from a principle already at hand—a basic element, so to speak, in the *style* of Christian morality: the doctrine of perfection.

One is tempted to grant, as Denomy argues, that a doctrine of double truth could have come into medieval thought in some indeterminate, secondhand way, even before 1179, when Averroës' *Philosophy and Theology* appeared. There are, however, two objections to this hypothesis. One is that we never *hear* of the doctrine of the double truth. In all that is written about love, in all that is said about its conflict with the love of God, no writer ever came out and proposed the doctrine by name. If Andreas had it explicitly in mind when he wrote of the "rejection" of love, he came no closer to saying so than in the vague phrase *duplicem sententiam*. Hence if the doctrine of the double truth had any part in courtly notions, it lingered far under the surface—something scarcely conscious, an emotion rather than an idea. And even granting that in some way this Arabic doctrine had filtered into the minds of twelfth-century Christians who concerned themselves with "love," how could the notion have gained acceptance; how could it be taken up by men who professed one revealed truth, plain and incontrovertible; what conditions in their own system of thought created any *need* for such an idea? A second major objection is that in courtly writings the duality of truth has nothing to do with systematic philosophy. It is solely a question of morality. Granted, there are two opposing systems—a God of Love over against a Christian God, a "religion" of love over against the Church, sensual indulgence over against the ideal of continence; but the purpose of all this was not, as it was in Averroës, to establish a principle about philosophizing. It established, instead, a principle about conduct: it opened up a way of enjoying the very indulgences that the Church forbade without having openly to controvert what the Church taught. It fostered, to put it differently, a highly formalized game of sensuality and practiced an elaborate and perhaps ironic "religion" of love which conflicted with Christian teachings but which did not openly or philosophically contend with them.

This "duality" of courtly love, I believe, formalized and ritualized a condition which had always existed in Christian thought. Everyone knows that the Church discouraged sensual indulgence, that it held virginity up as an ideal, that it regarded the passionate love of one's own wife as adultery.[17] Yet in accordance with St. Paul's grudging precept that it is better to marry than to burn, the Church taught—not without debate—that marriage was a sacrament and that men were commanded to be fruitful and multiply (Gen. 1:28). When we speak of "the Church" we most often think of the monastic and ascetic tradition; and it is true, probably, that the better part of writing on such subjects was done by monks. But there was another tradition, what we might call a *prelatical* one, which concerned itself with canon law

[17] See, for example, St. Jerome, *Adversus Jovinianum*, I, 49 (PL 23:281). For a convenient summary of theological positions on sexuality, see Lewis, pp. 14-17.

and with administrative problems touching marriage ceremonies, remarriage, bearing and raising children, and so on; this tradition was practical and dealt more with applications than with ideals.[18] Taken together, the two views show how in matters of sexual conduct, as in other things, the Church counseled an ethical ideal so lofty that few could be expected to follow it, but that it had at the same time specific laws and precepts which all *must* follow. This condition of medieval thought is nowhere better illustrated than in the Wife of Bath. As concerns her marriages she has obeyed the letter of the law; remarriage, she rightly argues, is not forbidden. But she is uneasy, and zestfully defensive, because she has not followed the "counsel" of virginity or widowhood.

Such a duality was formulated in the doctrine of perfection. "Perfection" was a relative term. It was different from holiness or sanctification; it existed within the limitations of human frailty, and those who attained it were still subject to venial sin. Christians had before them Christ's command "Be ye therefore perfect" (Matt. 5:48); yet it was understood that all men are subject to ignorance, concupiscence, and death—the punishments of original sin. Hence a certain limitation had to be put on the meaning of perfection. The Christian was expected to be righteous—was indeed commanded to be so—but he was only "counseled" to be perfect. And it was understood that some would be more perfect than others.[19]

[18] For this idea I am indebted to Professor Charles W. Jones.

[19] On perfection, see the article by Frederic Platt in Hastings' *Encyclopaedia of Religion and Ethics*, IX (1917), 728-737; and the article by A. Fonck in *Dictionnaire de théologie catholique*, XII, 1219-1251. See also R. Newton Flew, *The Idea of Perfection in Christian Theology: An Historical Study of the Christian Ideal for the Present Life* (London, 1934). For comments on the idea esp. of

Accordingly, in the various means by which perfection could be cultivated—poverty, virginity, prayer, and so on—there were degrees or grades. Of chastity, which is what concerns us here, there were three—marriage, widowhood, and virginity.[20] These were said to produce various rates of return, the Parable of the Sower (Matt. 13:3-23) being often applied to them. In this way the Pauline view that it is better to marry than to burn (1 Cor. 7:9) was developed into a system where marriage was an allowable and righteous state, but less meritorious than widowhood or virginity. The premise, clearly enough, is that intercourse for fleshly pleasure is wrong, whether in marriage or not;[21] St. Augustine had said that it was better if "even during the life of her husband, by his consent, a female vow continence unto Christ."[22] Yet it was understood that while men should try to attain higher degrees of perfection, they could not

---

degrees or grades of perfection, and for further references, see Morton W. Bloomfield, "Some Reflections on the Medieval Idea of Perfection," *FranS*, XVII (1957), 229-232.

[20] On the three grades of chastity, see Ambrose, *De viduis*, IV, 23 (*PL* 16:254-255), and *Epistola*, LXIII, 40 (*PL* 16:1251). See also St. Augustine, *On the Good of Widowhood*, secs. 1-5, in *A Select Library of the Nicene and Post-Nicene Fathers of the Christian Church*, ed. Philip Schaff, Vol. III (Buffalo, 1887), pp. 441-443 *et passim*. For a brief history of the concept, see Matthäus Bernards, *Speculum Virginum, Geistigkeit und Seelenleben der Frau im Hochmittelalter*, Forschungen zur Volkskunde, ed. G. Schreiber, Band 36-38 (Cologne and Graz, 1955), pp. 40 ff. See also Morton W. Bloomfield, "*Piers Plowman* and the Three Grades of Chastity," *Anglia*, LXXVI (1958), 227-253.

[21] St. Augustine, *On the Good of Marriage*, sec. 6 (ed. Schaff, pp. 401-402) and sec. 18 (p. 407). Cf. St. Jerome, *Adversus Jovinianum*, I, 49 (*PL* 23:281); and Chaucer, Parson's Tale, X, 903 f.

[22] *On the Good of Widowhood*, sec. 13 (p. 446). Cf. secs. 6 and 15 (pp. 443, 446-447), and *On Virginity*, sec. 4 (p. 418).

all be expected to follow such counsels: some would be "called" to higher states than others.[23]

Such a doctrine, it will be said, is "otherworldly," and this it is, at least in the sense that it puts a higher value on things eternal than on things secular. It was nevertheless a highly satisfactory way of solving the problem inherent in all systems of idealism: it took into account the difficulty of following the ideal without debasing that ideal or attempting to adjust it to human capacities. It is otherworldly only because its highest grade involves a renunciation of worldly things; it is at base a "worldly" doctrine because it concerns itself with human conduct in the World. The real conflict between Christianity and courtly love was to come, therefore, not so much with the Church's otherworldly ideal of chastity as with its worldly precept of marriage.

It is not difficult to see how, imbued as they were with this style of thinking, medieval men could have accepted the Averroistic doctrine of the double truth. But, quite *without* this doctrine, the peculiar duality of courtly love was able to take shape. Men knew, from the idea of perfection—or rather, from the "hierarchical" attitude which it embodied—that while chastity and renunciation were best, marriage was allowable and meritorious. Enthusiasts of courtly love could, then, in that foggier part of the mind where strict adherence to orthodoxy and logic does not loom large, have applied something like the pattern of inferior "grades," good of themselves but falling short of the ideal. We live (they might have reasoned) in an imperfect World where the highest

[23] Cf. *The English Text of the Ancrene Riwle*, ed. A. C. Baugh (London, 1956), EETS, 232, p. 43. It is never quite clear whether one should strive actively for higher degrees of perfection or wait passively to see if one is called. The Wife of Bath, for instance, seems to prefer the latter.

perfection is for those especially called; in theory it would be best for all of us to renounce the World and follow the highest counsel, but in fact few do so. Why not, if one is allowed lesser degrees of perfection, admit also among those lesser degrees this nonmarital love which ennobles?

It will be objected against this thesis that the doctrine of perfection dealt with legitimate, desirable activities—that marriage was a lesser perfection than widowhood but still a "perfect" state. Courtly love, being idolatrous, and often adulterous, was *im*perfect; how could it enter into such a gradation at all? But this is not my meaning. I am saying only that the doctrine of perfection furnishes a model, a precedent, for the curious behavior of such writers as Andreas, who agreeably lead the reader on at length in favor of love and then point him off at the end toward something holier. In the Middle Ages it was acknowledged that no mortal ever attained the ideal except by degrees, and the doctrine of perfection illustrates how this is so. Against such hierarchical patterns of thought, medieval knights and ladies would have seen love as something admittedly inferior to chastity, widowhood, or Christian marriage—but still superior, from an aristocratic point of view, to whatever was base, whatever lacked *courtoisie* or *gentilesse*: Hate, Felonye, and Vilanye were the first to be excluded from the garden of Love.

2. THE GAME OF LOVE

The dichotomy in medieval thought between a worldly code and an otherworldly ideal helps to explain the *duplicem sententiam* which one often encounters in courtly writings. It does not, however, explain to what extent that code was presented ironically or seriously.

This question, about the tone and style of courtly writings, rests in part upon our notions of what irony is and what kinds of irony there are. It has always been an easy game to argue that a literary work is ironic and so means something other than what it says, but the only test is a precise knowledge of the author's true opinions or, at least, those most characteristic of his age. With courtly love this is especially difficult because no one is quite certain whether courtly love was a theory, a practice, or a literary convention.

If we take it to be a theory, we are faced with the embarrassing fact that the only statement of that theory—Andreas' *Tractatus*—is itself an enigma. After two books of painstaking analysis, in which all the ramifications of the art of love are discussed and ruled upon, Andreas without explanation turns about and writes of the "rejection" of love, holding that no man who serves love can please God. To account for this strange reversal, it has been argued that the entire work is religious and the first two books "generally ironic." The definition of love is actually scriptural, the object of love being described in terms which recall the supreme fruit of the tree of Babylon as described by Hugh of St. Victor in *De fructibus*; and the solemn style and perversions of doctrine in the first two books are intended ironically as a literary device to condemn sensual love. The humor is directed against the follies of lovers. And the "rejection" at the end merely makes explicit what was implied from the start.[24] On the other hand, it has been argued that all three books are intended seriously, the contradiction between the first two and the last being possible through

[24] Robertson, "The Doctrine of Charity in Medieval Literary Gardens," p. 28; "The Subject of the *De amore* of Andreas Capellanus," *MP*, L (1953), 145-161; and *A Preface to Chaucer*, pp. 393-448.

the Averroistic doctrine of the double truth. This view holds that Books I and II contain outright heresies supported by arguments of reason and nature, whereas Book III proposes orthodox views of theology and faith, the author making no attempt to reconcile the two opposing doctrines.[25]

Each of these opinions assumes that the Chaplain had a clear, conscious intention—that he knew what he was about and proceeded to create an "integrated" work. For this the text itself presents little evidence. Andreas tells us that he has proposed a *duplicem sententiam*, and he is right. He seems to use Christian language in describing love, but it is not clear why he does so, and it is entirely possible that he does so accidentally. He says nothing about a doctrine of double truth, nor does he explain in any other way why he rejects the first two books in the third. It is indeed quite possible that he could *not* have explained it, that he had no consistent philosophical theory and no conscious program or plan; for the ambiguous style of the *De amore* may have been an imaginative stroke of genius, prompted by contradictions, doubts, and anxieties in the culture itself.

If this is the case, we shall have to think some about the social background of the *De amore*. Several students of the problem have put to one side the "theory" of courtly love and viewed it as an aristocratic practice—as a social convention or "game," like those behind the Provençal *tenzon* and the *jeu-parti*, which never really had a theory.[26] W. T. H. Jackson, for example, holds

[25] Denomy, "The *De amore* of Andreas Capellanus and the Condemnation of 1277," pp. 125-149. The discussion of Andreas which follows was written independently of the excellent study by Felix Schlösser, *Andreas Capellanus: Seine Minnelehre und das christliche Weltbild um 1200* (Bonn, 1960).

[26] W. T. H. Jackson, "The *De amore* of Andreas Capellanus and

that Andreas, in no way a philosophical thinker, was writing in the *De amore* a "not too serious text-book for certain members of [the] court—and in particular, a book for the ladies of that court." The dialogues are "not intended seriously, in the sense that the whole art they represent was not serious but an elaborate game"; they represent a practice rather than a theory and should not be used as a guide to "courtly love" in literature. The book is a collection of things heard in sophisticated court circles, with a strong feminine bias and an emphasis on persuasive techniques between those of unequal rank. And the last book, which Jackson characterizes as "a string of precepts," was added because Andreas "felt the need to express both sides of the question"; it lacks the skill and the light touch of the first two books, but it is neither more nor less sincere—in just the same way that the ladies themselves could have made "the sincerest protestations of repentance in church" and then returned light-hearted afterward to the game. I should be inclined to go a step further and say that while the first two books are ironic and gamelike, the last is no less so. The chaplain is spoofing the ladies with all his pedantic rules and heavy discussions, but he is also spoofing them when he turns upon them with an antifeminist diatribe and a

---

the Practice of Love at Court," *RR*, XLIX (1958), 243-251. Cf. William Allen Neilson, *The Origins and Sources of the "Court of Love,"* HSNPL, 6 (Cambridge, Mass., 1899), pp. 240-256; J. Huizinga, *The Waning of the Middle Ages* (Anchor ed., Garden City, N.Y., 1956), pp. 107-128; Thomas Frederick Crane, *Italian Social Customs of the Sixteenth Century and Their Influence on the Literatures of Europe* (New Haven, 1920), p. 38; Sidney Painter, *French Chivalry: Chivalric Ideas and Practices in Mediaeval France* (Baltimore, 1940), pp. 118-119, 162-163; Francis Lee Utley, *The Crooked Rib* (Columbus, Ohio, 1944), pp. 32-36; and John Stevens, *Music and Poetry in the Early Tudor Court* (London, 1961), pp. 154-202.

string of ascetical precepts. The turnabout itself is ironic. And the whole seems to spring from the style of life at court.

This social custom or game, with its tone of irony and its elevated literary convention, surely captured the imagination of medieval men, and we should be learning a great deal if we could understand why. In the pages that follow, I wish to examine the thesis that the "game" of love was a ritualized expression of anxieties about social class and sexuality, and that it provided medieval men with a morale-building ideology which assuaged their feelings of guilt and unworthiness.

This interpretation belongs to Herbert Moller. Studying courtly love against the social history of the period, Moller has suggested that the origin of courtly love can be explained by the growth of a lesser nobility in which males outnumbered females.[27] He finds a similar problem about the sex ratio in the background of Hispano-Arabic love poetry; and he points out that such a condition existed precisely in those places and at those times that courtly poetry of the earlier "spontaneous" kind flourished: in southwestern France in the twelfth and early thirteenth centuries and in southern Germany until the mid-thirteenth century. In those areas there occurred a restocking of the nobility from the class of *ministeriales* and lesser knights. This rise of men to the lower nobility, plus immigration of young knights into the south, created a large group of unmarried "bachelor" knights who, rather than jeopardize their status by marrying beneath them, wanted to marry into families of higher status. Such marriages were encouraged, since they often entailed economic advantages for the wife's family and were not thought to affect the rank of her house; but the

[27] Herbert Moller, "The Social Causation of the Courtly Love Complex," *CSSH*, I (1959), 137-163.

high sex ratio made them rare. The result was competition among members of the new nobility, the *ministeriales*, and the lesser knights.

These conditions brought about the development of a collective fantasy. Marrying heiresses, always a difficult pursuit, and the possibility of polyandrous relationships, against which the Church and the medieval social structure placed imposing prohibitions, became fantasy subjects for knights. For, Moller argues, courtly literature at base reflects anxieties about acceptance within a compatible group and approval by an authority figure.[28] Even the upper nobility had to redefine its existence in a changing world and justify its claim to social superiority: in addition to its claims of wealth and birth it had to show itself capable of a certain style of life. The troubadours verbalized these requirements. To the notion of restrained and "pure" love were often linked the notions of tournament, chivalry, and crusade. Hence the courtly poems were part of an "ethical or morale-building complex"; they "verbalized anxieties of rejection and at the same time helped to allay these anxieties." The underlying effect was to deflect biological energies into culturally desirable channels. And the lady was the guardian of the cultural demands imposed by this aristocratic society.[29]

One need not be a devotee of the behavioral sciences

[28] In "The Meaning of Courtly Love," *JAF*, LXXIII (1960), 39-52, Moller argues that the lady is the authority figure, suggestive of the maternal superego. This Freudian analysis of the content of courtly literature seems, though Moller does not say so, to support the view of courtly love as a "feudalization of love." On the lady as authority figure in a social group, cf. Lewis, p. 2, who remarks that French *midons* is etymologically "my lord."

[29] Moller, "Social Causation," p. 162 and "Meaning of Courtly Love," p. 49. On the element of fantasy in courtly love, cf. Painter, pp. 102-104.

to see that in these conjectures there is the soundest core of common sense. The evidence of Moller's demographic studies simply bears out what had been supposed nearly a century ago by Violet Paget and must be supposed by anyone who tries to picture the life of feudal lords in a medieval castle: that it was a world of men, gathered about a great lord who out of feudal necessity was married to a lady of a great family. She, the *domina* of the castle, is surrounded by a few ladies-in-waiting, poor relatives for the most part, and a number of lesser knights who in the castle act as servants at her table, as guards at her chamber. Extra women are replaced by men who can serve the lord in time of crisis. There is no space to be spared. The lady is a stranger in the castle, married not for love but for family ties and dowry; she cherishes the attentions of squires and lesser knights, for she receives, probably, little enough of this from her husband. The young knights look up to her, respect her, are educated in aristocratic niceties by her. There are no *un*married women for them except peasants—for virginity in unmarried women of the upper class is a prized possession. The lady's daughters are therefore kept out of the way, married and sent off in their early teens, or put in nunneries. Yet this lady is far too high-born for the knights to entertain hope of a sexual union; and their desire for it, if it takes root in their fantasies, conflicts with their sense of loyalty to the lord. They know, all of them, that the lord has the right to kill his wife if he finds her with a lover—and to kill the lover.[30] Thus it comes about that they must play at what they cannot do. In their fancies the high-born married woman becomes the impersonation of the feudal loyalty in which they are trained, and the idealization of their adulterous

[30] Painter, pp. 98-101.

fantasy becomes "the glorification of excellence within the compass of guilt."[31]

The lover's situation, it will be agreed, is not an enviable one. And in the most human way he develops a style which helps relieve his discomfort. For one thing, he presents his inferiority as if it were a virtue—he does not say "I don't care if I am inferior" but "This is the way I want it." His "humility" and his constant complaints about the lady's pride really express his feeling of social inferiority and his anxiety about her disdain. Probably the lady often relished her position as a pawn in the affairs of men and her ability to raise the social position of a suitor;[32] but since she was often at her father's mercy in making a marriage, her hauteur might well have been tinged with anxiety, too. The famous dictum of Andreas' treatise, that love can exist only outside of marriage, may express a pervasive anxiety about the making of marriage contracts, which was not wholly in the hands of either partner; and it states what must have been more often than not a fact about marriages thus contracted. Similarly, the emphasis in courtly literature upon courtesy reflects the young knight's anxiety about his station. While he is "unworthy" and "humble," he attempts to demonstrate his worthiness;

[31] Violet Paget [Vernon Lee, pseud.], *Euphorion: Being Studies of the Antique and the Mediaeval in the Renaissance* (London, 1885), pp. 346-388. Miss Paget believed that the situation in the castle which she so vividly described actually issued in a practice of adultery. The wife, she conjectured, was too powerful in her own family ties to be hampered by the objections of the husband, and the husband would be indulgent, having himself been a lover of another's wife in younger days. This fancy I think underestimates the harshness and possessiveness of feudal lords, especially in the earlier period; but it does explain the tolerance of Mark in Gottfried von Strassburg's *Tristan* and Arthur's tolerance in the last books of Malory.

[32] Moller, "Social Causation," pp. 156-159.

since he could not do this on the grounds of wealth and
birth, as the upper nobility could, he had to appeal to
a new mystique, a style of life which is—or should be—
characteristic of aristocracy. This anxiety about the basis
of class distinctions, certainly a dominant theme of
Andreas' first two books,[33] continues to appear well into
the sixteenth century in courtesy books and treatises on
"true nobility," which urged that humility was a distinguishing trait of a noble character. The prestige of
humility as a Christian virtue helped to reinforce the
mystique and to turn the suitor's feelings of social inferiority into an emblem of his worth.

To these anxieties about social status were added other
anxieties about sexual satisfaction. The ultimate "solace"
which the lady has it in her power to offer or withhold
is not the legitimate sexuality of Christian marriage, it
is adultery. It must be kept secret, it must not be given
too freely (or withheld completely), it must be regarded
with a devout awe—in short, it is a reversal of the sexuality which orthodox medieval social institutions approved, and certainly a reversal of the premium put on
virginity. It is the fantasy of a particular milieu in
southern France, in which polyandrous relationships
were desired (and "needed," because of the high sex
ratio), but forbidden. Perhaps the fantasy about adultery
is also an expression of the man's anxiety about achieving
sexual satisfaction in a marriage contracted out of economic and social motives.[34] Indeed, the underlying
theme of much courtly literature, that love has an

[33] *Ibid.*, pp. 159-162.

[34] Courtly love did not seem to diminish promiscuity or discourage
adulterous relationships with peasant girls. See Andreas, I, xi ("The
Love of Peasants"); and Moller, "Meaning of Courtly Love," p.
40. There is some question, though, whether the lesser nobility would
have felt so secure in this kind of predatory behavior.

ennobling effect, expresses both the social and sexual
anxieties of its other themes. The yearned-after relationship could itself raise the lover from the position of
social inferiority which hindered the relationship in the
first place; and his commitment to a "pure" love which
transcends the physical denies the initial anxieties about
a forbidden polyandrous relationship or a union, physical or marital, with the high-born.

From its beginnings, then, courtly love had the
character of a gamelike revolt against traditional morality. By the thirteenth century courtly writings had become conventional. They continued to be written and
read in the south even when the specific conditions of
upward social mobility among the lesser aristocracy no
longer existed, and they became fashionable in the north,
where such conditions had not existed at all. Along with
the conventional literature went a conventional kind of
behavior, *courtoisie*—the ritual adoration of ladies and
the habit of performing servant-like actions for them.[35]
This became, of course, an emblem of social superiority,
as did the profession of a belief in idealized love. But
was there, behind these outward, and recorded, manifestations, a clandestine practice of adultery in aristocratic
circles? In a later age Gerson exclaimed against bastards,
infanticides, and abortions;[36] but he was a priest and antifeminist, writing a polemic. There is little evidence
outside the romances that in the twelfth and thirteenth
centuries high-born ladies actually lent themselves to a
codified and "accepted" adultery, though where secrecy
is requisite evidence is bound to be scant. Undoubtedly
there was always the garden-variety, unritualized adultery. But, privacy being so difficult to attain in a medieval
castle, it would have been far from easy to consummate

[35] Moller, "Social Causation," pp. 145-148.
[36] Huizinga, p. 127.

the courtly game. One thinks of the machinations of Pandarus to find a private chamber; and one remembers that outside the door slept all Criseyde's ladies. Even private conversations in the daytime were not easily managed. The behavioral manifestations of courtly love—the game at court, the songs, the recital of romances—patterned themselves on an underlying habit of thought rather than on an established clandestine practice. The behavior and the literature, in other words, originated in common psycho-cultural needs: it was not that the one influenced the other but that they influenced and supported each other. This fantasy-directed behavior took conventionalized and approved forms: *courtoisie*, flirting which came to nothing, "courting" which ended in marriage, and talk or song about polyandrous and adulterous relationships. Not that fantasy precludes actuality—it is quite possible that courtly affairs of the prescribed extramarital kind may sometimes have been consummated; but this would have been an outcome of the entire complex, not its cause.

And what the fourteenth century inherited from earlier manifestations of this fantasy-directed behavior was a style—a style of life emblematic of social superiority, and a style of literature. In the later period, when upward social mobility among knights ceased to be an important concern, attention turned to the question of whether the knight was successfully maintaining the style of life which marked his social superiority. And, as with Chaucer's Franklyn, that style of life came to be emulated by the middle class. As for the literary style, it preserved the power to verbalize and allay anxieties even when the nature of the anxieties changed. It expressed the yearning and longing which men feel, in love and out of it. It dwelt upon emotions of tenderness and feelings of exaltation, along with the reverse side of such emotions—frustration, disillusionment. It made into a fashion the ambivalence of these feelings, expressing them with conventional ironies—that the lover's desire was hot and cold, that the lady was his sweet foe, that love was sweet pain or a living death. It had often an ironic tone which rises from the conflict of Christian ascetical ideals with actual fleshly conduct—and it is not always easy to know where the poet's sympathies lie. For at the heart of courtly writings, even before Andreas' time, and surely as late as Chaucer's, lay the conflict of these social and sexual preoccupations with the ascetic strictures of the Church. To a large extent the literature of courtly love has as its central concern the contrariety between love, which is idealized, and the lust of the flesh, which is proscribed. From this point of view, courtly literature has always a certain ascetical undertone—there is always a warning voice to remind us that all is vanity. This is just as true, in the obverse way, of many ascetical writings, in which there is a soft but lively voice which signals the enticement of the thing forbidden.[37] And this "ironic" style is hardly illustrated better than by Petrarch's sonnet *S'amor non è*—which Chaucer translated and put into the mouth of Troilus:

> "If no love is, O God, what fele I so?
> And if love is, what thing and which is he?
> If love be good, from whennes cometh my woo?
> If it be wikke, a wonder thynketh me,
> When every torment and adversite
> That cometh of hym, may to me savory thinke,
> For ay thurst I, the more that ich it drynke.
>
> "And if that at myn owen lust I brenne,
> From whennes cometh my waillynge and my
> pleynte?

[37] Cf. Huizinga, pp. 140-143.

If harm agree me, wherto pleyne I thenne?
I noot, ne whi unwery that I feynte.
O quike deth, O swete harm so queynte,
How may of the in me swich quantite,
But if that I consente that it be?

"And if that I consente, I wrongfully
Compleyne, iwis. Thus possed to and fro,
Al sterelees withinne a boot am I
Amydde the see, bitwixen wyndes two,
That in contrarie stonden evere mo.
Allas! what is this wondre maladie?
For hete of cold, for cold of hete, I dye."
(1, 400-420)

This style expresses the curious relation between love
and religion that had been a feature of courtly writings
from the beginning. The lover had always used the arguments of religion to persuade the lady. The Church
taught that one should not love rank and riches; the
knight (who perhaps had neither in abundance) argued
that he was worthy for better reasons. "Lady, heed not
Rank nor Riches in your treatment of me," wrote
Aimeric de Peguilhan: "he who exalts and upholds the
humble gains thereby the favor of God and friends and
fair renown."[38] So humility, the chief of Christian
virtues, came to be the distinguishing virtue also of the
courtly suitor. Chastity, at least where "pure" love was
concerned, was incorporated into the courtly scheme:
"fin' amors," love and erotic play without consummation,
was the higher form of love, a means to growth in
virtue.[39] Obedience, one of the points of the monastic

[38] *The Poems of Aimeric de Peguilhan*, ed. and trans. William F.
Shepard and Frank M. Chambers (Evanston, Ill., 1950), pp. 158-
159.
[39] Denomy, "Fin' Amors," p. 175.

rule, became part of the rule for lovers: the lover is the lady's "servant" and performs her whims. Like a monk, he lives in poverty, he fasts, even prays.[40] As in the *Roman de la rose*, courtly love built up a system of corresponding virtues and vices patterned on that of Christianity, with the lover placed in the role of worshiper and penitent. The setting and outward circumstances of love, too, often coincide with those of religion. The initial meeting may occur in a church, as in the *Filostrato* and the *Troilus*—not only because that was the most central and likely meeting place in medieval society[41] but because it was the locus of great spiritual experiences, of conversions.

This relationship of love to Christian morality is what distinguishes various styles of courtly literature. On one end of the spectrum stands Dante, in whose work love is totally idealized and merged with Christianity in its highest eschatological and ascetical aspects, the lady becoming symbolic of the very end of Christian life itself. At the other extreme, as in the *Flamenca* or the *Council of Love at Remiremont*, fleshly love is treated with broad humor and its incompatibility with the Christian life is flaunted. Between these extremes, with inevitable overlapping, love may be idealized and made compatible with Christian marriage, as in *Parzifal* or in all of Chrétien except the *Lancelot*.[42] Or it may be treated, as in the *De amore*, ambiguously and equivocally—praised and

[40] Moller, "Meaning of Courtly Love," pp. 41-43, suggests that the lady is a mother-figure, and that the hunger and fasting of the lover are a regression to the infantile identification of love and food. But it is surely indebted as well to the ascetic tradition, in which fasting was a frequent practice.

[41] See Griffin and Myrick, p. 15.

[42] See Tom Peete Cross and William Albert Nitze, *Lancelot and Guenevere: A Study on the Origins of Courtly Love* (Chicago, 1930), p. 67.

idealized, and yet shown to be dissatisfying and imperfect. Finally, it may be treated, with various degrees of irony, as something which exists in a non-Christian, "natural" world.[43] Into this last mold, more than any other, falls the *Troilus*. The lover's story may follow the pattern of the Christian life, but in a "natural" world where he seeks a pseudo-grace in a pseudo-Christian system. *Yvain* is a good example. Here, the knight finds in the forest a spring, with an iron basin hanging over it, beside it a stone. He is led to it by a monster, and he marvels "how Nature had ever been able to form such a hideous, ugly creature"; the spring is "shadowed by the fairest tree that ever Nature formed,"[44] its foliage green even in winter. When the knight pours water from the spring onto the stone, using the basin, there follows a terrible storm, after which the birds perch upon the tree and sing. There appears then a knight, whom he slays. This knight was the husband of the lady in the castle; and with her, on first sight, Yvain falls in love. After a certain hesitancy, she consents to marry her husband's slayer, because she needs protection: "Would you dare to undertake the defense of my spring for love of me?" she asks.[45] Of this strange narrative some would say, no doubt, that the motif of the spring is at base a fertility rite, the spring a womb-symbol, the situation conspicuously Oedipal. Yet the real point is that this rite would have suggested to the medieval Christian the baptismal rite itself—the water poured, as in baptism, from a metal receptacle, but upon

[43] On this last tradition, see the excellent treatment by Aldo D. Scaglione, *Nature and Love in the Late Middle Ages* (Berkeley and Los Angeles, 1963), esp. pp. 14-23.

[44] Chrétien de Troyes, *Arthurian Romances*, trans. and ed. W. W. Comfort (Everyman ed., 1958), pp. 190, 185. Other quotations are from this translation.

[45] p. 206.

a stone! The rite is in effect a pseudo-baptism which calls forth not the channels of Grace but the unleashed forces of Nature; it brings about the knight's entrance into a natural world where Love has the power to replace established social relationships, a world in which high-born husbands may be slain and the widows married forthwith, in which lions can be tamed and bodies exist without hearts.[46] Yvain then "sins" by staying at the tournament more than the year which the lady has allowed, is accused of "stealing" her heart; by suffering and knightly deeds he does a kind of penance and, on his knees, receives at length her absolution. "Lady," he says in the final scene, "one ought to have mercy on a sinner. I have had to pay, and dearly to pay, for my mad act. It was madness that made me stay away, and I now admit my guilt and sin. I have been bold, indeed, in daring to present myself to you; but if you will deign to keep me now, I never again shall do you any wrong." In this one sees precisely the requirements of penance: a confession of the wrong, a satisfaction through penitential acts, and an intention of amendment. But, in the anti-world of courtly love, the sinner is restored to the good graces of the lady rather than the Church; his hope is in this world rather than the next. "Lady," cries Yvain ambiguously, "so truly as God in this mortal life could not otherwise restore me to happiness, so may the Holy Spirit bless me five hundred times."[47]

Thus, while it is *not* true that every tale of love is an allegory on the doctrine of charity, it *is* true that in almost every line courtly writings of this "naturalistic" kind could—to the reader inclined to catch the implication—accuse and discredit love by the very violence of

[46] p. 214. On the allegory of the body and the heart, see Lewis, p. 31.

[47] pp. 268-269.

their dissociation from the most basic Christian doctrines. That was the most startling subject of fantasy in the courtly tradition—that there could be a Christianity of this World, a heaven on earth, human love for divine. The very enormity of it is what accounts for its appeal as fantasy. It could be taken seriously as a lovely game; it could be enjoyed as ironic badinage; it could be the subject of great poems; but it could never be believed in the way that the articles of the creed or the miracles of the saints were believed. It was in another and inferior realm.

3. THE LUST OF THE FLESH
   IN THE *TROILUS*

In Christianity one could fulfill all the requirements of a lower grade of perfection and still aspire to a higher one. That was the style of Christian morality. And it was the style of courtly love. Only, the grade in which love operated posited a world where nature was good and the objects of natural affections stable. That, of course, ran counter to the most fundamental medieval doctrine—that the natural order was corrupt and transitory, that the World and the things of the World were not to be loved but scorned. Hence love, at least in this naturalistic tradition, was doomed to failure: there was, as Andreas said in his last book, a whole order of reality higher and truer than the one in which love operated, and a man could never enter upon that order so long as he remained in the service of Love. The entire structure of courtly love hung upon the tender thread of an "if"— *if* it were legitimate to love an unstable object in a transitory World, *if* it were not infinitely more important to turn one's thoughts to God. Courtly love in its adulterous form could exist only in a fantasy world where Christianity did not warn men against the love of the

World; and even at that, only where Fortune did not remove its objects. Hence, in the *Filostrato* and the *Troilus*, the setting is in pre-Christian times, and, at least in Chaucer, love is often described in religious language, some of which normally applies to sin.

The love of Troilus and Criseyde takes place in the ancient world, before man gained the benefits of the Incarnation and Resurrection. Of this the medieval reader would have been acutely aware. C. S. Lewis has demonstrated how Chaucer added to the *Filostrato* a great deal of "historial" detail in order to make the story fade into its surroundings as part of the matter of Troy.[48] This "historial" treatment created an atmosphere which would have struck the fourteenth-century reader as distant, strange, perhaps shocking.[49] He would have understood himself to be in another world whose people had none of the benefits which he as a Christian had: they had not been adequately warned against the transitoriness of worldly things, had not been informed of the salvation possible to them in a life beyond; they had neither the sacraments of the Church nor the advantage of the Jews in the "old dispensation." They were "natural" men, therefore, under natural law, and their only chance of heavenly reward lay in using well the vestige of reason left to all men after the Fall. If

[48] C. S. Lewis, "What Chaucer Really Did to *Il Filostrato*," *E&S*, XVII (1931), 59-61. See also George Lyman Kittredge, "Chaucer's Lollius," *HSCP*, XXVIII (1917), 49-54.

[49] The point is discussed at length in John S. P. Tatlock, "The Epilog of Chaucer's *Troilus*," *MP*, XVIII (1921), 640-658. It is not necessary to accept Tatlock's thesis that this historicity is characteristic of the Renaissance and that the epilogue is a return from the Renaissance to the Middle Ages. Lewis, "What Chaucer Really Did to *Il Filostrato*," pp. 59-60, shows that this historicity would have held interest for Chaucer's audience as a "new bit of the Troy story" or even a "new bit of the matter of Rome."

through it they could attain righteousness, they could be saved among the "virtuous heathen,"[50] though their chances, it must have been felt, were *de minimis*.

Courtly love in the *Troilus* is, then, placed in a world where Christianity could have no effect upon the moral choices of people. This fact, however, while it affects the setting and atmosphere of the poem, does not alter the picture of courtly love in any way. The love of Troilus and Criseyde proceeds exactly according to the tradition as we find it in Chrétien, Andreas, and the *Roman de la rose*:[51] the God of Love is irresistible (1, 237-238) and conquers Troilus for his pride (204-217). Troilus, like other lovers, suffers inner torments,

---

[50] On this doctrine, see A. E. Taylor, *The Christian Hope of Immortality* (New York, 1947), pp. 96-98. For a general treatment of the background of the idea and for further references, see T. P. Dunning, "Langland and the Salvation of the Heathen," *MA*, XII (1943), 45-54. What follows was written without the benefit of T. P. Dunning's "God and Man in *Troilus and Criseyde*," in Norman Davis and C. L. Wrenn, eds., *English and Medieval Studies Presented to J. R. R. Tolkein* . . . (London, 1962), pp. 164-182.

[51] Cf. Lewis' argument ("What Chaucer Really Did to *Il Filostrato*," pp. 58-59) that Chaucer was "groping back, unknowingly, through the very slightly medieval work of Boccaccio, to the genuinely medieval formula of Chrestien." For Chaucer's indebtedness to the French tradition, see Charles Muscatine, *Chaucer and the French Tradition: A Study in Style and Meaning* (Berkeley and Los Angeles, 1960), esp. pp. 124-132. For a detailed demonstration of the characteristics of courtly love as they exist in the *Troilus*, see Alexander J. Denomy, "The Two Moralities of Chaucer's *Troilus and Criseyde*," *TRSC*, XLIV, ser. 3, sec. 2 (June 1950), 35-46. For comments on the manner in which Chaucer refines the sexuality of Boccaccio, see Karl Young, "Aspects of the Story of Troilus and Criseyde," *WSLL*, II (1918), 367-394. That Chaucer may have used a French adaptation of Boccaccio which itself makes the story more noble and courtly is argued by Robert A. Pratt, "Chaucer and *Le Roman de Troyle et de Criseida*," *SP*, LIII (1956), 509-539. Meech, pp. 165-177, shows physical and psychological symptoms of love in Troilus which are indebted to courtly tradition.

falls into despair, and wishes to die (519-553, 603-616). He attempts to conceal this woe (316-357), yet practices adoration and devotion to his lady (358-378). He suffers all of the usual symptoms—loss of color (441), sleeplessness (484), sighs and groans (360, 724), tears (543), and fainting (III, 1092). He takes advantage of a go-between, arranges first to see the lady, keeps a respectful silence and distance, and after a due period attains consummation of the affair, always observing the utmost secrecy. It is understood that marriage is not the object. This love is seen, moreover, to have an ennobling effect on him: he is fiercer in arms (I, 470-476), fights better, is friendlier, politer, and more generous—in fact is improved in all virtues (I, 1072-1085, III, 1772-1806), and wins reputation and renown for this excellence (III, 1716-1729). All this is the effect of love; for though he is "unworthy" he knows that he can improve through "heigh servyse" (1286-1288)—and he does. Troilus, because he is purer, gentler, more hesitant and more spiritual than other courtly lovers, seems less real. There is a nuance of irony in this portrait of Troilus as courtly lover: Pandarus and the narrator, as they view his conduct, point up what is extravagant and idealized in the courtly code—they acknowledge and assuage our incredulity.[52] Nonetheless, as Alfred David has shown, Troilus is the hero of the poem; we are expected to sympathize with him; and Chaucer has endowed him with qualities of honor, compassion, humor, and intelligence which make our sympathy feasible.[53]

Chaucer has therefore taken courtly love in its most traditional, most idealized form and depicted it *as though* it were part of the customs and religion of the ancient

[52] Muscatine, pp. 137-138.

[53] Alfred David, "The Hero of the *Troilus*," *Speculum*, XXXVII (1962), 566-581. See also Meech, pp. 402-410.

world. Surely it *was* pagan in its way, with its vows and
rites, and all its talk of Venus and Cupid. At the same
time this passionate, romantic love, occurring against the
smoky background of a doomed city, is recounted to a
Christian audience by a Christian narrator. We are
therefore, in the *Troilus*, at once in two worlds. One
is the world of the present, in which the narrator, a
bookish fellow with no first-hand experience of love, is
telling us an ancient tale gleaned from an unknown
"authority" named Lollius. The other is the world of
the distant past, strange and unreal with all its pagan
ways, its temples and gods, its language—even its lore
of a city, Thebes, as old again as Troy is to us. The
narrator moves us sometimes close to the "inner" story
so that we see things happening one by one as if we were
on the scene, and yet at other times draws us away, reminding us of the present moment, of the predestined
doom of the city which *we* know through hindsight, and
of the historical sweep and continuity which linked the
fall of Troy to the founding of the West.[54]

As he tells us his story, the narrator in some sense
leads the reader in the right reactions to it—he is fearful
for Troilus, expectant and hopeful of the blossoming
love, envious and overexcited at the consummation, woe-
begone at the hero's betrayal.[55] Only, *he* has read Lollius
and already knows the outcome. And he has warned us
of that outcome from the beginning: the "double sorwe
of Troilus" is his theme, and he twice tells us that those
two sorrows are Troilus' woe in love and his loss of
love's joy (i, 1-5)—they are the sorrows "Of Troilus in

[54] Morton W. Bloomfield, "Distance and Predestination in *Troilus
and Criseyde*," *PMLA*, LXXII (1957), 14-26.
[55] See Robert M. Jordan, "The Narrator in Chaucer's *Troilus*,"
ELH, XXV (1958), 237-257.

lovynge of Criseyde, / And how that she forsook hym er she deyde" (55-56). From this and the subsequent story, with all its references to Fortune, the Christian audience would have had no trouble in drawing the moral that worldly loves, being transitory and unstable, deserve to be scorned. In this, too, the narrator reacts as the audience is expected to react. He is at the beginning the servant of the servants of Love, who, for his "un-liklynesse," will only write of lovers' woes and pray for those who serve Love. He is sad, at the beginning, but his spirits revive as he gets further into his story. Only at the end does he learn from it that the Christian view of love is best. But just as long as he draws us away from the present and gets us involved in the love story, we remain in ignorance of its moral meaning. We are made to take the short view, to suspend our knowledge of the outcome.[56] For this reason the past, as we draw close to it, becomes like the present in the only way that present time really differs from the past: its future becomes unforeseeable. And just as the past comes to take on the immediacy and unpredictability of the here and now, its "pagan" customs turn out to be nothing more than the conventional courtly ones of the poet's age.

Hence the picture of ancient Troy is a kind of mirror image of Chaucer's own world, strange but familiar, lost in the past but rooted in the present. This blurring of the pastness of things accounts for the element of anachronism in the poem, and this we must pause to examine. There are, I think, three species of anachronism, and although in the poem they intermingle, we shall do best to pluck them apart for examination.

[56] That the narrator learns from his own story is a point made by Bloomfield, "Distance and Predestination," pp. 20-21, and Muscatine, p. 161. On the "multiconsciousness" required of the reader, see Muscatine, pp. 132-133.

Troilus and Criseyde

(1) Courtly love of the French school full grown in ancient Troy is of course a deliberate anachronism. It corresponds to Boccaccio's device of placing his own love for Maria d'Aquino among the Trojans. This is in no sense unfamiliar as a rhetorical device in literature—it is why Swift took Gulliver to strange lands and why Spenser placed *The Faerie Queene* in the long ago and far away. And Chaucer used the device elsewhere.[57] What he has done in the *Troilus* is to replace Boccaccio's autobiographical and personal motives with general and ethical ones. He has turned a *roman à clef* into a moral poem: Boccaccio in his conclusion shows that women (viz. Maria d'Aquino) are fickle; Chaucer shows that earthly loves are inferior to the love of God. That Chaucer really believed the ancients practiced love after the fashion of Eleanor of Aquitaine or Chrétien is out of the question, for he had too sophisticated a sense of history: "In sondry londes, sondry ben usages."[58] To his readers, however, the anachronism would not have seemed unreasonable: in all the literature of courtly love there was, as we have seen, a tacit admission that it was not appropriate to the Christian world. And in its "religion" of Venus and Cupid it did itself approach being an imaginative reconstruction of paganism.[59] Moreover, Chaucer knew Ovid and may well have seen the similarity between Ovidian and courtly *amor* better than he saw the difference. Besides, the Middle Ages was given to

[57] For example, in *The Book of The Duchess* and *The House of Fame* Chaucer used the device of a distant setting to dramatize a present application. Another use, though the point is debated, is in the Prioress's Tale: he changed the setting of his source to Asia, then at the end reminded his audience of the similar incident which had happened in England in the person of Sir Hugh of Lincoln.

[58] See Morton W. Bloomfield, "Chaucer's Sense of History," *JEGP*, LI (1952), 301-313.

[59] See Tatlock, pp. 646-659.

depicting ancient materials in modern dress—it allegorized Vergil and Ovid and turned the ancient gods into abstractions and planets. The procedure seems quaint to us when we find it in Chaucer or Shakespeare; we think less of it in a recent novel or film, where the modern element is easier to take for granted.

(2) Into this anachronistic courtly *amor* Chaucer injects the spirit, the doctrines, and the language of medieval Christianity. This is the "religion of love"—the familiar courtly practice of representing love as a pseudo-Church with pseudo-Christian dogmas, lore, and ritual.[60] At least twice Chaucer makes specific reference to Christian doctrines—once when he says of Fortune and the heavens that "under God ye ben oure hierdes" (III, 619), again when he says "What! God foryaf his deth" (1577). Elsewhere the Christian language is more metaphorical, for Chaucer obscures his (or his narrator's) Christianity until later in the poem.[61] Thus the narrator introduces himself as one who serves "the God of Loves servantz" (I, 15)—a phrase like that used of the Pope—who will advance his own soul best by praying for Love's servants and living in charity (47-49). He opens with a liturgical bidding prayer,[62] asking the reader to pray for Troilus, himself, and all lovers. Similarly, referring to the God of Love, he uses the language of the *gloria patri* (245).

Hence much of the information which we get from the Christian narrator about the characters, and even some of their speeches, echo Christian language. We are told that Troilus' sin against the God of Love is pride

[60] See Lewis, *Allegory of Love*, pp. 18-22; and Meech, pp. 262-270.

[61] Bloomfield, "Distance and Predestination," pp. 19-20 and n. 7.

[62] See Robinson, p. 814, note to lines 15 ff.

(210-217, 225, 230), which Troilus repents (318). Troilus seems to refer to Criseyde as a god (276), and hopes for "grace" (370) and pity (460). When Pandarus observes his conduct he jokingly suggests that he has fallen into "attricion"[63] and "holiness" (554-560). Later, in describing love, Pandarus uses the figure of a conversion from heresy "Thorugh grace of God" (1002-1008). And in Troilus' conversations with Pandarus in Books I and II there is an elaborate parallel with the Christian confessional, including the phrase *mea culpa* (II, 525), a prayer for forgiveness (526-539), and directions from Pandarus as priest for an act of contrition (I, 932-935).[64] In Book II we learn that Troilus is to be saved by faith (1503), and in Book III he is to attain the bliss of Heaven.[65] One could go on piling up such examples, but it would be pointless. Of those given more than half are original with Chaucer, and in many cases, as with the bidding prayer,[66] he has taken a tiny hint from Boccaccio and developed it at length. There is a great deal more of this Christian language in the first three books, while the love affair progresses; in the last two it is replaced in part by the frequent references to Fortune.

Chaucer used this Christian language, I am convinced, in full consciousness for an artistic purpose: while he presents his story of earthly love as something erotic, and beautiful, he wants to keep us in mind of the Christian ethos by which it is finally to be judged. Exactly as he asks us to suspend the present and regard the past, he

[63] See Robinson, p. 816 n. 557. The term had a technical sense in theology.

[64] Arthur E. Hutson, "Troilus' Confession," *MLN*, LXIX (1954), 468-470.

[65] See III, 704, 1204, 1251, 1322.

[66] See Lewis, "What Chaucer Really Did to *Il Filostrato*," pp. 66-68.

asks us to suspend our Christian strictures and be taken up with a "pagan" religion. Yet that pagan religion, as it turns out, is the courtly mode of the fourteenth century, and it is presented in an unremittingly Christian mold.

(3) There are other anachronisms which are not necessarily connected with the "religion of love" and probably not used consciously for any artistic purpose.[67] In part they simply involve proverbial language; Chaucer himself remarks that

> . . . in forme of speche is chaunge
> Withinne a thousand yeer, and wordes tho
> That hadden pris, now wonder nyce and straunge
> Us thinketh hem, and yet thei spake hem so.
>
> (II, 22-25)

It is exactly this *linguistic* difference between past and present which makes some amount of anachronism unavoidable. In dealing with former times the artist, like the historian, must talk about "prime ministers," "secret police," "tax collectors," and so on, even though such phrases bring with them modern attitudes and meanings; the alternative is to fill one's pages with foreign words. The same problem arises when the artist would show the everyday life of his characters or the way they talked. It is not especially strange, for example, that Criseyde and her ladies hear the tale of Thebes in what seems very much like a fourteenth-century scene (II, 82-84). By the same token it should not distress us that Pandarus uses clichés like "the devel have his bones" (I, 805) or "Fy on the devel" (II, 1737).

---

[67] For an instance of this unconscious anachronism, see H. M. Smyser, "The Domestic Background of *Troilus and Criseyde*," *Speculum*, XXXI (1956), 297-315. For anachronistic details about the setting, see Meech, pp. 195-196 and n. 46.

This unavoidable anachronism—what we might call "narrative anachronism"—is present throughout the *Troilus*. Since the tale is being told to a contemporary audience and is presented as an adaptation or translation of "Lollius," the reader should not be surprised to see some features of the ancient world translated into modern terms. We hear references to a relic (I, 153), heavenly love (979), saints' lives (II, 118), saints in heaven and fiends in hell (894-896), a bishop (104), the monastic life (759), the tonsure of monks (IV, 996), and the doctrine of accident and substance (1505). Some of this comes from the speeches of the characters, but there is nothing so surprising as to destroy the illusion of history—if anything it would have made the Trojan characters seem credible and familiar. That Chaucer puts into their mouths many references to a singular God may be taken as conventional or proverbial and not necessarily Christian. The line "As wisly verray God my soule save" (III, 1501) seems specifically Christian, but it should be taken for an everyday colloquialism, not a confession of faith—as when Unitarian ladies cry "Saints preserve us!" The most startling anachronism in the speech of a character, Criseyde's line "that God that bought us bothe two" (1165), is very probably a misreading for "wrought."[68]

On the whole Chaucer's method of referring to deities is characterized by Troilus' prayer which begins,

> . . . O Love, O Charite!
> Thi moder ek, Citherea the swete,
> After thiself next heried be she,
> Venus mene I, the wel-willy planete!
> (III, 1254-1257)

The invocation to pagan gods here *sounds* like the Chris-

[68] The reading "wrought" is given in Root's edition.

tian liturgy; God is love, two persons of God are invoked, the mother of God is mentioned. At the same time the god is love in an earthly sense, and his mother is Venus, associated in the medieval mind, as in the modern one, with fleshly love. She is identified, however, as a planet, which would have suited the medieval attitude to pagan deities. And the invocation of Charity, which has such a specific sense in Christian thought, has a certain ironic force: the pagan Troilus invokes "Charity" as he practices its opposite, cupidity.[69] The shock to the medieval reader would have enhanced his sense of the starkness, and wrongness, of the pagan faith; but because of its historical distance this picture of paganism would, I believe, have caused him to read the poem rather with curiosity and interest than with a sense of moral outrage.

This was Chaucer's technique for making the ancient world familiar enough to be credible but strange enough to seem distant. It is the problem of every imaginative writer who would treat events of ancient times and distant places. Chaucer solves it by making his characters most like his audience, presenting them most anachronistically, in those moments when his readers should empathize with them. Hence they are most like Chaucer's contemporaries in the first three books; in the last two they become more distant and foreign—there is less talk of familiar Christian notions and more talk of the pagan goddess Fortune. Even Troilus, with whom we are sympathetic till the end, becomes distant from us as he is removed from boudoir to battlefield. For this reason, in the earlier part the complicated process of

[69] Meech, pp. 204-207, 215-226, shows how Chaucer has added more "ancient" details about paganism and especially pagan gods, but has at the same time made such details anachronistic by using Christian language.

falling in love, with all its doubts and decisions, is described in terms of medieval psychology, i.e., in the terms used to describe the process of making moral choices. This is something which Mr. Robertson has shown, and it is an exceedingly important point.[70] Because Troilus and Criseyde seem to experience suggestion, delectation, and consent, they seem to be presented as sinners. From a strictly Christian point of view they *are* sinners; or at any rate Chaucer is clearly *not* recommending similar extramarital adventures to his Christian audience. But Robertson always speaks as though Chaucer wrote the *Troilus* with a library of exegetes and moralists at his elbow: Troilus is a lecher, Cupid is Satan, Pandarus a priest of Satan, Venus the goddess of lechery. Hence he represents Chaucer as taking throughout a harsh and disapproving, what we should now call a "puritanical," tone. But Chaucer was at pains to create a narrator as a vehicle for the tone, and that narrator is disingenuously sympathetic, interested in the love affair, and moved by its outcome; in the epilogue, where Chaucer's own attitude is apparent, the tone is far from harsh

[70] D. W. Robertson, Jr., "Chaucerian Tragedy," *ELH*, XIX (1952), 1-37, esp. pp. 8-11. Robertson intentionally exaggerates the "ironic" side of the poem. On p. 13 he says that Chaucer maintains "a sympathetic attitude on the surface, referring at times to his sources or pretended sources for confirmation, or calling attention to the antiquity of his subject. But this sympathy is tempered by a consistent irony. Since critical discussions of the poem sometimes carry the sympathetic attitude to an almost sentimental extreme, the present essay emphasizes the irony, not, however, with the implication that the sympathy does not exist." This should be kept in mind during my comments which follow. Robertson seems to feel, but perhaps does not mean to imply, that Chaucer had a single and explicit moral purpose in writing the *Troilus*. Many details which he uses to indicate this may be found in Boccaccio, but it is not clear whether he thinks Boccaccio had a similar moral purpose. For another treatment of the *Troilus*, drawn chiefly from the above, see Robertson, *A Preface to Chaucer*, pp. 472-503.

or puritanical. If *Troilus and Criseyde* is anything more than a chessboard of scriptural allegories designed to teach a moral lesson, then the psychological language of Christian morality is used in it not *primarily* to depict Troilus and Criseyde as sinners (though the implication may be found); it is used because it was the only psychological explanation which the Middle Ages had for demonstrating a moral act.[71]

The point is important because Boccaccio, while he also used a pattern like suggestion-delectation-consent, did *not* represent falling in love as a moral act. His Troilo does not hesitate once Pandaro has offered to fix things up; his Criseida hesitates only because she is worried about the suitor's sincerity and her own reputation—and that not for long. All of Pandarus' persuading and urging is considerably expanded in Chaucer's treatment; in Boccaccio, Troilo needs only a bit of friendly reassurance, and Criseida needs only reassurance and a promise of secrecy. From this point of view Boccaccio's Criseida is much closer to the medieval anti-feminist picture of womanhood: she is passion's slave, where Chaucer's heroine is a rational creature. Hence Pandaro's *carpe diem* argument hits the mark at once in the Italian work. When Pandaro warns her, "Non perder tempo, pensa che vecchiezza, / O morte, torrà via la tua bellezza," she replies, "Oimè, . . . tu di' vero, / Così ci portan gli anni a poco a poco" (ii, 54, 55). In Chaucer, confronted with the same argument, Criseyde beats her breast and cries, "Allas, for wo! Why nere I deed?" (ii, 409)—and reminds Pandarus that he, her best friend, ought to dissuade, to forbid her from love. The speech is based on a similar one in the *Filostrato*, spoken when Criseida learns it is Troilo who loves her;

[71] Cf. John Speirs, *Chaucer the Maker* (London, 1951), p. 66.

it is what people call defensive. Chaucer, with characteristic insight, puts the speech at the moment when Criseyde is most threatened—not when she learns who
loves her but when she senses her own desire for love.
To Boccaccio physical desires are taken for granted and
the decision to proceed with the affair is a matter of
arranging the circumstances—"hot desire" is his theme.
Chaucer mitigates this and substitutes the idealized love
of the French tradition. With infinitely greater perception, Chaucer understood that desires are ambivalent—
are "hot and cold"; and he recognized the role that
the unconscious plays in making decisions. Hence he
depicts moral choice not as a single occurrence of suggestion, delectation, and consent, but as a recurring
process in which a possible action is consented to little
by little, each consent bringing in new and further
suggestions.[72]

With Troilus, consent to *love* Criseyde, which comes
almost at once, causes desires to increase in him "like
fire"; then, at Pandarus' urging, he consents to *act* upon
his love. Troilus' pride against the God of Love suggests
the Christian notion that pride goes before a fall; and of
course the hero's fall is at once foreshadowed in the
narrator's apostrophe, "O blynde world, O blynde en-
tencioun!" (1, 211). But the actual suggestion comes
with his first sight of her—through the eyes, as sin was
often said to come.[73] "O mercy, God," he cries; and we

[72] The gradual process in which the sinner involves himself is not
unfamiliar to Christian writings. St. Augustine described the manner
in which sin increases desires, so that desires increase sin. On the
background of this idea, see Alfred L. Kellogg, "An Augustinian Interpretation of Chaucer's Pardoner," *Speculum*, XXVI (1951), 465-
469. See St. Augustine, *Enarr. in Ps. LVII*, 19-20 (PL 36:688), *De
civ. Dei*, XXI, 9, and *Sermo CLI*, 8 (PL 38:814-819).

[73] See Robertson, "Chaucerian Tragedy," 14-15; and Griffin and
Myrick, pp. 94-95.

are told that he hardly knew "how to loke or wynke" (301). It is the mental impression of her beauty that now holds him and enlivens his desires, a state very like "delectation":

> And of hire look in him ther gan to quyken
> So gret desir and such affeccioun,
> That in his hertes botme gan to stiken
> Of hir his fixe and depe impressioun. (295-298)

Love has converted him (308), and he repents that he had made fun of Love's folk (318-319). Returning home, he considers how much he ought to speak or hold in, and decides (it would have been taken seriously in the fourteenth century) to begin at once on a song. By this time he has consented with full determination, "For with good hope he gan fully assente / Criseyde for to love, *and nought repente*" (391-392—italics mine).

In what follows, we are shown how, after this act of consent, desire increases in him and makes him liable to Pandarus' arguments. The song itself, translated from Petrarch's *S'amor non è*, makes the point at once: "For ay thurst I, the more that ich it drynke."[74] Like many of Petrarch's sonnets, the language echoes that of moral theology:

> And if that at myn owen lust I brenne,
> From whennes cometh my waillynge and my
> > pleynte?
>
> . . . .
>
> How may of the in me swich quantite,
> But if that I consente that it be? (406-413)

---

[74] This line, and in general the fact that Troilus' desire increases, were used in the anonymous fifteenth-century *"Disce more"* to illustrate fleshly love. See Willis Wager, " 'Fleshly Love' in Chaucer's *Troilus*," *MLR*, XXXIV (1939), 62-66. Robertson, "Chaucerian Tragedy," p. 28, quotes Gérard of Liège on the point.

For it is his own consent to love which has brought upon him this "swete harm"; yet the sweetness of it keeps him from changing his mind. He is embarked upon an unknown sea, caught between his own hot desire and the cold indifference of the lady. Petrarch's famous image is supremely appropriate here to Troilus' plight:

> . . . Thus possed to and fro,
> Al sterelees withinne a boot am I
> Amydde the see, bitwixen wyndes two,
> That in contrarie stonden evere mo.
> Allas! what is this wondre maladie?
> For hete of cold, for cold of hete, I dye.
>
> (415-420)

Again and again in the lines which come after we are reminded of the sensual desire, the passion, burning within him: "So muche, day by day, his owene thought, / For lust to hire, gan quiken and encresse"; "And ay the ner he was, the more he brende" (442-448). Over and over it is described as a hot fire burning him, and it increases daily, spawning only more and more arguments that she should have compassion on him (465-468). Other fears leave him—"Both of th'assege and his savacioun" (464), a reference quite possibly to his safety,[75] but certainly with a strong moral overtone for any Christian reader. Hence at length he falls, as he confesses to Pandarus, into despair (605). Now all of this is the "religion of love," but it is still Christian language and still suggests Christian notions. In its single-mindedness, its burning and increasing, and in its self-torturing character, the love of Troilus is like the

[75] See Robinson, pp. 815-816 n. 464. In II, 486, the word is used with the same ambiguity.

Augustinian portrait of the sinner.[76] The pattern which Augustine describes, however, might apply to any moral act—the love of God had itself been described as burning and increasing.[77] For that matter, Boccaccio uses more images of heat and flame than Chaucer does[78] without ever implying that these desires are sinful. It is not necessary, therefore, to find in the passage a suggestion of sin. Rather it is the case that Troilus, because of an earthly love, finds himself amenable to the suggestion of Pandarus. That suggestion is made to seem so eminently sensible that we applaud Troilus' acceptance; only much later do we discover the falseness and uselessness of Pandarus' point of view. It is perhaps therefore only in retrospect that we make anything out of Pandarus' reference to "delight" and "reson":

> "No," quod tho Pandarus, "therefore I seye,
> Swych is delit of foles to bywepe
> Hire wo, but seken bote they ne kepe.
> Now knowe I that ther reson in the failleth.
> (761-764)

In the same way we do not at once perceive why it is significant, when Troilus repents at Pandarus' urging to

[76] On this tradition, see C. S. Lewis, *A Preface to Paradise Lost* (Galaxy ed., New York, 1961), pp. 66-81; and Kellogg, "An Augustinian Portrait," pp. 465-469. See also Donald R. Howard, "Milton's Satan and the Augustinian Tradition," in Allan Gilbert, ed., *Renaissance Papers* (Columbia, S.C., 1954), pp. 11-23. On the increase of Troilus' desire, see Meech, pp. 359-360.

[77] See Richard Rolle of Hampole, "The Love of God," as ed. in Mossé, *A Handbook of Middle English* (Baltimore, 1952), pp. 232-233. A number of verbal correspondences between the language used to describe the love of Troilus and that used by medieval mystical writers have been pointed out by Sister Mary Linus, O.P., in an unpublished essay.

[78] The point is demonstrated by Meech, pp. 346-363.

the God of Love (936), that he cries, "A, lord! I me consente."

With Criseyde, consent comes still more slowly and circuitously; her state of *delectatio* is subtler and lasts longer, and Pandarus must use a great deal more persuasion. Circumstance plays a greater role in her final acquiescence, and of course there is no initial arrow from Cupid and no stinging first sight of the lover. Rather, the initial suggestion comes from Pandarus. The scene occurs in May, and the opening lines, with the description of spring and the mention of the swallow's song, help prepare for the magnificent moment, later, when falling asleep she hears the nightingale's song of love.[79] When Pandarus arrives at her palace, she is listening to a maiden read a tale of Thebes—a legend as far in the past for her as her story is for us. The sense of history, of pastness, throughout the passage (the book opens with an invocation to Cleo) serves at once to underscore the romantic strangeness of the setting—"In sondry londes, sondry ben usages"—and to bring us up close to their world, to immerse us in it.

Pandarus' technique of persuasion in the scene is so familiar to all readers of the poem that there is scarcely any need to describe it in detail. Each suggestion, each joke, each subtly placed argument helps manipulate Criseyde into a receptive frame of mind. The passage (II, 97-385) is almost entirely original with Chaucer, and part of its effect is to draw the reader into Criseyde's thought and feelings, to make the reader experience the flood of suggestions directed at her and the cautious defense she sustains against them. Pandarus begins by ask-

[79] See Charles A. Owen, Jr., "Significance of a Day in *Troilus and Criseyde*," *MS*, XXII (1960), 366-370. Owen shows how the nightingale's song, echoing the earlier one, sounds a faint note of warning (p. 369).

ing whether the tale they are hearing is not one of love—"O, som good ye me leere!"—and she parries with, "Uncle, . . . youre maistresse is nat here." He good humoredly suggests that she throw off her widow's "barbe"; "lat us don to May som observaunce," he cries, but she answers, "God forbede! . . . be ye mad?" In reply he teases her with the promise of some good news, five times better than the end of the siege, but will not tell it. In the course of the varied talk which ensues, he praises—as if by the by—all the good qualities of Troilus in great detail, then concludes his encomium, as if bored, with "I wol gon henne." She bids him stay, to speak of wisdom, and the others give them privacy. And now Pandarus, in full earnest, advises her to end her mourning—dropping a passing reference to the fair "adventure" in store for her. She begs to know it, but he puts her off. Looking deep into her face he says "On swich a mirour goode grace!" which increases her curiosity further. He then launches into a philosophical discourse, the effect of which is that some "goodly aventure" is shaped for everyone at some time or other, but that one must be able to take advantage of the moment: "Cache it anon, lest aventure slake!" To allay her fears, he vows that he would never bring such a tale if it could do her harm. And now he is ready to tell her his news. In doing so, Pandarus cleverly associates Troilus with himself ("But if ye late hym deyen, I wol sterve—"), bursts magnificently into tears, makes a noble apostrophe against lack of pity, adds an avowal of his regard for her honor—"I am thyn em," he protests—and closes dramatically,

> But alwey, goode nece, to stynte his woo,
> So lat youre daunger sucred ben a lite,
> That of his deth ye be naught for to wite.

The whole passage is so intensely persuasive that it is somewhat anticlimactic, and funny, when Criseyde says to herself, "I shal felen what he meneth, ywis." Her reaction, which springs out of the fear and hesitancy we have seen in her from the beginning, marks the difference between Chaucer's treatment and Boccaccio's; in Chaucer she is genuinely shocked, and distressed, that her uncle (an older man, not a cousin and a contemporary, as in the *Filostrato*) should give her such counsel:

> ". . . Allas, for wo! Why nere I deed?
> For of this world the feyth is al agoon.
> Allas! what sholden straunge to me doon,
> When he, that for my beste frend I wende,
> Ret me to love, and sholde it me defende?"
> (409-413)

Pandarus, indignant, denies that he meant any harm or villainy and runs off to die, but she stops him. Now, she "wel neigh starf for feere"—she is the "ferfulleste wight / That myghte be" (449-451)—and out of her fear comes a certain pity for the "sorwful ernest of the knyght" and a cautious awareness that "It nedeth me ful sleighly for to pleie." It is here that she makes a choice. She agrees, with heavy conditions, to *be nice* to Troilus:

> But that I nyl nat holden hym in honde;
> Ne love a man ne kan I naught, ne may,
> Ayeins my wyl; but elles wol I fonde,
> Myn honour sauf, plese hym fro day to day.
> (477-480)

In deciding this she is, as she proclaims, constraining her heart against her "lust" (476).

The passage which follows is a detailed psychological analysis of the aftermath of her decision. Having given in, having made up her mind, she betrays a flush of

interest in Troilus, a flush of eagerness at the prospect
of a liaison. This is consistent with the theological principle that one wrong choice leads to others, that error
weakens the will; but such theological principles are
themselves based on the soundest observations of human
psychology. My point is that the emphasis in the passage
is not on any moral lesson about the inception of wrongdoing, but on the human response of a complicated and
interesting character. Having given the most cautious
and circumscribed consent, she begins to take delight in
the idea. Chaucer seems to have understood that while
delectation precedes consent, each act of consent is itself
a kind of auto-suggestion which leads to new delecta-
tions. "O good em," says Criseyde,

> "Tel me how first ye wisten of his wo.
> Woot noon of it but ye?"—He seyde, "No."—
> "Kan he wel speke of love?" quod she; "I preye
> Tel me, for I the bet me shal purveye." (499-504)

Then, expanding a few lines in Boccaccio, Chaucer
undertakes to explore her thoughts. She goes to her
closet, sits down as still as a stone, and reviews every
word in her mind. She assures herself that a man can
love a woman until his heart breaks "And she naught
love ayein, but if hire leste" (609)—the phrase of course
gets to the heart of the matter better than she knows.
Now, from outside, there is a shout, the people proclaim
Troilus in the streets, and looking out she sees him
riding from battle; she is so struck with the sight of him
that she turns red, says to herself "Who yaf me
drynke?"—and pulls her head in the window at once.
Chaucer takes pains to remind us here that it was no
sudden love, but had come upon her little by little.[80]

[80] Lines 666-679. Joseph A. Longo, "The Double Time Scheme

And to show her indecision further, he adds, from his "auctor," her long soliloquy (701-808): She tells herself first that it will be an honor to deal—*in honesty*—with so great a warrior; he is her king's son, and if she should avoid him he might have her in despite. She reminds herself of a sound ancient principle, that there is measure in all things. And he is, after all, an honorable man. She *is* beautiful, and young, she says, and she is her own woman; he loves her, and there is no reason why she should not love him if she wants to—keeping always her honor and name. But then some fearful thoughts shake her resolve. She will sacrifice her security and liberty if she loves, for always "som cloude is over that sonne"; and there is the danger of gossip, the natural malice of people; and men are untrue and often betray women. She does not really give an answer to these doubts. They come to the fore, they terrify her; and then her thoughts clear. She is still in doubt—"now hoot, now cold"—but her last words to herself, the last reassurance that she gives herself, echoes Pandarus' argument and his whole view of life: "He which that nothing undertaketh, / Nothyng n'acheveth, be hym looth or deere."

Here Chaucer leaves her thoughts and turns his attention to her feelings. The passage is great for its power to call forth in the reader Criseyde's frame of mind by implication rather than through explicit statement or soliloquy. A flood of impressions pours in upon her. She goes out in the yard. It is shadowed with blossoming green boughs. Her women are there, and she walks about with them. At length Antigone sings a song. The

---

in Book II of Chaucer's *Troilus and Criseyde*," *MLQ*, XXII (1961), 37-40, shows how Chaucer has used a longer indeterminate time span in Book II in order to emphasize how slowly Criseyde makes up her mind.

song tells of a maiden's infinite joy in love, despite the
ways envious folk defame it.[81] In answer to Criseyde's
question, Antigone says the song was made by the good-
liest maid of great estate in all Troy, who "let hire lif
in moste honour and joye." Criseyde sighs and asks if
there is such bliss among lovers. "Ye, wis," is the answer—no one who has ever lived can describe its bliss
but those who have known it. Criseyde replies that it
will be night soon—but she has taken note of everything,

> And ay gan love hire lasse for t'agaste
> Than it dide erst, and synken in hire herte,
> That she wex somwhat able to converte.

She goes to bed, and when all is quiet she lies still and
thinks of all that has happened. She hears a nightingale
under her window.

> A nyghtyngale, upon a cedir grene,
> Under the chambre wal ther as she ley,
> Ful loude song ayein the moone shene,
> Peraunter, in his briddes wise, a lay
> Of love, that made hire herte fressh and gay.
> That herkned she so longe in good entente,
> Til at the laste the dede slep hire hente.
>
> (918-924)

And it is really at this point that she is resolved to love.
What comes after, everyone knows. The letters, the
interview, the patient maneuvering of Pandarus, the
smoky rain, the dark chamber, the exchange of rings,
the final moment of consummation—all of it so circumstantial that one cannot imagine it otherwise, so inevita-

[81] Sister Mary Charlotte Borthwick, "Antigone's Song as 'Mirour'
in Chaucer's *Troilus and Criseyde*," *MLQ*, XXII (1961), 227-235,
shows how Antigone's song mirrors courtly love as opposed to
heavenly love and answers the objections of Criseyde in lines 771-805.

ble that one can hardly find any point where Criseyde
rationally and explicitly consents to the affair. Things
just seem to happen. But they would not happen thus if
she had not succumbed to love at first: as she embraces
Troilus she says, "Ne hadde I er now, my swete herte
deere, / Ben yold, ywis, I were now nought heere!"
What Chaucer shows is the fact—as we should now state
it—that such moral choices are prepared for, and finally
take place, not in our reasonable, verbalized thoughts,
but in less conscious ones. That is why the scene ends,
strikingly, in her dreams:

> And as she slep, anonright tho hire mette
> How that an egle, fethered whit as bon,
> Under hire brest his longe clawes sette,
> And out hire herte he rente, and that anon,
> And dide his herte into hire brest to gon,
> Of which she nought agroos, ne nothyng smerte;
> And forth he fleigh, with herte left for herte.

*

I have dwelt on these scenes at such length because I
believe that the manner in which Chaucer *shows* us their
decisions to love indicates a great deal about his own
moral position. For one thing, it shows us that Troilus
and Criseyde *do* have free will, *do* make a choice in
favor of love which they could have resisted *if they had
any reason to*. Their choices are made, as most choices
are, by a slow emotive process which brings into play all
facets of the mental life. Pandarus dissuades them from
their hesitancies and reinforces their inmost desires until
at last they can transform urges into actions; their
readiness is all.[82]

[82] On free will in their decisions, see Willard Farnham, *The
Medieval Heritage of Elizabethan Tragedy* (reprinted Oxford,

In the second place, the scenes show us that there *is* psychological realism in the poem, added by Chaucer to the material of the *Filostrato*. Recently, in a reaction against the post-Victorian estimate of Chaucer as a psychological realist, critics have seen much of the behavioral detail as conventional to the style of medieval literature or as grounded in moral theology.[83] And what they say is right. But there is psychological realism all the same. Medieval stylistic conventions and Christian moral theology themselves had great psychological aptness—both reflected the sensibility of medieval men, and sensibility is an expression of the emotional life. Besides, they embodied ideals and interpretations of conduct which influenced people's behavior. The writer uses traditional styles and ideas to represent reality; but the conventional element with which tradition colors his work cannot be thought to blind him to the individual psychology of his contemporaries. As for that, much of what we call individual psychology is itself conventional. Whether or not we feel enthusiasm for Chaucer's psychological "insight," and whatever its provenance, Chaucer here shows us the thoughts, actions, and feelings of people as people behaved then and, to a considerable extent, behave now.

Lastly, the examination of this process has put out of mind, for me at least, the possibility that Chaucer depicted the decision to love—either of Criseyde or of Troilus—*merely* in the terms of suggestion, delectation,

---

1956), pp. 145-147; James Lyndon Shanley, "The *Troilus* and Christian Love," *ELH*, VI (1939), 271-281; Howard R. Patch, "Troilus on Determinism," *Speculum*, VI (1931), 226-236; and Meech, pp. 233-238. Robert Kilburn Root, *The Poetry of Chaucer* (Boston and New York, 1906), pp. 115-119, says that if Pandarus had not intervened Troilus' love would have remained an ideal passion.

[83] See, for example, Muscatine, pp. 130-132; and Robertson, "Chaucerian Tragedy," *passim*.

and consent. He was not concerned to do this any more than he was concerned to present the process of falling in love merely in the terms of courtly doctrine. We can discern the patterns of courtly *amor* in the first two books, and we can discern some of the language and ideas usually applied to sin. But Chaucer has depicted Troilus and Criseyde, with profound understanding and meticulous detail, as human beings seriously involved in human affairs. Sinners they may be; but in Books I and II it is clear that we are not meant to reject their affair out of hand—we are meant to empathize. Why else would he have added to his source so much analysis? If they are sinners, their errors are not chiefly owing to sensual love; they have nothing better to turn to and have therefore no reason to avoid or repent their sensuality. They are "sinners" chiefly because they are pagans.[84]

It is Pandarus who persuades them to love, and Pandarus represents Chaucer's interpretation of the philosophy, or at least the morality, of paganism. This is to a large extent what makes Pandarus so interesting as a character; his wit, to be sure, is entertaining, and his vicarious interest in promoting the affair, with its slight neurotic edge, cannot fail to arrest one's attention and curiosity; his own inadequacy as a lover is amusing and in its way touching. But what seems like irresponsibility in him is more than a character trait; it is part of his philosophy. And that philosophy, I believe, is Chaucer's notion of paganism. It is part of the historical atmosphere, like the temples and rites of ancient gods. I am surprised that I do not find this opinion expressed in

[84] It is very important not to fall into the error of thinking that Troilus and Criseyde are Christians. Mr. Robertson, though he thinks Cupid is Satan and Venus is lechery, can then say "Troilus has defied the gods and placed Criseyde above them" ("Chaucerian Tragedy," p. 32).

those critical treatments of the poem which I know. It is, perhaps, a point so palpable that it is taken for granted. Something *like* it is presented by those critics who show what Pandarus thinks about Fortune, but there is more than this single Boethian principle. If we imagine Chaucer reading what he did of classical literature, we can suppose that he would have formed some notion of the attitudes of the pagan world; not any clear notion of Stoicism or Epicureanism, but something vaguely and preponderantly ancient in contrast to what he knew as contemporary and Christian.[85] This he did with great sensitivity. And the resulting view he attributes to Pandarus. Pandarus believes in taking advantage of Fortune, because it is fickle and because life is fleeting. Destiny will present us with *aventure*, and we should use it for our delight at once; we should "seken bote" (I, 763). This is the very opposite of Christian contempt of the World—and why should it not be? He does not know anything about the afterlife. Rather it is the *carpe diem* of classical thought; Pandarus in fact says what could be a translation of Horace's famous line when he tells Criseyde, speaking of her "good aventure," "Cache it anon, lest aventure slake!" (II, 291). In this he is not a cynic, and he is not "amoral"; he is far from being a priest of Satan—though he is sometimes like a

[85] On Chaucer's knowledge of Latin classics, see Eleanor Prescott Hammond, *Chaucer: A Bibliographical Manual* (New York, 1908), pp. 84-105; and Edgar Finley Shannon, *Chaucer and the Roman Poets*, HSCL, 7 (Cambridge, Mass., 1929). C. L. Wrenn, "Chaucer's Knowledge of Horace," *MLR*, XVIII (1923), 286-292, argues against Lounsbury (*Studies in Chaucer*, II, 261-264) that Chaucer knew the *Ars poetica* and had probably seen a manuscript collection of quotations including perhaps one or two odes. The notion of virtue as a mean was taken over from Aristotle by St. Thomas and other scholastics; see Thomas Aquinas, *Commentary on the Nicomachean Ethics*, II, lectio vii, 324.

priest of Venus—or even a tempter. He is a well-meaning uncle to Criseyde and a loyal friend to Troilus. He follows a courtly idea of behavior, for which Troilus shows gratitude. When he sees that he has done harm, he repents.[86] It is not that he has no idea of virtue—he has no *Christian* idea of virtue; one would be surprised if he had. His idea of virtue, like that of the classical world, depends not on restraint but on moderation— "the mene of it no vice is" (i, 689), he declares.

And this pagan philosophy is what directs the love affair. Criseyde accepts his philosophical arguments; she echoes his notions explicitly in her soliloquy (ii, 715, 807-808), and it could be argued that she continues to act upon them after leaving Troy. It is ironic when we hear Diomede using one of the same notions (v, 783-784)—but then he is a pagan, too. Troilus, on the other hand, accepts Pandarus *the man* as an advisor: "My lif, my deth, hol in thyn hond I leye" (i, 1053). He does not stop to dispute Pandarus' philosophical position; later he will give it much thought. Pandarus, we know, is the mastermind of the affair; it is he who brings each of them to the point of willingness. They have free will to decide one way or the other as much as any Christian

[86] The idea that Pandarus is a devil is proposed by Robertson, "Chaucerian Tragedy," pp. 16-17, and refuted by Charlotte D'Evelyn, "Pandarus a Devil?" *PMLA*, LXXI (1956), 275-279. On Pandarus' good intentions, see Eugene E. Slaughter, "Chaucer's Pandarus: Virtuous Uncle and Friend," *JEGP*, XLVIII (1949), 186-195. Robertson ("Chaucerian Tragedy," p. 26) cites the fact that Pandarus tells Troilus he would procure him his own sister if he wished it, and that Troilus later makes the same avowal. He offers this as evidence of Pandarus' moral delinquency and the error into which Troilus falls because of it. To be sure it is a stark and pagan avowal. But it is an avowal of good intentions and loyalty, not of depravity—an exaggerated protestation of friendship which in each case carries the implication that the friend would forbear to ask so much.

does. What they do *not* have is the right "doctrine." They have no better counsel than what they get from Pandarus, whose philosophy, though quaintly classical, is from a Christian viewpoint wrong-headed and therefore ineffective as a remedy against Fortune.

Yet while Chaucer has presented Troilus and Criseyde as if they were making moral choices by their own free will, while he presents them as if they could have avoided the error of their ways and its outcome had not Pandarus urged them on, he reminds us everywhere that their end was predestined.[87] What appears to be a courtly romance with some ascetical overtones thus becomes a *de casibus* tragedy. This suited very well the medieval way of viewing the problem of free will. Following Boethius, Chaucer would have believed that we are free to make moral choices but are *not* free to decide circumstances or to control the results of our choices. Seen as the fall of Troilus, the story follows this pattern. The pattern has been discussed at length by many critics,[88] and I shall do no more than summarize what they say. Troilus is the hero;[89] he rises and

[87] If Pandarus had not urged them, it is apparent that they would not have loved. But, since they are pagans, this would hardly have been a matter of moral virtue; for Criseyde it would have been the result of fear and propriety, for Troilus of courtly hesitancy.

[88] See especially Robert Kilburn Root, *The Book of Troilus and Criseyde by Geoffrey Chaucer* (Princeton, 1926), pp. xlviii ff.; Howard R. Patch, "Troilus on Determinism," pp. 225-243; Farnham, pp. 129-160; Walter Clyde Curry, "Destiny in Troilus and Criseyde," in *Chaucer and the Mediaeval Sciences* (rev. ed., New York, 1960), pp. 241-298; Theodore A. Stroud, "Boethius' Influence on Chaucer's *Troilus*," *MP*, XLIX (1951), 1-9; Bloomfield, "Distance and Predestination," pp. 22-26; and David, esp. pp. 576-581.

[89] By this I mean not only that he is, as stated, the principal character, but that he is a sympathetic character whom we are expected to admire and pity. See J. Milton French, "A Defense of Troilus," *PMLA*, XLIV (1929), 1246-1251; and David, pp. 566-571.

then falls on Fortune's wheel; and Criseyde is the unstable object of his worldly love.[90] Taken as a worldly
object, Criseyde is herself subject to the vicissitudes of
Fortune; Chaucer has made her, however, more than
the *donna mobile* of the *Filostrato* or the unstable temptress of antifeminist writings—he has made her understandable as a human being. Despite this, it is clear from
the beginning that their love, like any earthly love, is
mutable. Hence, Fortune's sway is central to the whole
atmosphere of the poem. It lies in and behind the opposing armies of the war itself:

> . . . and thus Fortune on lofte,
> And under eft, gan hem to whielen bothe
> Aftir hir course, ay whil that thei were wrothe.
>
> (I, 138-140)

It is nervously acknowledged, after the consummation,
by Pandarus:

> For of fortunes sharpe adversitee
> The worste kynde of infortune is this,
> A man to han ben in prosperitee,
> And it remembren, whan it passed is.
>
> . . . .
>
> For worldly joie halt nought but by a wir.
> That preveth wel it brest al day so ofte;
> Forthi nede is to werken with it softe.
>
> (III, 1625-1638)

It is echoed by the narrator:

> And thus Fortune a tyme ledde in joie
> Criseyde, and ek this kynges sone of Troie.
>
> (1714-1715)

[90] See Farnham, p. 145.

This motif of Fortune becomes central in Book ɪv, where its effects are felt. Book ɪv begins with a proem addressed to Fortune, who cast Troilus "out of his lady grace, / And on hire whiel she sette up Diomede." The doom of Troy and the fate of Troilus are suggested everywhere—in Calchas's prophecy (ɪv, 71-126), in the ransom of Antenor, who is to betray the city (197-210), in Troilus' complaint against Fortune (260-336), in Pandarus' mistaken notion that Fortune can be outwitted or ignored (380-427, 600-602), in Troilus' speech on predestination drawn from Boethius (958-1078), in Cassandra's "fewe of olde stories . . . how that Fortune overthrowe / Hath lordes olde" (v, 1457-1533). Destiny hovers over every moment of the tragedy; the reader knows from the outset that Troy is to fall, Aeneas to escape, the West to be founded. So, from the long view, we know that the love of Troilus and Criseyde must be a short and lovely interval in a longer and starker process of fallen cities, of battles lost, of peoples exiled and lovers separated, of heroes slain.[91]

That is what gives to Book ɪɪɪ its extraordinary tension. The electric sense of a "forbidden love" which we get from the consummation scene does not spring solely from the Christian prohibition against cupidity but from the human fact that time is ticking away and adverse chances taking shape.[92] At the heart of courtship—of the

[91] See Curry, pp. 249-251; George Lyman Kittredge, *Chaucer and His Poetry* (Cambridge, Mass., 1915), p. 120; and Root, *The Poetry of Chaucer*, p. 92. Robert D. Mayo, "The Trojan Background of the *Troilus*," *ELH*, ɪx (1942), 245-256, disputes the idea that the setting gives an atmosphere of impending doom. For an excellent analysis of the correspondence between the fall of Troy and the tragedy of Troilus, see John P. McCall, "The Trojan Scene in Chaucer's *Troilus*," *ELH*, xxɪx (1962), 263-275.

[92] See Roger Sharrock, "Second Thoughts: C. S. Lewis on Chaucer's *Troilus*," *EC*, vɪɪɪ (1958), 123-137. Sharrock sees this element of ordinary life in the poem as consistent with the "creatural

noble ritual of courtly gentilesse—is sexuality, and this aspect of it is from a Christian standpoint wrong. Book III puts us in mind of what is mistaken about "payens corsed olde rites"—but it does so from the lovers' point of view, as the epilogue does so from Chaucer's. Everything that will bring about their disenchantment will also, in the end, commend the rightness of Christian morality. But for the time, this Christian dimension of the story is carefully kept at the edges of the stage. We experience the love as they do, knowing that time's winged chariot is hurrying near, that things are going to go wrong as surely as the dawn ends their first night: "Go selle it hem that smale selys grave," cries Troilus to the light, "We wol the nought, us nedeth no day have"—but day comes.

Even before the lovers are brought together, the short interview between Pandarus and Troilus (III, 239-420) sounds a sobering note. Pandarus, with a feeling of hesitancy and guilt (based on notions of gentlemanly conduct and family loyalty which are not inconsistent with his paganism), warns Troilus that he must treat her honorably:

> . . . for shame it is to seye:
> For the have I bigonne a gamen pleye,
> Which that I nevere do shal eft for other,
> Although he were a thousand fold my brother.

He has become, he says, "betwixen game and ernest, swich a meene / As maken wommen unto men to comen"—not from covetousness, of course, but friendship. Still, he is her uncle, and if people knew that he had "in my nece yput this fantasie, / To doon thi lust and holly to ben thyn," they would say he had done the worst treachery ever. He therefore urges Troilus to observe secrecy, to avoid boasting. Troilus reassures him

realism" of late medieval style, pointed to by Auerbach and Huizinga.

with self-possession and perhaps a touch of humor:
"Thow woost how longe ich it forbar to seye / To the,
that art the man that I best triste" (365-366)—and he
swears not to betray this trust, adding that he does not
take what Pandarus has done as a "bauderye." But he
adds, since Pandarus has done him this service, "So, for
the love of God, this grete emprise / Perfourme it out,
for now is moste nede" (416-417). In this, of course,
there is a suggestion of hot Italian desire after the polite
English avowal, and it is hard to know whether it has
crept in or been ironically retained from the *Filostrato*.
(The phrase "grete emprise" has been added; it is *"il
mio disio"* in the source.) Again, before leaving him,
Pandarus tells Troilus, "Make the redy right anon, /
For thow shalt into hevene blisse wende" (703-704).
There is perhaps here a similar ironic note. Possibly we
may permit ourselves to be amused by the physical urgency which lurks beneath the "grete emprise," and by
the hyperbole about its bliss.[93] I do not think, however,
that these ironies constitute a procession of Christian
morals paraded before us with sounding brass—we are
too much caught up in the immediacy of their love for
that: they are an accompaniment to the main action,
whose harmony we shall not be sure of until the finale.
Just so, in what follows, we are gently kept in mind of
the dark side of love—the details, imagery, and language
before the consummation remind us over and over of
all the things that prohibit and interfere with love, that
make it go wrong. The rain which keeps Criseyde over-
night is brought by "Fortune, executrice of wyrdes"
(617). The story of Troilus' woe which Pandarus tells
her brings in the threat of jealousy and gossip—"Allas!

---

[93] In the Merchant's Tale (IV, 1637-1673), January similarly expects heavenly joys from love. On the nature of the irony in passages
such as these, see Muscatine, pp. 137-139.

conceytes wronge," she cries, "What harm they don"
(804-805). "O brotel wele of mannes joie unstable!" she
adds, and goes on (820 ff.) to speak of how transitory
joy is.[94] On the next day, Troilus returns to his palace—
happy, no doubt; but we are told that "Desir al newe
hym brende, and lust to brede / Gan more than erst, and
yet took he non hede" (1546-1547). Later he tells
Pandarus:

> I hadde it nevere half so hote as now;
> And ay the more that desir me biteth
> To love hire best, the more it me deliteth.
> (1650-1652)

These references to "delight," to lust increasing the more
it is satisfied (like the "thorn" which Criseyde is bidden
"pull out"—the thorn in the flesh, as it must be) are so
decidedly Christian that, whether by design or only
because they are part of the pseudo-Christian language
of love, they bring into the audience's mind the slight
echoing hint of Christian qualms. They help to prepare
for the Christian sentiment of the epilogue. But more
than that, they help prepare for the turn of Fortune's
wheel. On the next day, in fact, Pandarus himself makes
a point of warning Troilus about "fortunes sharpe
adversitee" (1625 ff.) and reminding him that "worldly
joie halt nought but by a wir."

Thus until the end it is everywhere suggested that the
love of Troilus and Criseyde is doomed just *because* it is
a thing of this world. Like the narrator's reactions, the

---

[94] In the same vein is the narrator's concluding comment on their
night of love: "It was byset in joie and bisynesse / Of al that souneth
into gentilesse" (III, 1413-1414). It is hard for those who remember the Franklyn's Tale here to avoid wondering whether
"gentilesse" is not used with a touch of irony.

reactions of Pandarus help to create the mingled feeling
of exaltation and doom; even at the height of Book III
Pandarus, like the narrator, is apprehensive about the
instability of earthly joy. And, when all is lost, both the
narrator and Pandarus are helpless and confused.[95] But
at this point the similarity of the narrator and Pandarus
breaks off. Here, in the moment of tragedy, Pandarus
drops out of the picture:

> . . . sory of his frendes sorwe he is,
> And shamed for his nece hath don amys,
> And stant, astoned of thise causes tweye,
> As stille as ston; a word ne kowde he seye.
>
> (v, 1726-1729)

He disappears into the lost world of ancient Troy, the
spokesman of a philosophy which has been shown false.
The narrator is of our world, Pandarus of theirs; and
the narrator here draws away from them, toward us. He
addresses us directly, and tells us that he was wrong in
his momentary flirtation with the pagan worship of
Love, that however beautiful and exciting it is, it is a
false love—or, rather, a love of the false things of the
World.

> Swich is this world, whoso it kan byholde:
> In ech estat is litel hertes reste.
> God leve us for to take it for the beste!
>
> (1748-1750)

And now we discover that the narrator *is* in fact Chaucer[96]
—Chaucer the enthusiast of courtly love (as he may

---

[95] The similarity in character and reaction between the narrator
and Pandarus is observed by Nevill Coghill, *The Poet Chaucer*
(Oxford, 1949), pp. 75-76, where the portrait of Pandarus is regarded as partial self-portraiture.

[96] I base this on v, 1799-1801. Chaucer speaks in his own person

well have been in younger days), who has now found
its essential wrongness. It is evidence of his genius that
in presenting the unreal and unstable joys of earthly
love, Chaucer adopts an unreal, and temporary, stance.
Knowing this we can go back and find some possibly
ironic lines, some places where Chaucer's final view
shows through the masquerade of the courtly enthusiast.
We can find an underlying stream of Christian references which in retrospect make the body of the story
consistent with the epilogue. We can find the whole
treatment of Fortune, a pagan goddess, which comes
only in the end to have its full Christian significance.
But while these elements of the poem prepare us for the
epilogue, they never mitigate the intensity of the love
itself or the sorrow of its outcome.

At the beginning of the present chapter I have shown
how in the epilogue Chaucer added to the *Filostrato* an
expression of contempt of the World, a reference to the
traditional three worldly vanities, and an emphasis on
"the blynde lust," opposed to the love of God. His procedure seems unaccountable. He tells us a story of a
predestined tragic love among pagans who had no notion
of Christian morality and no Christian hope of salvation;
then he draws the moral that the World is unstable, that
young people should abstain from worldly vanity and
worldly appetites and instead love Christ. Cold comfort
that would be to Criseyde in her new life with the
Greeks, or to Troilus wherever Mercury had sent him!
Of course we can argue that pre-Christian men could
have made right choices through the vestige of reason

---

and then says he will return to "my rather speche." The next stanza
begins "The wrath, as I bigan yow for to seye. . . ." Jordan, p. 255,
says the anonymous narrator *becomes* the poet Chaucer. On the
narrator, see Donald R. Howard, "Chaucer the Man," *PMLA*, LXXX
(1965), 337-343.

left them after the Fall. Chaucer might very well have
said this, if anyone had put it to him. But he was writing
about the pre-Christian world, not for it. And what he
is finally talking about when he deals with the "payens
corsed olde rites" is *not* paganism itself, which no one
of his audience practiced or indeed knew much of anything about, but the paganism *manqué* which they *did*
know about, that of courtly love. To follow courtly
practices, he suggests, is to put oneself into a pseudo-
pagan world where Christian doctrine and Christian salvation do not obtain, where the lusts of the flesh and the
primal reign of Fortune are men's harsh lot. In the end
courtly love takes its place among all earthly vanities;
and Chaucer reminds us, in an unforgettable image, that
the dead can laugh. But it is a fundamental quality of
Chaucer's style, and a measure of the grandeur and
complexity of his poem, that he presents this pernicious
pagan world as a thing of immense beauty, in its fullest
and most passionate magnificence.

4. THE WORLD OF THE *TROILUS:* CHAUCER AND THE HUMAN CONDITION

The style of the *Troilus* is grounded in the counterpoint-
ing of two different and contradictory worlds—the one
a specific action and setting chosen out of the past, rich
and passionate and filled with wit and delight, but withal
somber and a little frightening; the other a temporal
and natural order governed by conditions which began
at the Fall and will not cease until the Judgment, a
World lost by Adam and saved by Christ. This latter
world, governed by destiny, stars, and Fortune, is the
one in which the Christian narrator addresses his
Christian audience: it is the World they knew through
revelation. It is not quite the same thing as "the wicked
world" or "this wretched world"—for it is under the

sway of Providence, which is just and right. The "wicked world" is the World seen through the limited spectrum of vain human wishes; it is unstable and corrupt; it is the lust of the flesh, the lust of the eyes, and pride of life; it is not to be loved. Chaucer makes us discover here, as medieval man discovered again and again, that this transitory and wicked state, which we should renounce, is a part of the universal and right governance of all things. It is how he justifies God's ways to man. To do so he lets us see and experience the human wishes of the two lovers. While he shows their love in "historial" Trojan garb, it is the familiar game of love his audience knew. And at the end he makes us see its vanity.

Many of the specific effects which commentators have described in the poem go into the delineation of these two worlds. The dual time scheme which Henry W. Sams[97] demonstrated serves the purpose of distinguishing the action of the poem on the one hand as a human relationship in which the reader becomes involved, on the other hand as a series of events seen in perspective as a given time span in the inexorable predestined process of history. The reader is made aware of specific images which suggest the turning of one year, reflecting the joy and subsequent woe of the hero; at the same time the reader recognizes a passage of three years out of the past to be followed by other years bringing the events of recorded history. Charles Muscatine, approaching the poem from the viewpoint of conventional styles which go into the making of the work, finds two "perspectives" from which Chaucer views his story.[98] One of these is the courtly perspective of Jean de Meun and the French tradition. From it Chaucer "prizes courtly

[97] "The Dual Time-Scheme in Chaucer's *Troilus*," *MLN*, LVI (1941), 94-100.
[98] Muscatine, pp. 131-132.

idealism for its very real virtues, for its recognition of nobility, of beauty, and of spirit." The other is the perspective of Boethius, from which he sees "the imperfection inherent in any mode of life—be it practical or idealistic—wherein the end itself is *earthly* joy, and hence wherein the prize may at any moment be washed away by the same tides that brought it." The whole, as Bloomfield has shown,[99] is held in unity by the narrator, who becomes involved for a time in the events of the love affair and then withdraws from them into the present, toward the Christian audience, viewing the outcome as a predestined result of choices and drawing from it a Christian moral.

These two worlds are related because each unique event in history is part of the historical and universal course of things. Fortune, which brings about the tragedy, brings about the fall of Troy and the founding of the West—hence Chaucer reminds us in the epilogue, as Boccaccio had done, of the crucial death of Hector. In this respect the ending of the *Troilus* is like the beginning and ending of *Sir Gawain and the Green Knight*, where the events of the story are related to the meaningful flow of history. But beyond this medieval men believed that each individual's moral choices predisposed his future place in the universal order, so that each individual act in time had importance *sub specie aeternitatis*. That is why the story is not a mere exemplum: past events are real and tangible, though moral meaning may be seen in them. At the end the characters are dispersed and each one followed into his place in the subsequent course of history. Criseyde goes off among the Greeks— ironically repeating with Diomede the same process of hesitant acquiescence that she had experienced with

[99] "Distance and Predestination," pp. 14-19.

Troilus and Criseyde

Troilus. Troilus is killed and transported to the eighth sphere, from which he can scorn the World and laugh at the pursuits of worldlings. Pandarus is silenced, his story at an end.[100] And the narrator retreats into the present, among us, dropping his mask and revealing himself as Geoffrey Chaucer, Englishman, friend of the moral Gower and the philosophical Strode.

This disruption of the human relationships which have made up the inner world of the story has about it something which the modern reader will take as "tragic" in a modern sense. When Chaucer referred to his poem as "myn tragedye," however, he had in mind stories of the kind which Cassandra tells to Troilus or the Monk to the Pilgrims.[101] He did not have in mind Lear and Cordelia in their prison, Cleopatra in her monument, or Hamlet gasping his last wishes to Horatio. The "dark voyage" of tragedy, which leaves the audience struck with wonder and awe at the mystery of life, is not to be found at the end of the *Troilus*. We are two centuries too early for this, and we shall mistake Chaucer's final disposition of his tale very gravely if we find in it bits and patches of Shakespeare and Marlowe, not to say Pirandello or Arthur Miller. There are at least three reasons why this is the case: (1) Chaucer ends his story by reminding us of its historicity. We are not told to look upon the tragic loading of this bed; we are given specific details about the aftermath. We are told about the outcome of the war and about the deaths of Hector and

[100] Muscatine, p. 145, points out that for Pandarus silence is defeat.

[101] Robertson, "Chaucerian Tragedy," pp. 1-11. For further development of Chaucer's idea of tragedy, see R. E. Kaske, "The Knight's Interruption of the *Monk's Tale*," *ELH*, XXIV (1957), 249-268; Robert A. Pratt, " 'Joye after Wo' in the *Knight's Tale*," *JEGP*, LVII (1958), 416-423; and John F. Mahoney, "Chaucerian Tragedy and the Christian Tradition," *AM*, III (1962), 81-99.

Troilus. We are referred to Dares for further details. The poem itself is put into its place in history when it is bidden "kis the steppes, where as thow seest pace / Virgile, Ovide, Omer, Lucan, and Stace." Tragedy in the modern sense points to the human meaning and the human mystery of a catastrophe; here, the meaning is explained by a stated philosophy of history. (2) The *Troilus* ends with Criseyde, thus far a sympathetic figure, acting badly. Her letter is dreadful. Her giving Troilus' brooch to Diomede is worse. She becomes the fickle and treacherous woman of antifeminist tracts. And the only thing that keeps her from seeming utterly the villain of the piece is that she perceives herself in this state: "O, rolled shal I ben on many a tonge!" she laments. "And wommen moost wol haten me of alle" (v, 1061-1063). Even at that there is a touch of hypocrisy and a touch of what is now called self-destructiveness in her last speech:

> But syn I se ther is no bettre way,
> And that to late is now for me to rewe,
> To Diomede algate I wol be trewe.
>
> (1069-1071)

Cleopatra, to be sure, perceives her errors too, but she rises to the occasion with noble words, and asps. Lady Macbeth is crushed by her own failings, and we see her punished. For Criseyde it is not hard to *imagine* her becoming what she was to be in later treatments, a common prostitute and a leprous beggar. But that is not what Chaucer shows us. He shows her nervously settling down with the next knight that comes along. He even makes a joke at the end (v, 1779-1785) by warning women against men. (3) Chaucer ends the story by withdrawing Troilus from the World. The Elizabethans ended their tragedies with a lifeless body, a eulogy, a funeral march. We may *suppose* that Hamlet goes to heaven and Macbeth to hell, but we are never so informed. Devils come to get Dr. Faustus, it is true, in a grand moment of stage spectacle and horror; Iago on the other hand is only handcuffed and lowering, ready to be tortured. The Elizabethan character ends his life in this World, and the rest is silence—and surmise. The effect is one of mystery and wonder. But Troilus is followed off stage to the eighth sphere and put securely in the hands of Mercury; he is laughing once more; he has got his equanimity back.

Nothing could be more medieval than this ending. That it is *like* modern tragedy in some respects I would not want to deny. We see Criseyde decide to stay with Diomede in the same unconscious and frightened way that she had inclined to Troilus; we see Troilus pass from love's bliss into woe; the brooch, the letters, the inadequate counsel of Pandarus, the very consistency of their characters—all of it is what we now call tragic irony. At the end we are left with a feeling of exalted peace and with some sense that we can learn from the errors of the past. And we are made to feel that, in spite of human pain, Providence is just. But there is no hope for the future of the World—it is going to be like this again and again for everyone who will seek "feynede loves." There is nothing here comparable to the reconciliation of the Montagues and Capulets, or the new reign of Fortinbras, or the establishment on the throne of the heirs of Banquo. There is nothing to suggest that human action can be aided by human wisdom or human knowledge, nothing to suggest that we attain to heaven by using well the things of this World. The ending is uncompromising: we are to turn our thoughts to God.

Hence it is not merely the epilogue but the ending of the story itself which conflicts with the courtly or "romantic" element of the work. The ending shows the transitoriness of earthly things and praises that detachment which sees they are vanity. At the same time the *Troilus* is a poem in praise of love; in the story itself Chaucer removed to the background all Christian caveats and wrote of his lovers' ardors unchecked. Chaucer has strengthened *both* elements in his revision of the poem. Critics in their attempt to show how they are integral have often mitigated the one or the other, or have made one the subordinate of the other. Yet the two elements *are* contradictory, as much as free will and predestination, or past and present, and they are finally irreconcilable.[102] But they are both valid. In spite of its final Christian meaning, *Troilus and Criseyde* depicts love between man and woman as a natural and irresistible feeling, influenced by the stars—a part of the condition of human life. Even the pain it causes is *sweet* pain. Its inception and progress are presented often in the language of a religious or mystical conversion. The two people who experience it are admirable people: they are of the aristocracy and have the highest virtues of *gentilesse*, discretion, honor.[103] The "game" of love in which they come to take part is no Italianate seduction but a delicate, courtly ritual; it is full of depth, of subtlety, and of charm. It is entirely freed of the cynical sexuality of Boccaccio's poem; the restraint and discretion of the lovers is exemplary, so that the libidinal basis of the courtly ritual is left nearly to surmise. Moreover, once entered upon, love has an ennobling effect on the hero—he is a better warrior, more fearless, more courteous. The consummation scene is therefore exalted; it is, as Musca-

[102] See Charles A. Owen, Jr., "The Significance of Chaucer's Revisions of *Troilus and Criseyde*," *MP*, LV (1957-1958), 3.

[103] Cf. J. S. P. Tatlock, "The People in Chaucer's *Troilus*," *PMLA*, LVI (1941), 103-104.

tine has shown, in the high style;[104] and it is embodied
in an elaborate rite of vows and rings and tender words.
Whatever is mundane in it, whatever might catch from
us a glint of amusement or a raised eyebrow, is taken
into account by Pandarus' busyness and his sly commentary: Chaucer thus removes the danger of letting humor
despoil the sanctuary by admitting it and assigning it a
place.[105] Finally, the ending of the story is tragic not
because young ladies are fickle but because the objects of
all human striving fall under the sway of Fortune; the
narrator, in his role as one who serves the servants of
Love, shows admiration for their love and feels sorrow
for the inescapable tragic end.

When one returns from Chaucer's work to Boccaccio's
one is more than ever impressed with the difference between them. Critics have compared them in such detail
as to crowd and clutter the essential differences of purpose and outlook, on which all else depends. Boccaccio
wrote the *Filostrato* to make an impression on Maria
d'Aquino. His concern is, it may justly be said, the lust
of the flesh—*caldo disio*: the phrase is repeated over and
over like a *leitmotif*, echoed from the emphatic ends of
stanzas, enforced with images of heat and flame. The hot
desire of Troilo is his subject, Troilo being the poet
himself. The poem is about his own tormented passion,[106]
and this he takes—he is an Italian—to be a most important, and urgent, matter. There is scarcely an attempt
to mitigate the libidinal basis of the love affair: Troilo

[104] Muscatine, pp. 148-153. For a demonstration of how the consummation scene in Chaucer is less sensual than in Boccaccio, see
Meech, pp. 72-78.

[105] The point is made by Lewis, *Allegory of Love*, pp. 172-173,
and developed by Muscatine, pp. 130-131.

[106] Griffin and Myrick, pp. 18-22, show how the story ironically
foretold what was to be the actual course of events in the poet's
relationship with his mistress.

says he means no villainy (11, 31) but it is clear to everyone what he means; and Criseida herself is moved by
desire both to love and to leave him. There is at the
same time no suggestion at all that Boccaccio sees Troilo's
desires, or his own, from a Christian viewpoint. There is
scarcely a Christian overtone in the poem itself. No
Christian application is drawn from the workings of
Fortune. The moral is *la donna è mobile*. The ending is
an appeal to the lady. It is, while good for its intensity,
the stuff of Italian opera and *la dolce vita*; when we
turn to Chaucer's work, we are in another country.

Chaucer idealizes the love affair by softening its sexual
basis and ennobling the manner in which it is conducted.
What is *caldo disio* in Boccaccio becomes a "grete emprise" in Chaucer. Yet while he has idealized Boccaccio's
treatment of love, he has Christianized Boccaccio's moral.
His poem is at once more "historial" and more anachronistic than Boccaccio's; in it, Love is at once more noble
and more pagan. The *Troilus* is both more courtly and
more Christian than the *Filostrato*. Chaucer's purpose is
to explore the human and philosophical possibilities in a
great narrative of passion; he finds them in conflict. His
concern is not, as Boccaccio's was, fleshly lust—he reaches
beyond. His concern is the incompatibility of courtly
love with Christian love; and by courtly love he means
an experience, fleshly it may be, which brings man's
noblest features into play. Though the Christian message
at the end is not by any means an appendage, the love
of which he writes is more than a mere symbol of
worldliness. Chaucer sees in love the sadness, and
danger, which had been seen by Churchmen and by
exponents of love as well. Finally, his concern is the
incompatibility of all our worldly pursuits with our predestined otherworldly ends. In the simplest human
terms, he is writing about the limited happiness that is

in this World, as against the "pleyn felicite / That is in hevene above." In this he does not disqualify human happiness. He renounces "This world, that passeth soone as floures faire," but he does not deny the fairness of those flowers. It is as if to say, "Now we see through a glass, darkly; but then face to face."

What I have said here will not, I hope, be mistaken for a new idea. Many critics have argued the same or a similar opinion.[107] Many, perhaps most, would now hold,

[107] The chief variations appear to be these: (1) The epilogue and the poem are integral, owing to Chaucer's temperament or character. Thus Root, in *The Book of Troilus and Criseyde*, p. L, remarked that Chaucer's attitude "made for a serene Catholic temper, which could thoroughly enjoy and understand the world, while still recognizing its 'vanity.'" Patch, esp. pp. 238-240, argued that the poem has two layers of meaning, courtly and Christian: "It is an aspect of Chaucer's greatness and his breadth that he can enter as heartily into the love affair as into the vision of the limitation of earthly things and the supreme value of lasting idealism." Meech, pp. 420-421, 426-427, holds that Chaucer rejects love but maintains "a sympathetic if critical interest in it." (2) The epilogue and the poem are integral owing to Chaucer's use of various stylistic conventions and perspectives. See Muscatine, esp. pp. 161-165, and Sharrock, pp. 123-137. (3) The epilogue is conventional but nonetheless serious. Kemp Malone, in *Chapters on Chaucer* (Baltimore, 1951), pp. 139-140, regards the epilogue as a conventional recantation, remarking that "such an ending might be perfunctory, but in a serious major work the moral application of the story would have to be taken seriously."

Since Chaucer's own character and ideas, and the conventions and styles which he used, were all shaped by medieval ideas, there seems to me most sense in the argument (4) that the epilogue and the love story are equally serious, that it is unnecessary to make a choice between them, and that their unity is owing to ideas and attitudes inherent in medieval culture. This view was suggested by Karl Young, "Chaucer's Renunciation of Love in *Troilus*," *MLN*, XL (1925), 270-276, who argued that the epilogue is in the same ambiguous spirit as Book IV of the *De amore*, and by Farnham, pp. 154-155, who saw the intellectual conviction of the World's vanity

as I do, that the poem takes its emotional force and gets its profoundest artistic effect from the balance which Chaucer maintains between the two worlds of the poem. I have nothing to add but an explanation of why this balance had such strong poetical possibilities for Chaucer and his age. And my explanation is that this balance, taken as an element of Chaucer's style, and of *one* style of courtly love, is a fundamental aspect of the style of medieval moral discourse. It is consistent with a pervasive, unconscious pattern of medieval thought and feeling. And, to play my full hand at once, it is consistent with what Chaucer did in his other major work.

Nowhere does Chaucer evoke the "double truth" of courtly love so well as in the two worlds of the *Troilus*. That duality in courtly love, as I have tried to show earlier, was modeled on the familiar Christian idea that there are degrees of perfection. What Chaucer has done is to show that the system of courtly love—itself ennobling and beautiful, and carried out in the poem to its fullest and most poetic capacities—is a less perfect code, restricted to a "natural" world in which Christianity could not point the higher way and the consolation of its

---

as being in conflict with Chaucer's worldly interests. Shanley, pp. 271-281, emphasized the insufficiency of human pleasure as a theme of medieval literature and thought. Such a view is stated very persuasively by E. Talbot Donaldson, *Chaucer's Poetry* (New York, 1958), pp. 979-980, who shows that "the lines in which he condemns the world . . . poignantly enhance the very thing that he is repudiating." The point is developed by David, pp. 580-581: "Troilus' celestial laughter recognizes at the same time the absurdity *and* sublimity of human endeavor. . . . Man is forever striving after some such visionary beatitude as that held out by human love, and it is forever fleeing away from him. . . . The *Troilus*, in its largest sense, is an exemplum of Boethius' lesson that the life within time derives from and reflects the life beyond time." The remainder of the present chapter is intended as a contribution to this kind of interpretation.

philosophy could not preclude earthly woe. That was the medieval style—to set the temporary values of earthly life against the permanent ones of eternity and dispose them into a hierarchy. What is called love at court is the lust of the flesh *sub specie aeternitatis.* Yet with medieval writers one has always a sense of their looking back, with yearning and regret, to the inferior and transitory—to the snows of yesteryear, to the World "that passeth soone as floures faire." That is the feeling, and the ambiguity, of Chaucer's prayer: "God leve us for to take it for the beste!"

Chaucer ended the *Canterbury Tales* with the same ambiguity. The Parson's sermon on penitence and the author's own act of repentance make it clear that finally the pilgrimage is below and inferior to "thilke parfit glorious pilgrymage / That highte Jerusalem celestial" (x, 50-51). But that is not what everyone remembers. And it is not the thing to which Chaucer gave his best artistic efforts. We can, moreover, find the same pattern *within* the *Canterbury Tales.* I have attempted to show elsewhere[108] how Chaucer, in the Marriage Group of the *Canterbury Tales,* brought the argument about "sovereyntee" and about relative degrees of perfection in marriage to an apparent close in the Franklyn's Tale, and then sought to add one further tale which would give a final statement of the Church's highest ideal, of the highest grade of perfection. The Franklyn's compromise between courtly love and Christian marriage will seem to modern readers more appealing, and more satisfactory, than the Second Nun's Tale of chaste marriage and martyrdom; but this is no grounds for supposing a conscious preference on Chaucer's part—

[108] Donald R. Howard, "The Conclusion of the Marriage Group: Chaucer and the Human Condition," *MP*, LVII (1960), 223-232.

although it may have been an unconscious preference
immanent in the culture of his age. Chaucer does, there
is no doubt, show a good deal of interest in the Franklyn's
ideas, and I do not think he meant to reject them; but
he presents them, I believe, with irony and detachment.
And he acknowledges better ones. It is precisely so with
love, in *Troilus and Criseyde*. What is most often said
of Chaucer is most true: he had a comprehensive vision
of human life, a broad and tolerant humor. His genius is
for rendering what is of value, however limited, in all
things—whether in the raucous behavior of the pilgrims
on their way to the shrine at Canterbury or in the
sensuality of the pagan Troilus as he passes through
momentary bliss to sorrow, and beyond. Chaucer's evocation of human life—in the "comedy" of the *Canterbury Tales* or the tragedy of Troilus—rests upon his
ability to set the realities of human affairs against the
ideal of the Christian life without descending into cynical
mockery or indignant tongue-clicking.

This even-handed and in some ways ambiguous view
of the World is most often presented as an effect of
Chaucer's character or temperament. To an extent this
is perhaps true. Nevertheless, we can find in medieval
thought a precedent for the quality of the world he en-
visioned, and we shall do best to call it by its medieval
name: the human condition. The phrase—often wrongly
attributed to Montaigne—has in recent years become a
catchphrase among intellectuals; I hasten to declare
that I use it not in this fashionable way but in its historical, and original, sense. It was a major trend in late
medieval thought, one which Chaucer knew and used.
It is of course implicit in the "Boethian" attitude, but
it had its own literary tradition. The classic work of that
tradition, Pope Innocent III's *De contemptu mundi*—

158

which Chaucer tells us he had translated—was actually called *De miseria humanae conditionis*.[109] In it, Pope Innocent teaches—with all the trappings of scriptural citation, "etymologies," rhetorical flourish and bluster—that the human condition is one of misery. Its first book is organized around the terms "lust of the flesh, lust of the eyes, and pride of life." It describes the beginning, progress, and "egress" of man's life, from the first slime to the last ashes. Nevertheless, created things were the good creatures of a good God, and the human condition had therefore another aspect beyond its ineluctable misery: it had dignity. When the treatises on contempt of the World became extreme in their pessimism, there appeared some refutations called *De dignitate hominis*—in Italy, a few even during Chaucer's lifetime.[110] Indeed, Pope Innocent III, at the beginning of his great work, promised another essay on the opposite side of the question, arguing the dignity of man, *Christo favente*. Essential dignity limited by the human condition of weakness and of misery—that was the medieval view of man.

Contempt of the World therefore had, even in the structure of its most extreme expressions, an area of sentiment which favored created things. In the treatises on contempt of the World one may find five principal arguments or themes: (1) the mutability of earthly things, which makes them unsatisfactory as objects of affection; (2) the vanity of earthly things, which makes them dissatisfying even while they are still in one's

[109] *Legend of Good Women*, G prologue 414-415. On the title of Pope Innocent's work, see *Lotharii Cardinalis (Innocentii III) De miseria humane conditionis*, ed. Michele Maccarrone (Lucani, 1955), pp. xxxii-xxxv.

[110] Charles Edward Trinkaus, Jr., *Adversity's Noblemen: The Italian Humanists on Happiness*, CUSHEPL, 475 (New York, 1940).

possession; (3) the corruption of the natural order, in particular the body, which is subject to disease and death; (4) the expectation of an afterlife, which will reward or punish the deeds of earthly existence; and (5) the evils of the social order, which make worldly life unsatisfactory. Each of these themes, however, has its obverse of espousal. When writers spoke with sorrow of the mutability and vanity of earthly things, was there not the suggestion of an underlying and covert attachment to them? Thus the evils of the social order may be corrected, to make the World more nearly satisfactory. The afterlife grants reward and metes out punishment for the moral qualities of one's life in the World. Disease and death do not preclude partial health and temporary life. And the mutability and vanity of worldly things allow nevertheless the possibility of using well the things of this World while we have them, though without being foolishly misled into expecting from them permanence or unqualified bliss. The *Troilus* does not deal, except incidentally, with the corruption of nature, the afterlife, or the evils of the social order. It deals rather with the arguments of mutability and vanity. The worldly love of the hero does not last; nor does it satisfy him even while it does last—his desires increase as they are fulfilled. That is the human condition, and in it is the lesson of *contemptus mundi*. But there was as well the other, muted lesson: that Troilus as a human creature had dignity, and that he had a limited felicity—for a time.

CHAPTER FOUR

THE BODY POLITIC AND THE LUST OF THE EYES: *PIERS PLOWMAN*

For seuene synnes that there ben assaillen vs euere,
The fende folweth hem alle and fondeth hem to helpe,
Ac with ricchesse that ribaude rathest men bigyleth.
—*Piers Plowman*, B. xiv, 201-203

N THE opening lines of *Piers Plowman*—in the "Prologue" and in Passus I—there are two references to the Three Temptations. One, though rather covert and therefore debatable, occurs in the lines which describe the "feld ful of folk" as the dreamer first comes upon it.[1] Here, among "alle maner of men, þe mene & þe riche," he finds plowmen working to produce what "þise wastours wiþ glotonye destroiʒeþ," he finds some who "putte hem to pride," and he finds some who "chosen hem to chaffare." These are the first evildoers he encounters among all kinds of men from all three estates; and they are guilty of gluttony, pride and avarice. That avarice should come last may have a special significance, for in what follows the poet will put a heavy emphasis on those temptations which spring from purely economic motives—from the "lust of the eyes." In the first vision, Holy Church explains to the dreamer that God has created him and created the earth to supply his needs. She reminds him that "Al is not good to þe gost þat þe gut askiþ," and warns him,

> Leue not þi lycam for a liʒer hym techiþ,
> Þat is þe wrecchide world wolde þe betraye.
> For þe fend & þi flessh folewiþ togidere,
> And þat shendiþ þi soule. (A. I, 34-39)

The earth will supply the needs of the body, but the

[1] A. Pro., 20 ff. The A-text is quoted from *Piers Plowman: The A Version*, ed. George Kane (London, 1960), by permission of the Athlone Press, London, and Oxford University Press, New York; I omit his italics and brackets. My quotations from the B-text are from *The Vision of William Concerning Piers the Plowman . . .* , ed. W. W. Skeat (2 vols., reprinted London, 1924).

body—taught by World, flesh, and devil—will tempt men to misuse earthly things. This is the central conflict of the poem, as it is the central conflict of the Christian life.

The poem is to be a vision of a "feld ful of folk" halfway between the Tower of Truth and a deep dungeon—a vision of the World. The poet is dealing avowedly with what men do, and should do, in the *mundus* or *saeculum*—in the place where the needs of the temporal body must be provided for, in the time before each individual soul, and all souls, go to everlasting life. He will try to measure human affairs, and perhaps improve them, by applying Christian ideas and ideals to the corrupted currents of this World. It is a large subject, and the poem's "failure," of which critics are often quick to speak, ought to be measured against its ambitious and extraordinary scope. Its focus is on the World rather than on individual salvation or eternity. In this I do not deny that the poem deals with the scheme of individual salvation, but, as Morton Bloomfield has shown, this scheme is nonetheless "apocalyptic"—is social and historical as well as individual. The poem is "about" all these things, first, because Christianity is "about" them: in Christianity virtue and vice, life and death, individual salvation, judgment, eschatology—all are integrally associated, and no one can be dealt with divorced from the rest. As we have seen, the omnipresence of temptation and the possibility of sin or redemption applied both to the individual and to all of history. Into the life of each man came the legacy of the Fall and the Redemption, and the necessity of resisting the primal suggestions of World, flesh, and devil; but the final result of all individual choices was to come for all society and all history at the Last Judgment, not through an aggregate of saved souls but in a unified Kingdom of Christ.[2]

Piers Plowman, in dealing with so much, is dealing with the World in its traditional sense, a sense which links individual and society, time and eternity, good and evil. The poet recounts a series of dreams he has had which raise certain fundamental problems: How can a man save his soul? What does it mean to do well? How can the social order be made to function for the benefit of all? What relationship must the individual have to the social order? How should temporal goods be distributed? His method of answering such questions is to wander in the World and dream. Hence the structure of the work is that of recurrent dreams, which deal, repetitiously and circuitously, as dreams do, with the same problems. Everywhere there is a sense of searching, of yearning; the pattern of the poet's thought is a swirling and eddying, with all the hazy familiarity and inconclusiveness of dreams. And this kind of structure is announced in the opening lines with the figure of churning, merry waters into which he looks—a symbol, as some would say, of the unconscious.

The question "What is *Piers Plowman* about?" is therefore somewhat like asking "What are my dreams about?" They are about one's whole world, about all the troubles that perplex one and all the possible resolutions of these troubles. For Langland, of course, such anxieties are not personal, but cultural and in large measure intellectual.[3] He creates a dream world out of his mental life, in which, as in anyone's dreams, there is an area of centrality; just what that area is, however, remains a

[2] See Morton W. Bloomfield, *Piers Plowman as a Fourteenth-Century Apocalypse* (New Brunswick, 1961), pp. vii-x *et passim.*

[3] On the intellectuality of the poet and his audience, see C. S. Lewis, *The Allegory of Love* (Oxford, 1958), pp. 158-161.

matter of debate. Some years ago T. P. Dunning proposed that the theme of *Piers Plowman* is the right use of temporal goods.[4] No one has ever quite agreed with this, though many have admitted it as *one* theme. Surely the theme of such a poem is more inclusive: if the use of temporal goods is its theme, what are we to say of its attention to the contemplative life, individual salvation, apocalyptic ideas, eschatology? Nevertheless, while I do not think that the use of temporal goods is the theme of the poem, or even its subject, I do wish to show that it is the poet's central concern—that he sees human failings not primarily as the lust of the flesh (bodily pleasures) or the pride of life (status and power), but as the lust of the eyes. One who wandered in the world of fourteenth-century England, that time of plague, famine, and depopulation, would have been bound to think about economic questions, and a man of theological inclinations would see those questions in terms of human need and human avarice, labor and sloth. How, he asks, can men supply the primary needs of life if they will not submit to the toil of producing goods? How can they produce those goods without being lured by the lust of the eyes? How can the social order run smoothly without becoming corrupt? "How shall the world be served?"

We shall best verify what is central in *Piers Plowman* not by keeping score on allusions or symbols, but by determining how the poem is put together, what are its crucial and dramatic turning points, and what receives the weight of emphasis. This kind of dissection, which is not easily performed on a sonnet, is a staggering task for a poem with three divergent texts having the plan of dreams. Nevertheless I am going to proceed as if I

[4] T. P. Dunning, *Piers Plowman: An Interpretation of the A-text* (London and New York, 1937), esp. pp. 16-23.

knew what creature lies before us—though everything
I assume is a matter of convenience, not of fact. I am
going to assume that the A-text was written first,[5] and
that the B- and C-texts are subsequent revisions; that
these revisions were made by the same author ("Langland"); and that each revision was meant to have some
perceivable overall structure—was meant to be a single
poem, not a mere string of dream visions, and not two
poems, *Visio* and *Vita*, on the same subject.[6] I am going
to ignore the changes made in B of the lines included in
A. And I am going to eliminate the C-text from consideration altogether, on the grounds that it is easier to
slay a dragon if he has only two heads. If an excuse is
called for, it must be that I am writing a chapter, not a
book.

If we take the A-text as a finished work, we should
think of it the way the poet did, as divided into three
visions:[7]

Vision I   Introduction (Prologue and Passus I)
           Vision of Mede (Passus II-IV)
Vision II The Pilgrimage to Truth and the Plowing
           of the Half Acre (Passus V-VIII)
Vision III The Vita of Do-wel (Passus IX-XI)

The crucial turning points in this structure are the two

[5] Most students of the poem would now agree, but see Howard
Meroney, "The Life and Death of Longe Wille," *ELH*, XVII (1950),
20-33, where it is argued that A is an abridgment of B made for a
nonclerical audience.

[6] On this there is also general agreement, but see Dunning, pp.
184-194, where it is argued that the two parts are separate poems in
A and were made one by another author in B.

[7] See Thomas A. Knott and David C. Fowler, *Piers the Plowman:
A Critical Edition of the A-Version* (Baltimore, 1952), pp. 6-7; and
George W. Stone, Jr., "An Interpretation of the A-text of *Piers
Plowman*," *PMLA*, LIII (1938), 656-677. On the number and

scenes which link these visions. The link between the Vision of Mede and the following units is the scene in which the King determines to dwell with Reason and Conscience (IV, 144-158); it presents an ideal, and the rest of the poem explores that ideal and the reasons why it is not followed. The link between the second and third visions is the Pardon scene. These two scenes are fulcrums which balance the three major units against one another. Each part develops ideas and explores conflicts which have gone before: each problem is attacked by presenting an idea, which in turn poses a new problem. Nothing is ever wholly resolved, for every attempt at resolution raises new conflicts and new questions. That is why critics have described the structure of the work as "cumulative" or as being disposed in "ever-widening ripples."[8] It is also why any attempt to describe this structure in a strictly schematic fashion as a series of parallels or antitheses is doomed to failure. Our poet is a wanderer and dreamer, and we shall be misled if we expect the progress of a planned journey or the sequence of waking thoughts.

Because the poem is constructed in this way, it becomes more complex as it progresses and its emphasis becomes less distinct. At the beginning, however, the emphasis is clear: in the field full of folk, though many carry on the business of the World as they should, there are wrongdoers: some are wasters who destroy what others produce through gluttony (Pro. 20-22), some "putte hem to pride" in apparel (23-25), and some choose "chaffare" and devote themselves to getting money by wrong

---

division of the various visions, see Robert W. Frank, Jr., "The Number of Visions in *Piers Plowman*," *MLN*, LXVI (1951), 309-312.

[8] See, for example, John Lawlor, "*Piers Plowman*: The Pardon Reconsidered," *MLR*, XLV (1950), 450.

means, without working for it—among them friars, pardoners, and parish priests (31-83). Everyone is beset by temptation, and every good idea is going to fail as long as there are gluttons, wasters, and deceivers. That is why in her first speech Holy Church warns the dreamer to exercise "mesure" in supplying the needs of the body. Clothing, meat, and drink are necessities, but excess in any leads to wrongdoing. And this is a danger because the body itself, which initiates the need to sustain life, tempts men to sin:

> Leue not þi lycam for a liȝer hym techiþ,
> Þat is þe wrecchide world wolde þe betraye.
> For þe fend & þi flessh folewiþ togidere,
> And þat shendiþ þi soule. (I, 36-39)

At the beginning of the second vision, there is the same emphasis on temptation. Here, after Conscience's sermon, occurs the famous passage on the Seven Deadly Sins, in which each penitent reveals his fatal weakness. Part of the allegorical force of the passage is that some show how they will probably go back again to the sins they confess: Envy ends talking still about vengeance (V, 105-106), Covetise needs to pray that he be brought out of debt (145), and Glutton finishes with a reference to his Aunt Abstinence, whom he says he still hates (212). At the beginning of the third vision (the *Vita*), the friar warns Will that "þoruȝ þe fend, & þe flessh, & þe false world, / Synnes þe sad man seuene siþes in þe day" (IX, 38-39). Finally, at the point where the A-text ends, the B-text presents a fourth vision which shows Fortune followed by two damsels, the lust of the flesh and the lust of the eyes, with "pride of perfect living" following them both; and lust of the eyes especially plagues Will until Fortune turns and poverty pursues him in old age (B. xi, 1-61).[9] Each structural unit of the poem, at least in the A-text, begins therefore with a reference to the omnipresence of temptation and in all cases but one this is presented with reference to the three lusts of 1 John 2:16 or "the World, the flesh, and the devil."

What preoccupies the author most, however, is the temptation to avarice in men and, consequently, the unjust distribution of goods in society. In the prologue, while he mentions gluttony and pride (22-24), he puts avarice last and furnishes more examples of it. In Passus I, when Holy Church counsels "mesure," Will asks, "Ac þe mone on þis molde þat men so faste holdiþ, / Tel me to whom þat tresour apendiþ" (1, 42-43). Her answer is to render unto Caesar what is Caesar's and unto God what is God's; reason and kynde-wyt will teach one how to distinguish between them. Will asks her how he may save his soul, and she replies, "Whanne alle tresours arn triȝed treuþe is þe beste"—a line which she repeats twice thereafter.[10] "Treuþe" here is something other than knowledge; it is truth as conceived by a hierarchical, feudal society in which each man from king to peasant must fulfill his ordained place, Christ himself being "kingene king" and the angels his knights. It is nothing less than God's government of the World. The failure of obedience to this world order caused the Fall of Lucifer, she says; in such a plan, love is the most precious thing that God asks—out of love He let His Son

[9] Later in the B-text the tree of Virtues is to be plagued by three winds, the World, the flesh, and the fiend (B. xvi, 25-52).

[10] On the source of this phrase, see Greta Hort, *Piers Plowman and Contemporary Religious Thought* (London and New York, 1937), pp. 77-78; and cf. Sister Mary Aquinas Devlin, "Bishop Thomas Brunton and His Sermons," *Speculum*, xiv (1939), 343-344.

die for our misdeeds. But from this, Holy Church draws
an *economic* application:

> Forþi I rede þe riche haue reuþe on þe pore;
> . . . .
> But ȝif ȝe loue lelly & lene þe pore,
> Of such good as god sent goodlyche parteþ,
> Ȝe ne haue no more meryt in masse ne in houres
> Þanne malkyn of hire maidenhed þat no man desiriþ.
>
> . . . .
> Ȝe curatours þat kepe ȝow clene of ȝour body,
> Ȝe ben acumbrid wiþ coueitise, ȝe conne not out crepe;
> So harde haþ auarice haspide ȝow togideris.
> Þat is no treuþe of trinite but treccherie of helle,
> And a lering to lewide men þe lattere to dele.

(1, 149-173)

A society ordained by Truth, in which those who have
wealth give to the poor out of love—that seems to be
what Holy Church envisages. The remainder of the first
vision, the vision of Mede, explores the possibility and
difficulty of this ideal. Mede is the principle of reward
or recompense. By rights "mede" should be a thing indifferent, like riches or power—good or bad as it is used
well or ill. In theory Mede *is* this: she is the daughter
of Wrong and "Mendes" (exchange), and although she
is about to marry False, it is proposed that she marry
Conscience instead: under Conscience's sway she would
be used in accordance with Truth and Love. The King
proposes the marriage to Conscience, but Conscience refuses. His argument is that among fallen men Mede
cannot but be abused. There are *two* kinds of "mede,"
he says.[11] One is given by God to those who will work

[11] For a detailed account of the allegory of Mede, see A. G.
Mitchell, *Lady Meed and the Art of Piers Plowman*, The Third
Chambers Memorial Lecture, delivered 27 February 1956 (London,

in the World—and he advises the king not to interfere with this just recompense: "Tak no mede, my lord, of men þat ben trewe; / Loue hem & lene hem for oure lordis loue of heuene" (III, 222-223). The other kind, given to wrongdoers, is tainted by greed and injustice— the poet has already used the word in this bad sense when he said "Tak no mede . . . of men þat ben trewe." The wrong kind, says Conscience, is a "mesurles" mede which magistrates desire, and with which they maintain misdoers. What laborers and "low folk" get from their masters is not mede at all, but a measurable hire; nor is there mede in merchandising. Conscience seems to forget his original idea that there is a good mede governed by God—he now uses it to mean "graft," opposing it to "loyalty" (266-276). And that is exactly what has happened in the World. Mede starts out as a thing indifferent, good or bad as it is used; by *usage* it becomes bad—the thing, and so the word. The passage is an interesting example of the way allegory makes out of ordinary language personifications which correspond to experienced fact. In a World where men are beset everywhere by temptation, Mede cannot be anything but wrong. She must therefore be refused a place in the system, and the right government of the World must be established by a king who dwells with Reason and Conscience.

1956), esp. pp. 13-14: "The point that Conscience is trying to make is not that there are good sorts of reward and bad sorts of reward, but rather that there are only two things that deserve to be called by the name of Mede, reward, at all, namely the heavenly reward of God and the rewards given to wrongdoers. All other sorts of payment are not properly called rewards." See also the excellent study by John A. Yunck, *The Lineage of Lady Meed: The Development of Mediaeval Venality Satire,* NDPMS, XVII (Notre Dame, 1963), esp. pp. 284-306.

Just how this right government will work is the problem of the second vision. Characteristically the beginning
is very simple: Conscience gives a sermon telling everyone to do as they should, ending with a directive to pilgrims: "And ȝe þat seke seint Iame & seintes at rome, /
Sekiþ seint treuþe for he may saue ȝou alle" (v, 40-41).
It begins at once, with well-meant confessions from
everyone—they will join the pilgrimage and lead new
lives. But their confessions reveal what will spoil the
quest: most space is given to Envy, Covetousness, Gluttony, and Sloth, and each of the first three, in repenting,
shows just what in his make-up could lead him back to
his old ways. Thus handicapped, the pilgrimage starts
out; we are with somebody dressed like a pagan ("in
pilgrimys wyse"), bedizened with souvenirs of pilgrim-
ages, who ironically does not know the way to Saint
Truth—"Nay, so me god helpe," he cries, "I sauȝ
neuere palmere wiþ pik ne wiþ scrippe, / Axen aftir
hym" (vi, 22-24). A plowman appears, however, and
tells them the way—it is hard without a guide, they
murmur. The plowman is sorry, he has a half acre to be
plowed: "Hadde y erid þat half akir / I wolde wende
wiþ ȝow til ȝe were þere" (vii, 5-6). In a moment he
has set them all to work, each with some appropriate
duty—knights, priests, women—and the pilgrimage is
postponed. Why the delay? What is all this activity for?
It is *labor*, the never-ending activity required to supply
the needs of the body, *to sustain life*. "Þis," says the lady
in a veil, "were a long lettyng."

They are never going to return to the pilgrimage, for
plowing the half acre is more of a job than it seemed.
At prime, Piers "let þe plouȝ stande / To ouersen hem
hymself; whoso best wrouȝte" (vii, 104-105); and
while he stands watching them, like one of those ab-
stracted, serene plowmen in Brueghel, some of them

have sat down, and "sungen at þe ale, / And holpen to ere þe half akir wiþ 'hey trolly lolly.'" Piers, angry, warns them that this will be little help indeed, that they will get no benefit of the grain growing there. The "faitours" pretend to be blind, lame, sick—"ȝe ben wastours," cries Piers, "ȝe eten þat hy shulde ete þat eren for vs alle." No sooner said than Waster appears:

> A bretoner, a braggere, he bostide hym also,
> And bad hym go pisse wiþ his plouȝ: 'pilide shrewe!
> Wilt þou, nilt þou, we wile haue oure wil
> Of þi flour, and þi flessh fecche whanne vs likeþ,
> And make vs merye þerwiþ maugre þi chekis.'

> (VII, 141-145)

The knight courteously warns him, but Waster grumbles, "I was not wonid to werche . . . now wile I not begynne." To tame him, Piers calls on Hunger, who, being what he is, comes at once. Hunger and Waster fight; Piers intervenes, and the others, frightened, join him in the attempt to assuage Hunger: even "faitours" and hermits start to work, and we are wryly informed that a thousand blind and bedridden men have been suddenly cured. And now that everyone is working, Piers bids Hunger return home, first asking him for advice. Hunger's counsels are dreadfully stern—for beggars, he counsels a dole of unprepossessing food which will keep them thin (if they complain, he says, tell them to work); for those who are legitimately poor, he counsels charity; for those who have lain sick all week with stomachaches, he prescribes a moderate diet. But *all* must work at something:

> Kynde wyt wolde þat iche wiȝt wrouȝte
> Oþer wiþ teching, oþer telling, or trauaillyng
> of hondis,
> Actif lif oþer contemplatif. (231-233)

They are still waiting for Hunger to leave, but he stays on, asking to dine and drink. Although it is a bad season, some modest fare is fetched up for the time being, and at harvest time, when there is plenty, he is satisfied. But no sooner is all well than Waster refuses to work. Beggars demand white bread and the best brown ale. Laborers eat fresh vegetables and meat or fine fish, insist on high wages, complain about their work, curse the king and his laws which control their wages. The conflict is unresolvable. Waster will only serve while Hunger is master; and just for that reason Hunger is going to come back again and again.

That is why the erstwhile pilgrims must go on cultivating the half acre. Truth, hearing about the coming famine, bids them all go on plowing the land and presents a pardon to all who will help Piers in any way.[12] It is a wonderful pardon—*a pena et a culpa*—and will be offered to kings and knights, to bishops, to laborers, to pregnant women, to the old, the blind, and the sick who take their misfortunes meekly, even to merchants and lawyers so long as each performs his function properly, and to beggars so long as they have good reason to beg. Is it a true pardon? Yes, if people would do what it says. For if people would "do well and have well," what need would there be for the ordinary kind of pardon? "Pardon" here is like "mede"—it has a bad name not for what it is but for what men make of it. The best pardon is not a paper come all hot from Rome; it is the reward which God Himself offers good men. Even Chaucer's Pardoner granted the point:

> And Jhesu Crist, that is oure soules leche,
> So graunte yow his pardoun to receyve,
> For that is best; I wol yow nat deceyve.

[12] See David C. Fowler, "The 'Forgotten' Pilgrimage in *Piers the Plowman*," *MLN*, LXVII (1952), 524-526.

Hence, when he has waked the Dreamer tells us that he

> . . . demide þat dowel indulgence passiþ,
> Bienalis & trienalis & bisshopis lettres.

. . . .

> And so I leue lelly, lord forbede ellis,
> Þat pardoun, & penaunce, & preyours do salue
> Soulis þat han ysynned seue siþes dedly.
> Ac to triste on þis trionalis, trewely, me þinkeþ,
> It is not so sikir for þe soule, certis, as is do wel.

(VIII, 153-164)

The Pardon is nothing more than a declaration of God's grace, nothing but the promise of the Athanasian Creed that virtuous lives will be rewarded hereafter:

> . . . do wel & haue wel, & god shal haue þi soule,
> And do euele & haue euele, & hope þou non oþer
> Þat aftir þi deþ day to helle shalt þou wende.

(98-100)

From the idealist's point of view, such a pardon is all one could ask for. From the realist's point of view, there are degrees of virtuous living, and pardons exist not for saints but for sinners. If the World were not what it is, the Pardon would indeed be *a culpa*—that is the irony, that it could exist only by doing away with the Fall (which brought about human weakness) and the Redemption (in which God took the *culpa* upon Himself). The Pardon really has to do with the Last Judgment, not with sins which men inevitably commit (and may repent) from day to day.[13] That is why the priest impugns the Pardon—because it is too "otherworldly." He says what practical men and bureaucrats always say to idealists—"Where have *you* been?" "This won't work."

[13] See Bloomfield, *Piers Plowman*, pp. 115-116.

"You have a lot to learn." It is just the response, and just the sneering tone, one expects; and after viewing the fine little social order of the half acre one is hard pressed to feel much sympathy for the priest. Still, of course, he is right: the fine little social order of the half acre failed. The Pardon is a noble *idea*, but something else is needed to make things work in the World. And when Piers tears up the Pardon he does not deny this fact any more than he denies the Athanasian Creed or a declaration of God's grace—he accepts it, angrily.

Critics of the poem have seen in Piers' tearing of the Pardon either a rejection or an acceptance of the priest's objections: either Piers must be angry at the priest for impugning a true pardon, or angry at himself for having accepted a false one.[14] But such a choice is not necessary. The priest is not wrong, but unappealing—because he has lost touch with Christian idealism; nor is the Pardon false, but "unrealistic"—because it ignores human limitations. Piers pulls it asunder "for pure tene"—just plain anger and frustration and indignation of the kind which everyone has felt upon waking from certain dreams. Then, declaring "I will fear no evil for Thou art with me," he resolves to give up sowing and work less hard, to give less attention to his livelihood, to worry more about prayers and penance, not to care about sustenance. He is a little sulky, perhaps, but his intentions are of the best. What enrages him when he tears the Pardon is the ineluctable fact that an ideal social order, a just

[14] Robert W. Frank gives a useful summary of previous opinions about the Pardon in "The Pardon Scene in *Piers Plowman*," *Speculum*, XXVI (1951), 318-319. See also Frank, *Piers Plowman and the Scheme of Salvation*, YSE, Vol. 136 (New Haven and London, 1957), pp. 24-29. Since Frank's article, see D. W. Robertson, Jr., and Bernard F. Huppé, *Piers Plowman and Scriptural Tradition* (Princeton, 1951), pp. 91-99, and John Lawlor, *Piers Plowman: An Essay in Criticism* (London, 1962), pp. 70-82.

way of providing the necessities of life, is never going to work in this wicked World. And he is further enraged because people like the priest calmly accept this fact. Piers is all taken up with ideals and hopes; the priest is all taken up with practical measures and necessities. There is no resolution of their conflict. They confront each other with two complementary points of view— one stridently idealistic, surging with hope and spirit, impatient of compromise; the other niggling, literal-minded, and a little sour. It is impossible not to feel that the poet's sympathies lie with Piers. But that is not what he shows us. The priest and Piers stand arguing with each other and exchanging insults; they "aposid" each other. And through their words the dreamer wakes.

The Pardon, indeed the very existence of pardons, illustrates a fundamental dichotomy in medieval thought: that while men ought to strive for perfection and are commanded to be perfect, they are by nature flawed and therefore bound to be *im*perfect. The poet has begun by raising a question about the distribution of temporal goods, and he attempts to solve it by formulating an ideal society. But everything that makes the World wicked and corrupt makes the ideal impossible. Turn fallen men loose to plow a half acre and you get greed, avarice, and sloth. The weakness of the Pardon, as Nevill Coghill has most intelligently shown, is that it represents justice without mercy.[15] It is for perfect, not for fallen, men.

2. THE SEARCH FOR DO-WEL

In the *Vita*, the poet's concern turns from his initial economic preoccupation to a larger question. If the World

[15] Nevill Coghill, "The Pardon of *Piers Plowman*," *PBA*, xxx (1944), 316-320, 356-357.

itself by its very nature prohibits perfection, should we
attempt through some compromise to do with it what
we can, or should we renounce it altogether? What, in
a word, does it mean to "do well"? It is this phase of
the poem which has most occupied critics; and of course
it is this which draws the poet away from the problem
of lust of the eyes to larger, spiritual questions.[16] Even
in the *Vita*, however, the A-text harkens back at the end
to its initial concern. After the long examination of
Do-wel, Do-bet, and Do-best, at the point where the
dreamer wakes, the whole inquiry is brought back, in
the discourse of Scripture, to a simple principle about
temporal goods—that they should be distributed in charity and in mercy. Poor men who practice patience and
penitence, Scripture says, have their heritage in heaven,
and not the rich. Christians must love God and their
neighbor, and this means that "we shuln ȝiue & dele /
Oure enemys and alle men þat arn nedy & pore." We
are bound to honor our fellow Christians "And ȝiuen
hem of oure good as good as oureseluen," and to be kind
to heathens "in hope hem to amende." In the last analysis mercy will make the social order work well, and it is
mercy, in man and in God, which will win us a heavenly
reward:

> For *Michi vindictam et ego retribuam.*
> I shal punisshen in purcatory or in þe put of helle
> Eche man for his misdede but mercy it make.
>
> (A. xi, 255-257)

After this, the dreamer, observing that he is no closer
to knowing Do-wel, rejects his intellectual search. His

[16] A. C. Spearing, in "The Development of a Theme in *Piers
Plowman*," *RES*, n.s. xi (1960), 241-253, has shown how in treating
the theme of hunger and using the symbol of bread the poet has seen
an economic problem finally as a spiritual one.

name was entered in the "legende of lif" long before he was born, he says, and his salvation must depend on God's Grace, not on any learning. The sin of curiosity, of "vain learning," leads men to error—it is, as we have seen, a phase of "lust of the eyes." Quoting St. Augustine, he concludes,

> Arn none raþere yrauisshid fro þe riȝte beleue
> Þanne arn þise kete clerkis þat conne many bokis,
> Ne none sonnere ysauid, ne saddere of consience,
> Þanne pore peple, as plouȝmen, and pastours of bestis,
> Souteris & seweris; suche lewide iottis
> Percen wiþ a *paternoster* þe paleis of heuene
> Wiþoute penaunce at here partyng, into þe heiȝe blisse.   (308-313)

Salvation is easiest for those who fare worst in this World, who are least led astray by riches and plenty: the answer to the problem of distributing and using temporal goods is therefore not to have them.

This renunciation of the lust of the eyes, by no means the last word on the subject, is the germ of the expanded *Vita* in the B-text. At the close of A one seems to glimpse the poet faltering in the tangle of his own ideas, then stumbling upon the solution: not to *know* the good but to *do* it. The notion is developed very slightly in the "John But passus," sometimes found at the end of the A-text—a false start, as it actually is, to the development of the B-*Vita*: while Hunger and Death plot against Life, Will is told to stay in the World for a while longer, to "do after dowel whil þi dayes duren, / Þat þi play be plentevous in paradys with aungelys" (XII, 94-95). Similarly, in the *Vita* of B the dreamer turns from speculative to practical considerations. Only

now, as John Lawlor has said, "is he ready to apprehend as vision what eluded him as discourse."[17] This
emphasis on *doing* was, in ethics, what distinguished
Christianity from its classical antecedents. Platonism had
insisted that to know the good was to do the good, that
evil was ignorance. St. Augustine, perhaps following
Philo of Alexandria and the Stoics, understood that
knowledge of the good was by itself nothing without the
rational determination to *act* upon that knowledge.[18] In
the concept of *will* St. Augustine centered his difference
with Platonism: to do the good is not merely to seek
knowledge of it but to make a choice in favor of it, and
the will is the faculty of choice. It is in exactly this
respect, for the evildoer, that suggestion and delectation
differ from consent. But too much seeking can weaken
the will and lead one into error—in *Piers Plowman* we
have seen St. Augustine quoted on this very point. For
all the seeking of the dreamer is going to accomplish
nothing if he is merely amassing bits of intellection;
that would be the lust of the eyes. His purpose, rather,
is to find out what he must *do*, what right actions he
must *choose*;[19] it can hardly be an accident—or if so,

[17] John Lawlor, "The Imaginative Unity of *Piers Plowman*,"
RES, n.s. VIII (1957), 119.

[18] The concept of will seems first to have been stated by the Cynic,
Antisthenes. See Eduard Zeller, *Outlines of the History of Greek
Philosophy* (13th ed., New York, 1931), pp. 108-112.

[19] Cf. Hort, pp. 86-87: "The dreamer had assumed that to know
is the same thing as to do, and he had at the same time omitted to
endow man with a will. In his further search for Do-Well, the
dreamer does not at first see his mistake; on the contrary, he makes
it worse by introducing the idea of a perfectly free will coupled with
knowledge, both of which were given to man by God and both of
which are in man's possession, before he sets out in his search for
God. . . . With the introduction of wit and free will, Langland
begins his second and fuller description of man. By taking wit and

a happy one—that the dreamer's name is Will.[20] This change of emphasis accounts for the different structure which the B-text assumes. The B-text comprises the first two visions of the A-text (with some alterations) ending with the Pardon, plus a series of visions which expand the *Vita* of A, making it equivalent in length and development to the *Visio*. The new balance puts a heavier emphasis on the Pardon scene: it now marks a major change in the dreamer from a passive observer of the World's problems to an active seeker for their solution.[21]

The area where the ideal and the practical come into conflict is the World, and we know the World only by knowing ourselves—by knowing what we feel and perceive about the World. Langland's method was therefore to explore his own inner world, to examine the jumble of concepts, ideals, perceptions, emotions, and memories which seemed to explain why men do not *do* what they ought. The result is chaotic, as one would expect; but Langland, subject to a ubiquitous tendency of his age, attempted to make order out of chaos by equating the various strands of his inner life with established three-fold categories. We have seen the habit tediously at work in Chapter Two above. Whatever else made such triplicities appealing to the medieval mind,

---

free will into account his view of man is considerably altered, and consequently a new direction is given to his search for God."

[20] On the dreamer's name as a pun, see B. F. Huppé, *"Petrus Id Est Christus*: Word Play in *Piers Plowman*, the B-text," *ELH*, XVII (1950), 190.

[21] See Bloomfield, *Piers Plowman*, p. 5. On the Pardon scene as a crucial point in the structure of the work, see Henry W. Wells, "The Construction of *Piers Plowman*," *PMLA*, XLIV (1929), 123-140; T. P. Dunning, "The Structure of the B-text of *Piers Plowman*," *RES*, n.s. VII (1956), 225-237; and Lawlor, *"Piers Plowman*: The Pardon Reconsidered," pp. 449-458.

there is little doubt that the threefold nature of God exerted a powerful influence. Man, in the image of God, could be analyzed in three parts;[22] and history could be disposed into three ages corresponding to the Trinity.[23] Because Langland attempted to equate as best he could his own vision of the World according to a triplex form, many critical treatments have attempted to prove that one or the other is dominant, or that a particular association is the main one and others subsidiary. The problem is, obviously, that the three states—Do-wel, Do-bet, and Do-best—exist in the ragbag of the mind and are revealed through the slippery logic of dreams. They are psychological states: the *Vita* is a movement of the mind into itself.[24] For exactly this reason, *Imaginatif* becomes a key figure. In medieval psychology the *vis imaginativa* "mediated between the world of senses and the intellectual world"; it was the faculty of the mind which made pictures, formed ideas, and produced dreams.[25] The three states have therefore the misty disorder of dreams and prophecies. They enlist, but do not satisfy, the reader's curiosity.

[22] See St. Augustine, *De Trinitate*, x, 11-12 (*PL* 42:982-984) and *De civ. Dei*, xi, 26.

[23] See Bloomfield, *Piers Plowman*, pp. 65-67, 101-102, and "Joachim of Flora: A Critical Survey of His Canon, Teachings, Sources, Biography, and Influence," *Traditio*, xiii (1957), 264-271. Frank, *Piers Plowman and the Scheme of Salvation*, pp. 16-17, argues that the Trinity is the organizing principle of the *Vita*, the gifts of its three members constituting the scheme of salvation.

[24] See Bloomfield, *Piers Plowman*, p. 64. Cf. Henry W. Wells, "The Philosophy of *Piers Plowman*," *PMLA*, liii (1938), 341, 348-349. On the whole problem of identifying the three ways of life, see the excellent remarks of E. Talbot Donaldson, *Piers Plowman: The C-text and Its Poet*, YSE, Vol. 113 (New Haven and London, 1949), pp. 156-161.

[25] H. S. V. Jones, "Imaginatif in *Piers Plowman*," *JEGP*, xiii (1914), 583-588; and Bloomfield, *Piers Plowman*, pp. 170-174.

I shall attempt to summarize this material, as it has been variously elucidated, under what seem to me the major kinds of associations which the poet includes and the critics discuss:

(1) *The life of the dreamer and of mankind*. The materials of the *Vita* seem to be ordered in a way which corresponds to the author's intellectual development. Thought represents his own general knowledge; Study, his schooling; Clergy, his experience in a clerical order—and so on.[26] In B. Passus xx we see him growing old, losing his teeth, and becoming impotent. The dreamer, who is to be identified with the poet,[27] is also meant to depict mankind in general: hence the progression of his life can be understood as the three ages of man—youth, middle age, and old age. The first of these, as John F. Adams suggests, is governed by animal spirits, the second by reason, and the third by "qualities of becoming" which end in eternity. These three ages were associated elsewhere in medieval literature with the flesh, the World, and the devil; Langland (in B. xvi, 26-52) reverses this tradition, associating the sins of the World with youth and those of the flesh with middle age.[28]

(2) *The history of the world*. Beginning with B. Passus xvi, the *Vita* depicts in order the events of Holy Week—a sequence which rises to a magnificent climax in

[26] Otto Mensendieck, "The Authorship of *Piers Plowman*," *JEGP*, IX (1910), 404-420. Mensendieck sees in A. XI, 128 ff. a reference to the trivium and quadrivium. Wells, "Construction of *Piers Plowman*," pp. 137-138, regards the *Vita de Do-wel* as an attempt of the poet to trace his mental development. Cf. Gordon H. Gerould, "The Structural Integrity of *Piers Plowman* B," *SP*, XLV (1948), 60-75, who sees the work as a pilgrimage in time and the *Vita* as tracing the religious education of the dreamer.

[27] See R. W. Chambers, "Robert or William Longland?" *LMS*, I, 3 (1948 for 1939), 442-451.

[28] John F. Adams, "*Piers Plowman* and the Three Ages of Man," *JEGP*, LXI (1962), 23-41.

Piers Plowman

Passus xviii when the dreamer wakes and finds it is Easter. This is followed by an account of Pentecost (xix). At the same time, the poet suggests—parallel to his own decline in age—the decline of the World[29] and emphasizes the coming of the Antichrist, the Harrowing of Hell, and the Last Judgment. In this, as Bloomfield has shown, he draws upon medieval apocalyptic notions and associates Do-wel, Do-bet, and Do-best with an age of God, an age of Christ, and an age of the Holy Ghost.[30]

(3) *Relationships of ideas and mental states.* The three "lives" are expressed in the simplest and most compelling way by the use of a grammatical relationship among their names—well, better, best.[31] "Well" is simply opposed to "ill"; "better" and "best" (which come in English from a different base) are variations and extensions in meaning of the fundamental concept of goodness. The *search* is for Do-wel; better and best are a part of the answer. These three states suggest, of course, the three grades of perfection.[32] In B. xiv they are associated with contrition, confession, and satisfaction. In their most direct applications, they refer to the "purgative, illuminative, and unitive" stages of the spiritual life,[33] and to the "active, contemplative, and

[29] See Bloomfield, *Piers Plowman*, p. 127.

[30] Bloomfield, *Piers Plowman*, esp. pp. 116-126. Cf. Wells, "Construction of *Piers Plowman*," pp. 132-136; and Frank, *Piers Plowman and the Scheme of Salvation*, pp. 16-18.

[31] On the use of grammatical analogies in scholastic thought, see Bloomfield, *Piers Plowman*, p. 119. Cf. Frank, *Piers Plowman and the Scheme of Salvation*, pp. 41-44.

[32] See Morton W. Bloomfield, "*Piers Plowman* and the Three Grades of Chastity," *Anglia*, LXXVI (1958), 227-253, and *Piers Plowman*, pp. 44-67.

[33] See Dunning, *Piers Plowman*, p. 174; Wells, "Philosophy of *Piers Plowman*," p. 344; Meroney, pp. 10-15.

mixed" vocational states.[34] Recently Father Dunning has shown that, because the "active" life is itself spiritual, these two applications are compatible.[35] And these states are symbolized by the mysterious figure of Piers himself, first presented as a simple plowman, then as a learned clerk, and finally as Christ Himself.[36]

From this complex structure, which includes a number of passages on the use of temporal goods, I should like to fasten attention upon two scenes. My claim for their importance is based on their position—one at the end of the *Vita de Do-wel*, the other at the end of the poem. Both of these scenes deal with the imperfection inherent in worldly things, which puts our best ideals beyond our grasp. In both, this basic observation is centered in the problem of temporal goods; both present the virtue of temperance or *mesure* as an ideal solution to that problem; and in both the ideal is understood to be impossible of fulfillment.

In the B-text the *Vita de Do-wel* ends with the splendid figure of Hawkyn, the active man. After all the definitions of Do-wel, Do-bet, and Do-best, presented in a discursive and accumulative way which, though it defies remembrance, gives us a clear feeling for the three

[34] See Wells, "Construction of *Piers Plowman*," pp. 132-135, and "Philosophy of *Piers Plowman*," pp. 341-349; Nevill Coghill, "The Character of *Piers Plowman* Considered from the B-text," *MA*, II (1933), 108-135; R. W. Chambers, *Man's Unconquerable Mind* (London, 1939), pp. 102-106, 123-130, 149-155; Frank, *Piers Plowman and the Scheme of Salvation*, pp. 7-11. Elizabeth Zeeman, "*Piers Plowman* and the Pilgrimage to Truth," *E&S*, n.s. XI (1958), 1-16, compares the process of finding God within, personified in Piers, with Hilton's *Scale of Perfection*.

[35] Dunning, "Structure of the B-text," esp. pp. 233-237.

[36] Howard William Troyer, "Who is Piers Plowman?" *PMLA*, XLVII (1932), 368-384, and Coghill, "The Pardon of Piers Plowman," pp. 347-357, both suggest that the figure of Piers may be understood as a developed four-level allegory.

states, the figure of Hawkyn draws to a focus the essential problem of doing well with respect to the *vita activa*. Hawkyn is a minstrel who can play no instrument; his name is *Activa-vita* and his occupation is to supply wafers to "trewe trauaillours and tilieres of the erthe" (B. xiii, 239). These wafers are food, physical sustenance. They are presumably eucharistic wafers as well, but we should bear in mind that he provides the material substance used in the mass, not the spiritual consecration. And he provides it through labor:

> For ar I haue bred of mele ofte mote I swete.
> And ar the comune haue corne ynough many a
>   colde mornynge;
> So, ar my wafres ben ywrouȝt moche wo I
>   tholye.   (261-263)

In time of plague people complain about the lack of his wafers—he mentions a famine in 1370. Thus Hawkyn the active man symbolizes the labor of providing the necessities of life, a high function, so important that the mass itself cannot be celebrated without it. Then the dreamer looks at Hawkyn's coat. It is a "coat of Christendom," but besmirched with all kinds of sins (274-313), especially with the desire to please the people and have their praise. Because the active life seems to involve a pernicious compromise with the World, the poet here reminds us of that most uncompromising Christian principle, that no one can serve two masters. Conscience points out the flaws and spots on Hawkyn's coat, which Hawkyn acknowledges—wrath, envy, lying, tale-bearing, and many another sin. Covetousness, gluttony, and sloth, the sins which most hinder the active life, are the last to be mentioned; the poet then concludes with a discourse on the use of riches:

> Clerkes and kniȝtes welcometh kynges ministrales,
> And for loue of the lorde litheth hem at festes;
> Muche more, me thenketh riche men schulde
> Haue beggeres byfore hem the whiche ben goddes
>   ministrales. (437-440)

At the end of Passus XIII, Conscience asks Hawkyn why he had not washed his soiled coat, "or wyped it with a brusshe." Passus XIV begins, therefore, with Hawkyn's confession. He pleads that he has but one coat, and a wife and children as well; the coat has been cleaned many times by penance, but he keeps soiling it "with syȝte or sum ydel speche, / Or thorugh werke or thorugh worde or wille of myn herte" (XIV, 13-14). Conscience shows Hawkyn how he may clean his coat by contrition, confession, and satisfaction—here equated with Do-wel, Do-bet, and Do-best. Patience reminds him "We shulde nouȝt be to busy a-bouten owre lyflode" (33), offering instead *fiat voluntas tua*: "Haue, Haukyn!" he cries, "and ete this whan the hungreth" (49). He recommends, in short, that the active life be much less of this World: *Si quis amat Cristum, mundum non diligit istum*. This principle is presented in economic terms.[37] *Mesure* and patient poverty will permit us to supply worldly needs without falling into sin:

> For-thi Crystene sholde ben in comune riche none
>   coueitouse for hym-selue.
> For seuene synnes that there ben assaillen vs euere,
> The fende folweth hem alle and fondeth hem to
>   helpe,
> Ac with ricchesse that ribaude rathest men bigyleth.
>   (200-203)

---

[37] On the danger that temporal goods incite men to sin as an element in the passage on Hawkyn, see Stella Maguire, "The Significance of Haukyn, *Activa Vita*, in *Piers Plowman*," *RES*, XXV (1949), 97-109.

Patience shows (215-256) how the rich are more susceptible than the poor to each of the seven sins, and explains
(279-319) a text from Vincent of Beauvais' *Speculum
historiale*, x, 71, on the virtues of poverty. Then
Hawkyn breaks into tears, lamenting his sinful life, and
the vision of Do-wel ends:

'So harde it is,' quod Haukyn 'to lyue and to do
    synne.
Synne suweth vs euere,' quod he and sori gan wexe,
And wepte water with his eyghen and weyled the
    tyme,
That euere he dede dede that dere god displesed;
Swowed and sobbed and syked ful ofte,
That euere he hadde londe or lordship lasse other
    more,
Or maystrye ouer any man mo than of hym-self.
'I were nou3t worthy, wote god,' quod Haukyn 'to
    were any clothes,
Ne noyther sherte ne shone saue for shame one,
To keure my caroigne,' quod he and cryde mercye
    faste,
And wepte and weyled and there-with I awaked.
                        (322-332)

The *Vitae* of Do-bet and Do-best, which follow, are
a development of the higher grades of perfection suggested in the *Vita de Do-wel*. They are divided, as
redemptive history is divided, by the Resurrection: at
the end of Passus xviii the dreamer wakes to find it is
Easter. In the following passus he falls asleep—during
the Easter mass—and dreams of Pentecost and the
establishment of the Church. Piers comes to be identified
with Christ and the Apostolic Succession; he sows the
cardinal virtues and builds a house called Unity, making
of baptism and the Holy Blood a mortar called Mercy.

But again, just as everything seems to be going well, the ideal is disrupted. Pride opposes; a brewer turns against the idea of *redde quod debes* and protests that he will cheat the people; a priest, mistaking the term "cardinal virtue," protests against the abuses of Cardinals; a lord argues that he may take from his reeve whatever his auditor or steward advises. At last there appears a king, who declares that he will rule the *comune*, defending Church and clergy against evil men; he is the head of the body politic, the people being its members, so that his demands on them are just. Conscience agrees, so long as he will rule in reason: *Omnia tua sunt ad defendendum, set non ad depredandum.*

Here we find ourselves exactly where we were at the end of the first vision. A king will rule the *comune* under the guidance of Conscience and Reason—but men will not submit to this rule. Passus xx, the last vision, singles out the central problem. Not knowing where to eat, Will comes upon Need, who accuses him of intemperance and makes a speech in praise of poverty. He falls asleep and has a vision of the Antichrist, who comes followed by friars, with Pride bearing his banner, to overturn the truth. Old Age overcomes Will, taking his teeth, giving him the gout, making him bald, deaf, and—to his wife's displeasure—impotent. Death draws near him; Will, quaking with fear, asks Kynde to help him—Kynde's advice is "Lerne to loue." As the dreamer has been shown to decline, the Church has been traced from its glorious beginnings down to its corrupted present:[38] the friars now enter the picture. Being the most corrupt among the orders, and in some ways a monastic one at that, their reform is a key to the reform of the World, for monasticism is the most perfect state of life.

[38] See Lawlor, *Piers Plowman*, p. 182.

Their besetting sin is avarice: they do wrongs for the
sake of gain—"Thei wil flatre, to fare wel folke that
ben riche" (234). Envy has sent them to school to learn
logic and disputation, and to preach communism, which
goes against the commandment *Non concupisces rem
proximi tui.* They are easy in giving penance in order to
reap profits from the large numbers who go to them
(271-291). What they have done, Langland suggests, is
to violate the order of nature through intemperance—
they are guilty of avarice, and they have, in their extraordinary expansion, exceeded their "proper number."[39]
Thus Conscience, pointing to the examples of St. Francis
and St. Dominic, promises them enough bread, clothing,
and other necessities if they will "leue logyk and lerneth
for to louye" (249). Need itself, Langland suggests, has
tempted the friars, as it tempts all men, to an intem-
perate love of worldly goods.[40] The solution, the same
one presented in the passage on Hawkyn, is *mesure*.

The poem ends with this counsel, but it is presented,
as are all ideals in the poem, with the sad reminder that
men will ignore it. Friar Flatterer shows up with letters
from the Bishop, to hear confessions; Peace refuses him
admittance, but Hende-speche helps him get in. He

> . . . goth and gadereth and gloseth there he
>   shryueth,
> Tyl Contricioun hadde clene forʒeten to crye and
>   to wepe,
> And wake for his wykked werkes as he was wont
>   to done.   (366-368)

[39] On this last notion see B. xx, 252-265; and Bloomfield, *Piers
Plowman*, pp. 145-147.

[40] On this message of temperance with respect to the friars, see
Robert W. Frank, Jr., "The Conclusion of *Piers Plowman*," *JEGP*,
xlix (1950), 309-316; Robertson and Huppé, pp. 227-233; and
Bloomfield, *Piers Plowman*, pp. 69-72, 121, 145-149.

"The frere with his phisik this folke hath enchaunted," declares Conscience, and announces that he will become a pilgrim. He will

> . . . walken as wyde as al the worlde lasteth,
> To seke Piers the Plowman that Pryde may destruye,
> And that freres hadde a fyndyng that for nede flateren,
> And contrepleteth me, Conscience. (379-382)[41]

He is off again in search of Piers the Plowman. He cries aloud after Grace. And the dreamer wakes.

*

The problem of riches, of using temporal goods, of supplying the body's needs without permitting those needs to tempt the soul—all this is resolved by commending love, mercy, and temperance. The solution, though it seems simplistic when thus summarized, attains a towering dignity in the poem because it is a phase or corollary of an elaborate ideal. This was the ideal of a Christianized *mundus*, a hierarchy in which the *comune* is protected and ruled by a king who is in turn obedient to the precepts of the Church—a vicar of Christ who is the head of the "body politic" as the pope is the head of the "mystical body of Christ."[42] It proposes a subservience of *mundus* to *ecclesia* and commends the extension of ascetic and eremitic ideals into secular life, with all men living in "apostolic poverty." That ideal had been a lost cause since the early twelfth

---

[41] On the reading of these lines, see R. E. Kaske in *JEGP*, LXII (1963), 205-206.

[42] On the background of this ideal, see Ernst H. Kantorowicz, *The King's Two Bodies: A Study in Mediaeval Political Theology* (Princeton, 1957), esp. pp. 42-86; and Otto Gierke, *Political Theories of the Middle Age*, trans. F. W. Maitland (Boston, 1958), pp. 7-37.

century; by Langland's time the growing separation of church and state had in fact become a dichotomy. The "mystical body of Christ," a term usually applied to the mass, was now applied to the Church; and the "body politic" theory of the state, modeled on this notion of a unified and centralized Church, illustrates the growing independence of state from church, the two being seen now as separate bodies.[43] Langland, in urging a hierarchical relationship of the two, is appealing to an old and impossible ideal, in his own time still charged with emotional and sentimental power, though bereft of feasibility. This ideal was essentially feudal. It conceived of Christ as the "king of kings," so that each king on earth is like a subinfeudated vassal, Christ Himself being pictured as a feudal overlord, a great warrior whose Crucifixion is a triumphant joust or tourney.[44] The virtues it commended were therefore the virtues of a Christianized feudalism—*treuthe* and *leauté*.

The key passages of the poem adumbrate this feudal ideal. In Passus I, Holy Church commends Treuthe as the best treasure, and by it she means a compliance with the constituted order of things—obedience to God and love of one's neighbor. The passage on Mede (Passus II–IV) develops this principle with respect to society. If Mede can be kept from interfering with the system, Reason will rule by law, through one Christian king to whom all shall have *leauté*:

[43] See Gerhart B. Ladner, "Aspects of Mediaeval Thought on Church and State," *RP*, IX (1947), 403-422, and "The Concepts of 'Ecclesia' and 'Christianitas,' and their Relation to the Idea of Papal 'Plenitudo Potestatis' from Gregory VII to Boniface VIII," *MHP*, XVIII (1953), 49-77; Norman F. Cantor, "The Crisis of Western Monasticism, 1050-1130," *AHR*, LXVI (1960), 47-67. See also Kantorowicz, pp. 15-16, 193-232; and Bloomfield, *Piers Plowman*, pp. 102-104.

[44] See B. XVI, 160-166; and cf. Kantorowicz, pp. 72-73.

Shal no more mede be maister on erþe,
But loue & louȝnesse & leaute togideris;
And whoso trespassiþ to treuþe, or takiþ aȝeyn his
    wille,
Leaute shal do hym lawe and no lif ellis.

(A. iii, 266-269)

When Mede is banished from court, the King agrees to
live with Reason and Conscience:

'Be hym þat rauȝte on þe rode,' quaþ resoun to þe
    king,
'But I reule þus þi reaum rend out my ribbes,
Ȝif it be þat buxumnesse be at myn assent.'
'And I assente,' quaþ þe king, 'be seinte marie my
    lady,
Be my counseil ycome of clerkes and Erlis.
Ac redily, resoun, þou shalt not raike henne,
For as longe as I lyue lete þe I nile.'
'I am redy,' quaþ resoun, 'to reste wiþ ȝow euere;
So consience be of ȝour counseil, kepe I no betere.'
'I graunte,' quaþ þe king, 'godis forbode he faille!
As longe as I lyue libbe we togideris.' (A. iv, 148-158)

The plowing of the half acre depicts such a society from
the viewpoint of the common people, who must labor
to produce food, under the protection of the knights and
with the prayers of the clergy:

Kynde wyt wolde þat iche wiȝt wrouȝte
Oþer wiþ teching, oþer telling, or trauaillyng of
    hondis,
Actif lif oþer contemplatif. (A. vii, 231-233)

This "functionalism," with its feudalized hierarchy
under God and its facile balance of *ecclesia* and *mundus*,

is centered in the figure of Piers.[45] As the simple farmer, Piers exemplifies the qualities which workers must have in order for society to supply its economic needs. As a teacher and leader, he shows how such a society will work, what its various members must contribute, and how they must be coerced or rewarded. As he is identified finally with the apostolic priesthood and with Christ Himself, he shows what place this worldly order has in the scheme of things eternal. Hence the *Vita* explores this Christianized feudalism in two opposing perspectives; it examines the qualities in the life of the individual necessary to the success of the proposed social system, and it examines the limitation of this system when seen against the scheme of things eternal. The virtues of *treuthe* and *leauté*, in "pure" feudalism, were blind qualities expected of any vassal for good or for bad—it was not for him to quibble over the right or wrong of his lord's decisions. Hence, as we shall see in the next chapter, the feudal or "chivalric" virtues gave rise, in practice, to profound emotional conflicts. But in *Piers Plowman* feudal ideals are freed, or potentially so, from all conflicts. *Treuthe* and *leauté* cannot exist without love or charity toward God and one's neighbor, mercy toward the imperfections and miseries of one's fellow men, and temperance in the use of property and temporal goods. But imperfect men, as Langland knew, do not have these qualities; they must strive to attain them and must repent their failures to do so. That is why Conscience, at the very end, starts out once more in search of Piers the Plowman.

This ideal of a Christianized *mundus*, a potential solution to the problem of supplying temporal needs and

[45] See Rufus William Rauch, "Langland and Mediaeval Functionalism," *RP*, v (1943), 441-461; and see Gardiner Stillwell, "Chaucer's Plowman and the Contemporary English Peasant," *ELH*, vi (1939), 285-290.

using temporal goods, is applied to different spheres of thought. We are made aware of the right conduct for the individual, the right government of society in its process of becoming the kingdom of Christ, and the final disposition of all in Eternity. These spheres are tropological, allegorical, and anagogical matters, and it would not surprise many if the poet had in mind the theory of allegorical interpretation, especially in building up the all-encompassing figure of Piers. It *is* true that he had in mind some specific symbols of the exegetical tradition.[46] Whether such scriptural symbols entered the work unconsciously as part of the poet's mental content, or were selected and planned as part of an elaborate allegory, is a point more open to debate than to solution. Robertson and Huppé suggest, for example, that the figure of the Plowman is a scriptural symbol which stands for the true followers of the prelatical life, that the food he produces is the spiritual food of the Church, that gluttony and wasting are the misuse of worldly things and hunger the loss of "spiritual food" (i.e., excommunication), that clothing in general is the kind of lives men lead, and so on.[47] It seems unlikely that the poet selected such figures only because they had

[46] How he used these has been demonstrated, with respect to some specific examples, by Alfred L. Kellogg, in "Satan, Langland, and the North," *Speculum*, XXIV (1949), 413-414; "Langland and Two Scriptural Texts," *Traditio*, XIV (1958), 385-398; "Langland and the 'Canes Muti,'" in Rudolf Kirk and C. F. Main, eds., *Essays in Literary History presented to J. Milton French* (New Brunswick, 1960), pp. 25-35; and by R. E. Kaske, notably in *"Gigas* the Giant in *Piers Plowman,"* JEGP, LVI (1957), 177-185; "Langland's Walnut-Simile," *JEGP*, LVIII (1959), 650-654; " '*Ex vi transicionis*' and Its Passage in *Piers Plowman,"* JEGP, LXII (1963), 32-60; "The Speech of 'Book' in *Piers Plowman," Anglia*, LXXVII (1959), 117-144.

[47] See Robertson and Huppé, esp. pp. 17-19, 82-91, 169-176, 245-246.

in the tradition of exegetical writings such-and-such a value which he needed for his argument. Granted that some *ideas* must have suggested particular symbols. But in other cases the figures or images which his experience and imagination presented to him had, from traditions of exegesis, the power to suggest a second, "spiritual" meaning, and he took advantage of this fact at times. The poem, everyone agrees, is no mere jigsaw puzzle of allegorical figures, but a controlled work of art; and the question is, why are some symbols from the cornucopia of exegetical tradition more powerful than others? My answer is that some symbols are more powerful because in that tradition, as elsewhere, they were more relevant to medieval culture and to human life in general. The symbolic meaning of the plowman, for example, can be found in exegetical writings alongside the symbolic meaning for all kinds of creatures and objects. If we go beyond "scriptural" symbols into the more inclusive bric-a-brac of medieval iconography, we can find symbolic meanings even for bagpipes and lewd gestures, for kings and quite possibly for cabbages. While this tradition doubtless lent force to literary symbols, the image of the plowman, the food he produces, the famine he averts—these, as they emerge in the context of the work, have immediacy because they suggest the most pressing and fundamental problem of everyday life, that of sustaining life itself. Such images conjure up in the most unlettered mind the association of needed sustenance and the labor required to provide that sustenance. They are powerful images because they touch upon a fundamental ambivalence which no man has not felt: we desire, and must have, the food which sustains us, but we weary of the toil and trouble of obtaining it. There was, it is certain, something about the figure of the plowman which touched an area of great sensitivity

in the medieval mind. Chaucer himself used the plowman as a symbol of right living. As late as Brueghel we
can find plowmen in art, and we can still respond to
those trudging, purposeful figures with a strong sense
of the necessity, the usefulness, and yet the tedium and
futility of their labor. We consume at once what we toil
long to have; and this fact, which will never change,
gives to the labor of plowing and producing food a possibility which few other human actions have: the possibility of suggesting, by its very nature, the temporality
and brevity of human life, the ultimate futility of mundane labor, the longing for a life free of toil and trouble.

If I am right that the problem of supplying the needs
of the body is the central concern of *Piers Plowman*,
then this image is perhaps what accounts for the ever-
widening circle of the poet's thought. His theme is the
quest for salvation, individual and social; but his central
concern is more mundane. For labor itself is transitory
and seems futile; the body for which such labor provides nourishment is sustained only temporarily; and
the body has within it always the lusts that draw us
farther and farther into worldly preoccupations, farther
and farther away from our final end beyond time and
earthly vanity. All this reminds us of our spiritual, non-
temporal needs. The figure of the plowman as laborer
suggests in the most natural, most pristine way the
image of the plowman as cultivator of spiritual nourishment. A man of learning in the fourteenth century (a
clerk more likely than a knight) would, I believe, have
been aware of the scriptural dimension, the artifice and
the learned content, of this image, and of others. In this
I agree with Professors Robertson and Huppé; I differ
with them about the degree to which the poem's effect
and meaning would have depended for a fourteenth-
century reader, and must therefore depend for us, upon

the identification of these major, dominant symbols from the tradition of biblical glosses. The central and powerful symbols of *Piers Plowman* have a cogency of their own. Imagine a knight of the fourteenth century confronted with the poem; a knight was no scholar, and we may suppose he did not study the Bible or read the exegetes—did not perhaps read at all. Somewhere in the back of his mind, from the Gospels and Epistles of the mass or the fancy language of priests in sermons, he might have caught an echo of that scriptural tradition. But the image itself was powerfully suggestive; and the feeling which it engendered did not come about as a result of its presence in exegetical writings—if anything, it may have been that feeling which led exegetes to see in plowing, sowing, or reaping their similarity with higher, spiritual activities.

This is why the central concern of *Piers Plowman*, for all its mundane and limited attention to the simplest and vainest needs, has inherent in it such poetical and intellectual possibilities. But there is more than that. The very ideal by means of which Langland defines the right use of temporal goods, the very doctrine of a Christian community by which he places earthly labor in the scheme of things, suggested the most profound conflicts of the medieval ideology—conflicts so touching on the life of man that they could be resolved again and again by intellectuals, through the citing of authorities or the application of logic, and yet trouble once more the man who would think of them.

The most fundamental of these conflicts is the fact that "Al is not good to þe gost þat þe gut askiþ" (A. 1, 34). The World is the existence which most men lead in their earthly bodies; and the body is a central image in the poem. Need, which must be supplied by labor and satisfied in temperance, originates of course in the body, but it is felt as well in the body politic, of which the king is the head and his subjects the members. The poem proposes at length an ideal system for supplying these needs. But what makes the ideal impossible springs from the body, too. Need causes men to labor, but when their needs are fulfilled and they are weary, they will shirk and grasp. Thus life, individual and social, becomes a battle between need and sloth, between Hunger and Waster. And the one virtue which would stabilize this oscillation of human motives, *mesure* or temperance, is baffled by the nature of the World itself—by "the World, the flesh, and the devil" and especially, with respect to these material needs, by the lust of the eyes.

Because the World is a transitory and corruptible state, because the body politic is as malignant as the flesh itself, Langland points the reader, beginning with the Pardon scene, to higher orders of perfection—higher spiritual needs, the "contemplative" and "mixed" states, and higher stages of the spiritual life. But perfection, as we have observed, was a relative term, attainable only in degrees. Men were, as the result of the Fall, laboring under the punishment of imperfection. Christ's command "Be ye therefore perfect" had on this account to be interpreted as a counsel for all Christians constantly to rise above their imperfections, not as a command that all be saints or martyrs. It was understood that some are "called" to higher states than others. So it is with Hawkyn: there is nothing of itself wrong with the active life, but just because there are higher states, this lower one is the more corruptible. Hawkyn can justly defend his state of life and feel satisfied with it; but as it is less perfect, it is more likely to draw spots which he must clean by penance; hence doing well was never as good as doing better or best. This did not mean that any *kind* of higher state was better than any kind of lower one—

he who practiced the lower grade (marriage, say) with probity was better than he who practiced the higher one, chastity, without success. Because perfection was relative in this way, the inner life of the medieval Christian, so often depicted as a moral seesaw forever tipping on one end or the other, was much rather a continuous struggle in which, though one might tumble, one was drawn, as long as he was up, in two directions—toward temptation and toward higher perfection. The three grades of perfection look, from our convenient distance, like an elegant hierarchy free from the tensions of the modern world; it is only when we try to imagine what it was like to *live* the life of perfection that we sense how much there was in it of struggle and flight.

The grades of perfection, though conventionally arranged by three's, express the polarity in medieval thought between the worldly and the ascetic. The Church had developed a body of moral precept and canon law which established norms to maintain righteousness, and it had developed a body of ascetic and eremitic ideals which encouraged saintliness. It was understood that not everyone would follow these ascetic and eremitic ideals, though the hope that many or most would do so was entertained with some fervor until the twelfth century and was, as with Langland, periodically warmed over. But everyone *was* expected to maintain righteousness and to stay within the bounds of the lowest grade of perfection. In the World the *vita activa* was allowed and delimited. It was legitimate, and desirable, that men should attempt to improve their lot. Charity called for the healing of the sick and for giving alms to the poor; natural law demanded the provision of necessities. But just as soon as Langland had thought out a plan for improving men's lot, he saw in it the danger of an excessive attachment to worldly things. Hence in the

Pardon scene, Piers withdraws from the business of plowing:

> . . . 'Si *ambulauero in medio umbre mortis*
> *Non timebo mala quoniam tu mecum es.*
> I shal cesse of my sowyng,' quaþ peris, '& swynke
>   not so harde,
> Ne aboute my belyue so besy be namore;
> Of preyours & of penaunce my plouȝ shal ben
>   hereaftir,
> And beloure þat I belouȝ er þeiȝ liflode me faile.
> Þe prophet his payn eet in penaunce & in wepyng
> Be þat þe sauter vs seiþ, & so dede manye oþere.
> Þat louiþ god lelly, his liflode is þe more:
> *Fuerunt michi lacrime mee panes die ac nocte.*
> And but ȝif luk leiȝe he leriþ vs anoþer,
> By foules, þat are not besy aboute þe bely ioye:
> *Ne soliciti sitis . . .* (A. VIII, 102-113)

And hence Hawkyn is warned against the active life:

> . . . if men lyued as mesure wolde shulde neuere
>   more be defaute
> Amonges Cristene creatures if Crystes wordes ben
>   trewe.
> Ac vnkyndnesse *caristia* maketh amonges Crystene
>   peple,
> And ouer-plente maketh pruyde amonges pore and
>   riche;
> Ac mesure is so moche worth it may nouȝte be to
>   dere,
> For the meschief and the meschaunce amonges men
>   of Sodome
> Wex thorw plente of payn and of pure sleuthe;
> *Ociositas et habundancia panis peccatum turpissi-*
>   *mum nutriuit.* (B. XIV, 70-76)

Langland knew that the virtues which gain us salvation
are the same ones which will improve earthly life. Love,
mercy, and temperance will keep us from sin and gain
us Salvation; they will also do away with greed, sloth,
and envy—with, that is, whatever malevolence in men
has hindered the formation of an ideal Christian state.
He also knew that their value to the World must always
be written off as incidental when compared with their
heavenly rewards. And yet the World can never be
overlooked, for it is the corrupted World itself which
cripples temperance, love, and mercy—which makes salvation a struggle rather than a fact, and which makes
the ideal Christian economy, though immanent as a possibility for the World, impossible as a reality.

3. THE WORLD OF *PIERS PLOWMAN*: THE DREAMER'S MOMENTS OF AWAKENING

These conflicts in the poem, although they are disposed
into hierarchies, are never resolved. Every hope, every
ideal, every commended virtue is presented finally as a
lost cause. At the end Conscience becomes a pilgrim in
quest of Piers the Plowman, and Piers, though he seems
always within reach, is elusive and beyond our grasp.
This feeling of circuitousness, of wandering—this frustrated sense of seeking without finding, of perceiving
without understanding—is what gives the poem its
curious hold on the reader. Critics have remarked that
the poem is a "powerful presentation of the inner life,"[48]
that it is, especially in the *Vita*, a movement of the mind
into itself,[49] that it communicates "not a cumulative
effect of discursive thinking, but the very pressure of

[48] Wells, "The Philosophy of *Piers Plowman*," p. 348.
[49] Bloomfield, *Piers Plowman*, pp. 64 ff.

experience itself."[50] But how? Surely with Langland there is an intensely personal feeling of intellectual struggle; the contradictions, the repetition, even the very tedium of the search have an intensity which haunts, but baffles, the reader. Where he derived this intensity, I am going to suggest, was not from literary convention alone, or from the miscellaneous remembered scraps of intellection which he labored to synthesize, but from the form and "language" of dreams. I do not mean this in any narrow or even "Freudian" sense. Dreams reveal the sense of a "face swelling into reality," that intensity in human experience which poetry too communicates—an incalculable wholeness and complexity, and an inseparable union with the inner life.

The "dream vision" was of course a conventional literary form with which Langland would have been familiar. He would, too, have known something of medieval theories about dreams.[51] If one can judge from the Nun's Priest's Tale, the meaning of dreams was a frequent topic of discussion in fourteenth-century England. Langland stays, moreover, much closer to the tradition of dream vision than, for example, Chaucer did in *The Book of the Duchess*. In *The Book of the Duchess*, as G. L. Kittredge remarked,[52] Chaucer departed from the convention of dream allegories by using true dream psychology to write an elegy. *The Book of the Duchess* evokes the feelings which attach themselves to love, death, and mourning—it is the farthest thing in

[50] Lawlor, "Imaginative Unity of *Piers Plowman*," p. 126.

[51] Cf. his treatment of "Imaginatif," the faculty said to produce dreams; and cf. Bloomfield, *Piers Plowman*, pp. 170-174. On the influence of dreams and dream convention on the style of the poem, see Elizabeth Salter, *Piers Plowman: An Introduction* (Cambridge, Mass., 1962), pp. 58-64.

[52] George Lyman Kittredge, *Chaucer and His Poetry* (Cambridge, Mass., 1915), pp. 58, 66-72.

the world from an intellectual poem, and it is not a personification allegory.[53] Its literary force derives from its ability to evoke the dreamlike feeling of a nameless and unfathomable grief, an unresolved perplexity. But Langland is not even trying to attain such an emotional effect. He *is* writing an allegory, for which dreams were the conventional framework; his figures, far from being nameless, *are* personifications; and his purpose, as in allegory, is intellectual. Langland departs from convention in only one fundamental respect: he manages to give to his own intellectual striving the puzzling and distressing circularity of real dreams—to represent his own intellectual world under the guise of the emotional life. This element of psychological realism in the poem may be comparable to the realism of the "popular" style, which we find, for example, in the confession of the Seven Sins. But it is still far from being "realistic"— who ever dreamed a unified allegory complete with Latin quotations? Rather it is a literary device about which we must suspend our disbelief: we are to deal with the intellectual conflicts of Langland's age *as if* they were the private conflicts of an individual dreamer.

The dreams of the poem therefore represent in large measure the author's mind in its *conscious* workings. Dreams do, in fact, contain elements of rational, conscious thought as well as id-impulses, repressed wishes, and the like.[54] The dreamworld of *Piers Plowman* seems preponderantly to reenact the mental process by which learnt ideas are brought to bear on ideological and cultural conflicts. For example, we are made aware early in the first vision of the virtue of *leauté* (A. III, 266-

[53] That it is an allegory at all is doubtful, but see Bernard F. Huppé and D. W. Robertson, *Fruyt and Chaf: Studies in Chaucer's Allegories* (Princeton, 1963), pp. 32-100.

[54] See Erich Fromm, *The Forgotten Language* (Evergreen ed., New York, 1957), pp. 30-46.

269), and at the end of the first vision the King is shown dwelling with Reason and Conscience; but the solution is developed only in the long passage on the plowing of the half acre. There it takes root in our thoughts and we begin to associate it with the problem which it can solve. Until now it has scarcely been conscious at all.[55] And then only after it has become consciously associated and applied do we see, in the Pardon scene, its stumbling blocks and limitations. In the same way, the Latin quotations represent the association and application of learnt ideas to ideological conflicts. They are suggested by a certain train of thought; they clarify it or resolve it; and they furnish the suggestion for further thoughts. They represent the convergence upon our mental life of remembered precepts and scraps of intellection as they enter and leave our inner stream of imagery and verbalization.

The poem dramatizes this movement from unconsciousness to consciousness by representing moments of intellectual enlightenment as moments when one wakes from dreaming. At the moment of waking the dreamer is confronted by the most intense, most meaningful point of his dream. It may be, as at the end of the first vision, a pleasant wish-fulfillment. It may be, as in the Pardon scene, an unresolvable and troubling conflict, an expression of anxiety. Or it may be a final illumination, a sudden unfolding of reality. More than that, our dreams, as they succeed each other from one night to the next, tend to dwell upon specific themes. They show a course of development parallel with the changes and developments of a dreamer's waking life, and they can embody a process of integration.[56] This aspect of the dream-

[55] See Coghill, "The Pardon of Piers Plowman," pp. 332-337, who calls these foreshadowings "foretastes."

[56] See Thomas M. French, *The Integrative Process in Dreams*, in

world, which Langland simulates in the poem, accounts for the "cumulative" effect of the visions—their quality of having unity and development beneath their apparent chaos and circularity.

In what follows I am going to explore this phase of the structure of *Piers Plowman* by examining the dreamer's moments of awakening in isolation. It will mean omitting a great deal; but the experiment will be at least partially justified if, as I suspect, the most important and climactic moments of the poem occur at the ends of the visions, and if, as I hope to show, there is a demonstrable structure in which they are disposed.

In the *Visio* the dreamer wakes twice, first in a moment of hope and then in a moment of anxiety. In A. v, 3 he awakes at the encouraging moment when the King has agreed to dwell with Reason and Conscience as long as he lives. The King and his knights have gone to mass together, and the dreamer, regaining consciousness, wishes that he had slept sounder and seen more. The next moment of awakening (A. viii, 128), generated by this wish-fulfillment, is by contrast troubled and somewhat frightening. The dreamer has seen the pilgrimage to St. Truth interrupted; the plowing of the half acre has been instituted by Piers and then spoiled by Waster; Waster and Hunger have been seen in an unresolvable conflict; and now the priest has impugned Piers' pardon and Piers has torn it asunder in a rage. As the dreamer wakes, the priest and Piers are exchanging harsh insults; they "aposid" each other. This intense moment of conflict, of a kind familiar in everyone's dreams, leaves the dreamer perplexed, "Musyng

The Integration of Behavior, Vol. ii (Chicago, 1954), pp. 3-17, 287-289.

on þis metelis" as he wanders about the Malvern Hills. The same pattern—a dream of hope followed by a dream of anxiety—is repeated at the end of the poem.

In the *Vita* the first two lives, those of Do-wel and Do-bet, are knit together by several structural parallels. In each, the dreamer wakes from a dream-within-a-dream; these "inner" dreams present to him a fundamental truth which is the theme of the dreams to follow. In the *Vita de Do-wel* he wakes from the inner dream with Reason reminding him that men

> . . . most woo tholye
> In fondynge of the flesshe and of the fende bothe.
> For man was made of suche a matere he may nouȝt
>   wel astert
> That ne some tymes hym bitit to folwen his kynde;
> Catoun acordeth there-with *nemo sine crimine viuit*.
>   (B. xi, 390-394)

This fact of man's weakness, the fact that all are subject to the temptations of the fiend and the flesh and that no one is therefore free of sin, is the dominant preoccupation in what follows. When the dreamer next awakes he has heard a long explanation of salvation from the important figure Imaginatif. What Imaginatif tells him is that salvation depends not on the mere formula of baptism but on the works of man and the Grace of God. There is baptism of the font, and baptism of blood and fire. Hence Trajan was saved because he was "a trewe knyȝte" (B. xii, 280)—and *trewth*, the quality praised by Holy Church at the beginning of the poem, is here held up as obedience to God's law, as virtue itself. This focuses consideration on the problem of human imperfection, which hinders virtue. And the *Vita de Do-wel* ends with a personification of that imperfection—Hawkyn. Hawkyn is the Active Life, the provider of food; he is necessary to the World, but, being so much *of* the World, he is repeatedly cleansing his soul by penitence and repeatedly lapsing back into sin. When the dreamer wakes, Hawkyn, made aware of his ill success, is wailing in horror at his imperfections.

There is another "inner" dream toward the beginning of the *Vita de Do-bet*; from it the dreamer wakes seeing Christ crucified. Christ is presented here as a knight who "iusted in Ierusalem" (B. xvi, 163), which recalls the figure of knighthood associated with Trajan and with the crucial virtue *trewth*; and this reminder of the Crucifixion foreshadows the description of the Resurrection in Passus xviii. We are working toward a solution to the problem of human imperfection, and that solution is to be in God's grace. In the next waking moment, at the end of Passus xvii, the dreamer has been hearing a long speech by the Samaritan, which ends with a detailed explanation of the basis of human frailty—in the wicked flesh, in sickness and sorrow, and in "coueityse and vnkyndenesse." But she reminds Will of the possibility of virtue:

> For there nys syke ne sori ne non so moche wrecche,
> That he ne may louye, and hym lyke and lene of
> his herte
> Good wille and good worde bothe wisshen and
> willen
> Alle manere men mercy and forȝifnesse,
> And louye hem liche hym-self and his lyf amende.
>   (B. xvii, 344-348)

Now that the Samaritan has given this message, the two following dreams end in moments of great hopefulness. The dreamer wakes (B. xviii, 422 ff.) hearing Truth singing *Te deum laudamus* and Love singing *Ecce quam bonum et quam iocundum*; it is the day of the Resurrection and Will goes to the Easter mass. Here he falls asleep and dreams of the Resurrection, Pentecost, and the establishment of the Church militant. This dream ends with Piers the Plowman building the house called Unity. A King comes forward (B. xix, 462 ff.) to rule the *comune* and to defend the Church and the clergy from evil men; Conscience makes the condition that he rule with reason. The King gives no answer, though the implication is that he would agree. But at the same time we see what would hinder this just rule: a brewer, a clerk, and a lord (representing the three estates) have already declared themselves unwilling to resign their private interests. The dream ends in a mood of dubious expectancy.

The last passus is the vision of Do-best, a single dream concerned with Need, the Antichrist, and the necessity of Love. The friars are once more underfoot, as they must always have been in fourteenth-century England. The poet makes their reform symbolic of the reform of the World—but it will not be easy. Friar Flatterer is about plying his deceptions; Contrition forgets to cry and weep and wake for his misdeeds; Sloth and Pride assail Conscience, who—dogged, impervious—vows to become a pilgrim, to seek Piers Plowman through the World. The dreamer wakes as Conscience calls for grace; and with that image, as central to the Christian life as any image can be, the poem ends. We are once again at the unresolvable point where an ideal has been envisaged, then seen to crumble. In the last waking moment we are confused and uncertain, caught between hope and despair.

Taken singly, these moments of awakening, more than anything else in the poem, bring us close to its essential poetic force. They are those moments of euphoric hope, of intellectual clarity, of troubled uncertainty, of terror, which touch us most deeply and which stay with us longest. This is perhaps so because they seem like oases in the desert of this rambling work; yet what gives them this force is, to a great extent, the fact that they bring into focus the diffuse, chaotic content that precedes them. For modern readers the effect is more easily understood than enjoyed. We need always to remember, though, that what seems mere padding and filler to modern tastes would have had interest and merit to Langland's audience—that economy was not a virtue in a medieval work, and that medieval poets raised and discussed questions, important to them, which may seem beside the point to us. Take away the prolixity, the meandering, the circularity—all the qualities for which Langland is so often blamed—and you take away part of an effect which his audience would have admired. But *Piers Plowman*, though it may sprawl, stands together. These moments of awakening have structure and logic. They reveal a pattern which oscillates between Christian ideals and worldly imperfections; and this tension is what generates the widening concern of the poem, its cumulative manner of bringing to bear upon the practical problems of this World the vast system of Christian thought in its social and eschatological aspects.

The world of the poem, centered in these moments of awakening, encompasses therefore the temporal World itself. The specific figures—Glutton, Waster, Hawkyn, Piers, even Will himself—though they are all visible and concrete, are personifications of abstract qualities and general truths. They stand for states which are often in opposition to each other—as with Piers and the priest in the Pardon scene, or Hunger and Waster, or Hawkyn and Conscience. They are the embodiment of intellectual and emotional conflicts which the author experienced in his attempts to understand and live the Christian life. Such figures *can* occur in dreams; dreams can express and even resolve conflicts implicit in religious beliefs.[57] And dreams are at once specific and abstract; they reflect circumstantial details in the life of the dreamer, but also reveal general qualities of his character and even of his culture. Hence that element of the poem's style which mingles the concrete and the abstract, often treated as a function of personification allegory, is quite naturally a characteristic of dreams. The world of the poem, while it is the temporal, macrocosmic World, is also intensely personal. It would not be unreasonable to argue that Hawkyn and Conscience are projections or *alter egos* of the dreamer himself. The moments of anxiety or discomfort—the Pardon scene, the remorse of Hawkyn, the final determination of Conscience to become a pilgrim—are moments of the most intense feeling on the part of the author-dreamer. But the personal element of the work, its sense of intense inner pressure, is counterbalanced by its general, universal applicability. Will is the dreamer and the author, but he is Everyman as well; and this is so because every conflict that he feels, every solution that he unravels, every disappointment that he suffers, is true of the Christian life for all Christians—is true of the World. In just the same way that the momentary sin of Adam and Eve is the universal imperfection inherited by man, in just the same way that the point of time in which Christ died on the Cross is the universal fact of God's mercy and man's salvation—so every circumstantial moment in the poem has overtones that reach to the bounds of time, and beyond.

This can be said of most medieval works, and to this

[57] See the evidence presented in C. G. Jung, *Psychology and Religion: West and East*, Bollingen Series xx (New York, 1958), pp. 23-33.

extent most medieval works are "allegorical." It is of course a property of all literature to find the general in the particular, the abstract in the concrete; but there is a huge difference in the kind of general truth which, for example, Proust could discover in his minute anatomy of the "vast structure of recollection," and there is a huge difference in the method by which he does so. Troilus laughing from the eighth sphere at worldly vanities, Piers the Plowman returning as clerk and as Christ and then trailing off into the unknown where Conscience must seek him—neither would be possible in modern times. Troilus and Will are both Everyman; both exemplify universal truths of man's search and the World's vanity. But we have been told this so often that we need almost to be reminded of the contrary: Troilus and Will, though both are Everyman, are also Troilus and Will. They are unique, specific individuals bound like all of us by time and the World. And like many at isolated moments in their lives, Troilus and Will both experience single, unique moments of comprehension in which the World is understood *sub specie aeternitatis.* They both learn that this World, like the world of dreams, will pass away—the very lesson which, as Everyman, they illustrate. Troilus as Everyman shows us that earthly love is disappointing and inferior; and this is precisely what he learns in and after death. Will as Everyman shows us that a mere intellectual search will avail us nothing in our search for perfection—that the search must be carried out in action and that in this imperfect World it can be but imperfectly rewarded; and that is the lesson which he himself learns after the Pardon scene. For Langland—and this is true of few medieval poets—the evanescence of the World is expressed *within* the work but not at the end of it. Where Troilus is removed from the World, Will is returned to it. Where Troilus sees all and laughs, Will wakes to find Conscience searching still. For Chaucer the final comprehension of truth comes only in that moment when he can disperse the reality of his story, remove his hero from its world. For Langland all comprehension is bound by the World of time, and all our striving by the little world of the body.

CHAPTER FIVE

CHIVALRY AND THE
PRIDE OF LIFE:

SIR GAWAIN AND THE
GREEN KNIGHT

"Bot here yow lakked a lyttel, sir, and lewté yow
                                                   wonted;
Bot þat watȝ for no wylyde werke, ne wowyng
                                                   nauþer,
Bot for ȝe lufed your lyf; þe lasse I yow blame."
        —*Sir Gawain and the Green Knight*, 2366-2368[1]

HEN THE Green Knight explains to Sir Gawain why his neck has been nicked, he names Gawain's failing with such courtly *delicatesse* that it comes out nearly a compliment. "Here you were a little lacking, sir, and fell short of loyalty; but that wasn't because of any guileful deed, nor because of wooing, neither, but because you loved your life"—and, he adds with gallantry, "the less I blame you." The effect on Gawain seems all out of proportion. He stands silent "in study" for a long time, inwardly crying, anguished. Then all the blood of his breast streams into his face, and he "altogether shrinks" for shame. When he finally speaks he is a bit irrational: "Corsed worth cowarddyse and couetyse boþe! / In yow is vylany and vyse þat vertue disstryeȝ"—and grabbing off the girdle he flings it fiercely at the knight. It is only after this surprising, and comic, bit of projection that he admits his own failing: cowardice, he says, taught him to give in to covetousness and to forsake his nature, the "larges and lewté þat longeȝ to knyȝteȝ" (2381). He will wear the girdle, he declares, not for its beauty or price, "Bot in syngne of my surfet," as a reminder of "þe faut and þe fayntyse of þe flesche crabbed" (2433-2435).

Gawain's fault is presented, apparently, in religious terms. The girdle will warn him against pride, remind him of the failing and weakness of the flesh. The Green Knight grants that it was not any "wylyde werke, ne wowyng nauþer," and Gawain vows that he will wear

---

[1] The text used is *Sir Gawain and the Green Knight*, ed. J. R. R. Tolkien and E. V. Gordon (Oxford, 1930). By permission of the Clarendon Press, Oxford.

the girdle for neither its price nor its beauty: it is not the lust of the flesh or the lust of the eyes that has threatened him, but pride of life. But this pride is not the spiritual pride which was said to endanger the holiness of monks. It is pride "for prowes of armes" (2437); it led him into cowardice and covetousness, he tells the knight, "for care of þy knokke," and on that account he forsook the "larges and lewté" which befits a knight. It was, in other words, a transgression against the knightly code, and it can be conceived in religious terms only because the chivalric virtues themselves were, in part, Christian ones.

In some measure Gawain's fault is owing to the contradictions of chivalry itself: the chivalric "system" made rival claims on knights and so gave rise to moral conflicts. "System" and "code" we call it; but we must not be seduced into picturing chivalry as a club with bylaws. It was an ethos which, evolving spontaneously, reflected contrarieties inherent in medieval culture itself. "The peculiar charm of the chivalric ethos," as Curtius remarks, "consists precisely in fluctuation between many ideals, some of them closely related, some diametrically opposed. The possibility of this free interplay, of freedom to move within a rich and manifold world of values, must have been an inner stimulus to the courtly poets."[2] For chivalry was only the manners of the upper class, its code their mores. Hence the difficulty of tracing its "decline": it can be said to have declined only when the aristocracy itself began to lose power and centrality, when men not properly knights—Chaucer's Franklyn or the *bourgeois gentilhomme*—began to emulate its manners and modify its ideas. Most of the reasons as-

[2] Ernst Robert Curtius, *European Literature and the Latin Middle Ages*, trans. Willard R. Trask, Bollingen Series XXXVI (New York, 1953), pp. 535-537.

signed to the "decline" of chivalry—its overrefinement, say, or its disregard of the common people[3]—were really by-products of this changing class structure. Falstaff and Baron Ochs do not need to enter the picture, for there had always been decadent knights, as there had always been impoverished ones. Indeed the practice of chivalry was, in the strictest sense, decadent almost from its beginning. The earliest glimmerings of the chivalric ideal were intended for such as the Knights Templar, who were in effect monks; the feudal knighthood found the code or ethos of chivalry an ideal whose internal conflicts made it impossible of fulfillment.[4] And this, as nearly all critics agree, is the theme of *Sir Gawain and the Green Knight*—that because of human frailty *no* knight can be perfect, and that in striving for perfection one must therefore learn humility.[5]

The chivalric ideal was no doubt modeled upon the Church's notion of perfection; yet chivalry was at base a worldly institution. It originated in feudalism, and its chief concern from the outset was self-interest. The ideal of loyalty to a feudal overlord was born out of the need to combat mutual enemies—Saracens, Slavs, Magyars, Danes. When in the eleventh century those invaders were beaten off, there was a real danger that Christian

[3] Cf. A. T. Byles, "Medieval Courtesy Books and the Prose Romances of Chivalry," in Edgar Prestage, ed., *Chivalry: A Series of Studies to Illustrate Its Historical Significance and Civilizing Influence* (New York, 1928), pp. 200-201.

[4] For a good summary of the reasons for the decline of chivalry, see F. J. C. Hearnshaw, "Chivalry and Its Place in History," in Prestage, pp. 25-27. A. B. Taylor, *An Introduction to Medieval Romance* (London, 1930), pp. 195-200, compares the chivalric ideal with the ascetic strictures of the Church.

[5] The chief dissenter among recent critics is Alan M. Markman, "The Meaning of *Sir Gawain and the Green Knight*," *PMLA*, LXXII (1957), 574-586, who holds that the theme of the poem is loyalty, i.e., one's duty to others.

lords would turn upon each other. What prevented this internal devastation was the repression by overlords of private warfare among petty nobles;[6] that, and the Crusades—a happy accident, probably, rather than (as sometimes suggested) a clever scheme for preserving feudal unity.[7] The Crusades did not, however, turn knights into monks. Loyalty among knights was maintained for the protection of power and property, not to say for booty or ransom, and deeds of arms were pursued for the sake of individual glory. Glory as a motive for warlike deeds, an inheritance from the early Middle Ages, had by the fifteenth century replaced the profit motive.[8] Even in its noblest form the ideal of the perfect knight had therefore an edge of worldly vanity—for perfection was rewarded not only by salvation in the next world but by prestige and reputation in this one, by an earthly immortality of fame.[9]

To these worldly aspects of chivalry the Church was consistently opposed. Warfare was disapproved except when waged against aggressors or evildoers. Tournaments were forbidden by the Council of Clermont (1130) because they led to homicide. Plunder was prohibited (except against the unjust, who St. Thomas said had no right to property). Glory was permitted as a motive for just deeds, otherwise it was "vainglory." And, of course, courtly love was condemned.[10] These strictures were by no means consistently observed or enforced, but they are

[6] Sidney Painter, *French Chivalry: Chivalric Ideas and Practices in Mediaeval France* (Baltimore, 1940), pp. 17-19.

[7] See Hearnshaw, in Prestage, pp. 4-7.

[8] See Painter, pp. 34-37. See also F. S. Shears, "The Chivalry of France," in Prestage, pp. 69-70.

[9] The *locus classicus* for the notion is Froissart's *Chronicles*, e.g., in the opening chapters.

[10] See Painter, pp. 85-90, 149-162.

emblematic of the underlying conflict between the chivalric tradition and the Church. The virtues of the knight—valor, honesty, generosity—were not of themselves inconsistent with Christian teachings; but they had to be tempered by the specifically Christian virtues of faith, humility, charity, and (preferably) chastity.[11]

On the other hand, the Church made common cause with the feudal knighthood. From the time of Urban II, who instituted the first crusade (1095), the Church insisted that a true knight must be a true Christian. This notion, a phase of the "renaissance" of the early twelfth century, became at once associated with the literature of chivalry (the *chansons de geste*)[12] and with "fin' amors." The true knight fought for the Church against infidels, led a holy life, did charitable deeds, sought justice; his profession was instituted by God, wrote St. Bernard, because he had the capacity to bring peace, and ideally he was comparable to a monk in his way of life.[13] He was bound by oath to serve the king, but his first duty was to protect the Church.

The chivalric code is therefore a microcosm of more general historical conflicts. For one thing, the knight's loyalty is divided between religious and feudal obligations. In *Raoul de Cambrai* this conflict receives a most dramatic treatment: the hero Bernier is bound by oath to serve Raoul, but Raoul is an unholy evildoer who devastates an abbey, burns a nunnery (poor Bernier's

[11] For a comparison of feudal and Christian virtues, see Henry Osborn Taylor, *The Mediaeval Mind: A History of the Development of Thought and Emotion in the Middle Ages* (2 vols., London, 1930), Vol. I, pp. 545-547.

[12] E. F. Jacob, "The Beginnings of Medieval Chivalry," in Prestage, p. 45.

[13] St. Bernard, *De laude novae militiae ad milites templi*, PL 182: 921-927. Bernard had in mind the Knights Templar.

mother is one of the nuns!) and wages war against Bernier's own family. The hero finally breaks with his lord and does battle against him, but his great moral struggle in doing so shows that the feudal tie was a powerful rival even against blood relationships and religious obligations, and that such a conflict was viewed as a profoundly tragic circumstance. Beyond this, courtly love, when it entered the ethos of knights, set the lust of the flesh against ideals of chastity, pure love, and marriage. In part this merely repeated, at a refined level, the older conflict between the nobility's predatory sexual mores and the Church's law against adultery. Yet it introduced the further conflict between feudal obligations and lovers' vows—as with Tristan or Lancelot.

But, putting to one side the difficulty of maintaining religious, military, and courtly obligations all at once, there is a more fundamental dilemma about chivalry. Even in its most perfect form, even where the system could be followed without conflicts, chivalry was by nature a thing of this World. The earliest chivalric orders were formed, ideally, to protect pilgrims to Jerusalem from worldly harm. And as a more general code for knights, its purpose, even ideally, was to maintain and protect the power and property of the Christian Church and of Christian rulers.[14] It was therefore the embodiment par excellence of the active life. It called for perfection in *worldly* things—in arms, in courteous speech, in generous deeds. It called for preservation of earthly body as well as immortal soul. And it must have called for something else—for a certain self-esteem or confidence without which prowess must collapse and skulk away. Hence, in the quest for knightly perfection, it seemed impossible to escape the "pride of life."

[14] Cf. F. Warre Cornish, *Chivalry* (London and New York, 1901), pp. 223-224.

Moreover, the very *idea* of perfection put the practical below the ascetical, the active below the contemplative. There was accordingly in the idea of knighthood itself a certain reservation about its adequacy as a mode of life. The world of the knight was everywhere bounded by otherworldly horizons: the symbolism of his garments, his prime duty to the Church, the necessity of daily religious observance, the ideal of chastity, and behind it all his awareness that salvation was more important even than the highest earthly goals. So, in literature, there are for knights the constant temptations, the wandering and homelessness with none but God as protector, and the quest of all quests, after the Holy Grail.

In *Sir Gawain and the Green Knight* this essential dilemma of chivalry, that it was a worldly institution founded upon otherworldly ideals, is the central concern. While the poet addresses himself to the conflicts inherent in the knightly code itself, the ultimate problem, more basic and less resolvable, is not merely whether any knight can be perfect, but whether any *man*, if he seeks perfection, can afford to remain a knight. This would seem to ask whether knighthood is possible at all, whether it is a good state of life. Yet in all the highest literature of chivalry the life of the knight becomes finally a symbol of the Christian life itself; and the question is whether one can put any value upon *any* of the imperfect deeds of this transitory life while entertaining the hope of ultimate perfection in a life beyond.

2. SIR GAWAIN AS SINNER

The practice of chivalry, then, put the knight in the way of several conflicts: service to his feudal lord might conflict with service to God, and service to his lady might conflict with either. In critical discussions of *Sir Gawain and the Green Knight*, this fact about the chivalric ethos has often been allowed to pass out of sight. One critic would have Gawain fall not so much through amorousness as through a reflection on his reputation for courtesy;[15] another would have the poem deal chiefly with loyalty;[16] another with the juxtaposition of primitive and brutal forces of nature against the demands of civilized restraint.[17] Yet Gawain is tested for *all* the virtues of knighthood, and in a degree he fails in all. George J. Engelhardt has shown how the knight's religious, military, and courtly obligations required of him corresponding virtues—piety, valor, and courtesy.[18] Although Engelhardt does not emphasize the background of these virtues in the chivalric ethos, or the conflicts among them, he points once and for all to the central fact about the poem, that Gawain's failure in one respect leads him to failure in others. In accepting the girdle Gawain fulfills his obligation of courtesy to the lady, but he must then break faith with the lord. In breaking faith with the lord and keeping the girdle, he safeguards his body by magic and his soul by a false confession. At the final test he flinches. And when the meaning of the test is explained to him, says Engelhardt, he "rails like the misogynists." Thus he fails in loyalty, in piety, in valor, in courtesy. To be sure, he goes on valiantly to carry out the adventure, he remains chaste, and he is courteous for

[15] Francis Berry, "Sir Gawayne and the Grene Knight," in *The Age of Chaucer*, Pelican Guide to English Literature, Vol. I, ed. Boris Ford (rev. ed., London, 1959), pp. 148-158.

[16] Markman, p. 586.

[17] William Goldhurst, "The Green and the Gold: The Major Theme of *Gawain and the Green Knight*," *CE*, xx (1958), 61-65. See the objections to this latter view by Morton W. Bloomfield, "*Sir Gawain and the Green Knight*: An Appraisal," *PMLA*, LXXVI (1961), 16.

[18] George J. Engelhardt, "The Predicament of Gawain," *MLQ*, XVI (1955), 218-225.

all but a moment. Nevertheless, he has shown imperfection in several ways, and we shall want to know why and in what respects.

To the question "why" the poem gives two explicit answers. One is Gawain's explanation that the imperfection springs from the weakness of the flesh (2435-2436); but then that is what all imperfection springs from. The other is the Green Knight's, that Gawain loved his life (2368). This more particular answer is harder to accept, and one cannot help wondering whether it is not just more trickery on the Green Knight's part. True, when we think back, it *was* the promise of safety that made Gawain take the girdle—"Myȝt he haf slypped to be vnslayn," he had thought to himself, "þe sleȝt were noble" (1858). But does this mean that the poet is holding up self-preservation as an evil, as a cause for moral imperfection? St. Thomas, on the contrary, had put self-preservation under natural law, along with the impulses to procreate, know truth, and live in society.[19] Surely the *impulse* by itself does not lead Gawain astray—how could any knight perform any worthy deed if he did not protect his existence? Yet that is what the Green Knight says, and Gawain does not contradict it.

Gawain's *tangible* wrong is taking the girdle. A mere impulse to self-preservation is not of much use by itself, for self-preservation requires worldly means. No knight goes into battle without weapons and shield; in fact, one of the conditions of knighthood was having the means to provide armor.[20] Perhaps for this reason Gawain's clothing, weapons, and armor are described in the most

[19] *Summa theologica*, I, ii, q. 94, art. 2. See Odon Lottin, *Psychologie et morale aux XIIe et XIIIe siècles* (6 vols. in 8, Louvain and Gembloux, 1942-1960), Vol. II, part I, p. 96.

[20] Painter, p. 2.

voluptuous terms—they are of costly silk, bright fur, well-worked and highly polished steel adorned with gold. His helmet, the last garment he puts on (kissing it as a priest might kiss the stole) has a silk cover embroidered with gems, encircled with diamonds. His garments and armor are also *useful*—they are "alle þe godlych gere þat hym gayn schulde" (584). No symbolic significance is attributed to them, though a knight's garments, like a priest's, were often given symbolic values.[21] His shield alone is made an emblem of moral perfection, and the description of it is saved until the end, where it is more pointed and dramatic. By making this one symbol contrast with all the costly and elaborate equipage of knighthood, the poet managed to underscore the fact that a knight's valor is dependent on worldly goods.

After hearing mass, the knight puts on his helmet and takes up his shield. Here the manuscript makes a division with a colored capital,[22] and the poet, pausing, declares that he will tell why Gawain wears the pentangle. On the outside of his shield, the pentangle, or "endless knot," represents Gawain's perfection in his five senses and his five fingers, his faith in the five wounds of Christ and the five joys of the Virgin, and his possession of the five knightly virtues—franchise, fellowship, purity, courtesy, and pity.[23] On its inside is the image of the

[21] On the symbolism of the knight's garments, see Edgar Prestage, "The Chivalry of Portugal," in Prestage, p. 145. Cf. A. T. Byles, "Medieval Courtesy Books and the Prose Romances of Chivalry," Prestage, p. 192; and Painter, pp. 83-84.

[22] At line 619. See Tolkien and Gordon, p. viii.

[23] See Robert W. Ackerman, "Gawain's Shield: Penitential Doctrine in *Gawain and the Green Knight*," *Anglia*, LXXVI (1958), 254-265. Ackerman suggests that the reference to the five wits would have called up fourteenth-century writings on auricular confession, so that the passage is consistent with the later theme of penitence.

Blessed Virgin, which will remind Gawain of her five joys and so renew his courage.[24] These virtues correspond in a general way to the chivalric virtues of valor, piety, and courtesy and represent his military, religious, and courtly obligations. That is the meaning of the pentangle; the shield and its pentangle device are a single object, of course, but the shield itself has a significance of its own. It contrasts with the girdle: shield and girdle suggest two ways of accommodating the worldly aims of knighthood to the otherworldly ends of the Christian life. The symbolism of shield and girdle is symbolism of a different kind than that of the pentangle. The pentangle has an *assigned*, allegorical value; it is put into the poem in order to stand for an abstraction, like Sansfoy and Sansloy, or Sin and Death. It tells us that Gawain is the "pentagonal man," the ideal knight.[25] The shield and the girdle, however, take their symbolic meaning from the situation, the use they are put to, the attitudes and emotions which people show toward them, and their juxtaposition one against the other. They remain just as much girdle and shield as Desdemona's handkerchief remains a handkerchief. While the pentangle is a painted sign—it appears on the knight's coat-armor (637) as well as on his shield—the shield and girdle are real objects and function in the poem as living, articulate symbols, dynamically paired.

The pentangle shield, of course, evokes the chivalric

[24] See Engelhardt, pp. 218-220.

[25] On the pentangle, see Vincent F. Hopper, *Medieval Number Symbolism*, CUSECL, 132 (New York, 1938), pp. 124-125; and Edgar De Bruyne, *Études d'esthétique médiévale* (2 vols., Bruges, 1946), Vol. II, pp. 349-350. On the armor and shield as "scriptural" symbols, see Hans Schnyder, *Sir Gawain and the Green Knight: An Essay of Interpretation*, Cooper Monographs, 6 (Bern, 1961), pp. 53-54; and Richard Hamilton Green, "Gawain's Shield and the Quest for Perfection," *ELH*, XXIX (1962), esp. 126-135.

ideal. With its images on either side, it functions in two directions—to the knight as a devotional reminder, to the world as an emblem of his inner moral perfection. It is at base a worldly object, a part of his warlike gear, designed at once to protect his body and remind him of his immortal soul, so that it suggests at once his knightly valor and his spiritual indifference to destiny. To the World the shield shows what spiritual strength lies beneath Gawain's rich trappings; to Gawain it shows what ultimate spiritual meaning lies beneath the World's bright lures. Yet it is to have this devotional and spiritual meaning precisely in those moments when he is most the knight, when he is most given to worldly deeds and most reliant upon the shield as a made object. It thus points up the proper attitude for a knight: to be indifferent to one's life in the World and yet preserve it, to use the World well and yet love it little.

Later, after the temptations, when Gawain is ready to leave the castle for the Green Chapel, the poet again describes the arming of the knight. This time, however, he says nothing about the shield; instead he ends by explaining why Gawain wears the girdle:

> Bot wered not þis ilk wyȝe for wele þis gordel,
> For pryde of þe pendauntez, þaȝ polyst þay were,
> And þaȝ þe glyterande golde glent vpon endeȝ,
> Bot for to sauen hymself, when suffer hym
>   byhoued,
>   To byde bale withoute dabate of bronde hym to were
>   oþer knyffe. (2037-2042)

As the shield is emblematic of Gawain's knightly virtue, the girdle is emblematic of his fault. The whole movement of the story hangs on his yielding to temptation, accepting the girdle, and having his failing revealed to him. In the end Gawain himself makes the girdle a symbol of his "surfet" and of the weakness of the flesh. A girdle was an ordinary article of clothing, a belt or cincture from which one hung objects like keys or a purse. Because of its function it was a convenient symbol for worldliness—the *Oxford English Dictionary* in fact reports such a metaphorical usage in the fifteenth century. *This* girdle, however, has the added lure of being rich and finely wrought in its own right: it is made of green silk, embroidered about the edges, and hung with pendants of highly polished gold.[26] More than that, it has powers of its own—not merely an emblematic meaning, like that of the shield's device, but remarkable "costes þat knit ar þerinne" (1849), magical properties to save the wearer from being slain. The author carefully reminds us that Gawain accepts the girdle for these powers, not for its richness. He actually tells us what the knight thought before accepting it, that he would like to be "vnslayn" (1855-1858). And Gawain, when he proposes to wear it as a memento of his failing, himself denies any interest in either its worth or its beauty:

> 'Bot your gordel' quoþ Gawayn 'God yow forȝelde!
> Þat wyl I welde wyth good wylle, not for þe
> wynne golde,
> Ne þe saynt, ne þe sylk, ne þe syde pendaundes,
> For wele ne for worchyp, ne for þe wlonk werkkeȝ,
> Bot in syngne of my surfet I schal se hit ofte,
> When I ride in renoun, remorde to myseluen
> Þe faut and þe fayntyse of þe flesche crabbed,
> How tender hit is to entyse teches of fylþe. . . .'
>
> (2429-2436)

Gawain has taken the girdle, then, not to own it for its value or wear it for its beauty, but simply to save his

---

[26] See lines 1830-1833, 2037-2039, 2430-2432.

life. It is as worldly an object, and used for as worldly an end, as the shield; but unlike the shield, it is magical, it is used solely for a selfish reason, and accepting it requires that he break faith with the lord. Gawain is guilty not because he desires "to sauen hymself," but because in order to do so he uses worldly means in the wrong way.

*

The circumstances under which Gawain accepts the girdle are, in the simplest terms, an elaborately ritualized temptation. It occurs against a background of impending death, with a characteristically medieval feeling of the mutability of earthly things, and this points up the urgency of his desire to save his life. The work begins with a Christmas feast, colorful and overflowing with good cheer: the knights and ladies have gathered, we are told, "with alle þe wele of þe worlde" (50). But into their midst comes the hideous knight with his peculiar request. Gawain deals the blow which topples the man's head across the floor, and there is both horror and humor when the stranger retrieves it and gives Gawain, before returning the dreadful blow, "respite, / A twelmonyth and a day" (297-298). From that point one has a feeling of the brevity of Gawain's life, the closeness of his destiny; and the horrid figure of the headless knight, "þat vgly bodi þat bledde" (441), remains as a precursor of Gawain's fate, an image as hideous and menacing—and as grimly humorous—as a Death's head. The second section of the poem enhances this feeling, beginning as it does with a description of the passing of the seasons: "A ȝere ȝernes ful ȝerne, and ȝeldeȝ neuer lyke, / þe forme to þe fynisment foldeȝ ful selden" (498-499). The coming of winter, especially cogent in England where winter has always been a hardship, creates a particularly foreboding effect:

> Þenne al rypeȝ and roteȝ þat ros vpon fyrst,
> And þus ȝirneȝ þe ȝere in ȝisterdayeȝ mony,
> And wynter wyndeȝ aȝayn, as þe worlde askeȝ,
> > no fage,
> > Til Meȝelmas mone
> > Watȝ cumen wyth wynter wage;
> > Þen þenkkeȝ Gawan ful sone
> > Of his anious uyage. (528-535)

And when Gawain leaves there is heavy grief—"much derue doel" (558)—among the people of Arthur's court:

> Þe knyȝt mad ay god chere,
> And sayde, 'Quat schuld I wonde?
> Of destinés derf and dere
> What may mon do bot fonde?' (562-565)

The knights take farewell, bemoaning the loss of so noble a man. Gawain hears mass, is commended to Christ, and embarks on his journey. On Christmas he prays that he may hear mass, "And cryed for his mysdede" (760).

To a large extent the emphasis on nature in the poem enhances this theme of mutability. The point is crucial because it accounts for whatever elements of folklore or myth may be seen in the poem; those which have been suggested all touch on nature and natural processes— myths of fertility and vegetation, of a journey into the underworld, of the balance between winning and wasting, growth and deliquescence, civilized humanity and brutal nature.[27] Certainly it is true that the revolution of

[27] For treatments of this kind, see Bloomfield, pp. 12-14. Recent treatments include John Speirs, *Medieval English Poetry: The Non-Chaucerian Tradition* (London, 1957), pp. 215-251; and William A. Nitze, "Is the Green Knight Story a Vegetation Myth?" *MP*,

the seasons and the struggle of man against natural forces without or natural instincts within are dominant features of the poem. Yet to the medieval mind this emphasis on the natural order would have suggested the temporal and mutable World. Sublunary Nature, corrupt as a result of the Fall, suggested the moral lesson of *contemptus mundi*: that the objects of earthly loves, being transitory, deserved to be scorned.

This feeling of the instability of worldly things would not seem so specifically Christian if Gawain did not accept the girdle after three temptations. That these temptations correspond to the lust of the flesh, the lust of the eyes, and pride of life—the temptations of Adam and Christ in the patristic tradition—was first recognized by Alfred L. Kellogg.[28] For some time I was convinced that the poem was based upon this exegetical concept—

XXXIII (1936), 351-366. For the journey into death, see Heinrich Zimmer, *The King and the Corpse: Tales of the Soul's Conquest of Evil*, ed. Joseph Campbell, Bollingen Series XI (New York, 1948), pp. 67-95; and A. H. Krappe, "Who *Was* the Green Knight?" *Speculum*, XIII (1938), 206-215. Goldhurst sees the contrariety between the natural and the civilized carried out in the Green Knight, Gawain's temptation, and in the green and gold of the girdle itself. John S. Lewis, "Gawain and the Green Knight," *CE*, XXI (1959), 50-51, supports Goldhurst and adds that the colors green and gold traditionally symbolize vanishing youth, so that the Green Knight's appearance suggests the transitoriness of life. See also Berry, pp. 152-155, and Markman, pp. 579-581. For a judicious summary of this aspect of the study of the poem, see Francis Lee Utley, "Folklore, Myth, and Ritual," in Dorothy Bethurum, ed., *Critical Approaches to Medieval Literature*, English Institute, 1958-1959 (New York, 1960), pp. 86-92.

[28] Professor Kellogg's study of the poem was presented in preliminary versions at the University of Kentucky Foreign Languages Conference in 1957 and at the Modern Language Assoc. in 1958; it contained valuable analysis not only of the exegetical background but of several highly significant analogues. There is also material on this element in the poem in Schnyder, pp. 60-63.

that the poet was consciously applying it to the story of Sir Gawain. Of this I am now less certain. While the temptations of the poem seem to correspond with those of the exegetical tradition in a general way, the correspondence is thrown off in several respects, and it seems likelier that the temptations of Adam and Christ are very lightly, almost unconsciously, suggested. They are, as in life, elusively intertwined, at the threshold of one's attention, with more palpable realities. On the other hand, the tradition would imply the suggestion-delectation-consent formula and the problem of distinguishing between temptation and sin, certainly important in gauging the extent of Gawain's fault. The motif of the knight tempted by a seductress occurs again and again in romances, but no analogue to the temptation is so congruent with the patristic tradition as that of our poem.[29] And, having nothing like a source, we cannot say what the poet "added." In a general way chivalry was symbolic of the Christian life, so that any temptation of any knight can be read in some measure as a Christian reference. The *Gawain* poet could, then, have depicted the temptation of his hero, and have given it some Christian overtones, without necessarily calling on the patristic tradition. There are, to be sure, *three* temptations; but triplicities were common in the Middle Ages[30] and are frequent in storytelling throughout western culture. Moreover, there is a fourth temptation in the poem, though it is made by the servant who accompanies Gawain to the Green Chapel, not by the lady.

As to the temptations themselves, the first is the lust of the flesh beyond a doubt—she bluntly offers her

[29] See the introduction by Mabel Day to the edition by Sir Israel Gollancz, EETS, o.s. 210 (reprinted London, 1957), pp. xxiv-xxv. On the analogues, see George Lyman Kittredge, *A Study of Gawain and the Green Knight* (reprinted Gloucester, Mass., 1960), pp. 76-104.

[30] See Curtius, p. 511.

body!—and the third is pride of life at least in the limited sense of the desire not to die. The second temptation, however, does not quite seem like the lust of the eyes: the lady asks Gawain to teach her "some tokens of true love's ways" because of his superior knowledge, adding the taunt, "Why! ar ȝe lewed, þat alle þe los weldeȝ?" (1528). The lust of the eyes is traditionally avarice for possessions and honors and, as we have seen, sometimes involved "curiosity," i.e., love of learning. Perhaps in the second temptation the lady is luring Gawain into a boastful display of knowledge or a desire for honors and renown ("los"), but there is no mention of possessions, and, to say the least, there is still a noticeable element of sexuality. On the other hand, in the *third* temptation she offers him first a ring "worth wele ful hoge" (1820), then the girdle, finely wrought of silk and gold; and he refuses both gold and treasure— "Nauþer golde ne garysoun" (1837). Certainly if the poet had the patristic tradition in mind, he rearranged the three temptations; but as we have seen, the tradition allowed a certain fluidity. Moreover, the poet had a sound artistic reason for this redistribution: by putting the temptation to riches forward into the third part he made it unalterably clear that it was the magic power of the girdle *alone* which attracted the knight.

On the whole it seems difficult to deny that the poet was using the exegetical treatment of the three temptations at some level of consciousness. Yet the poet's departures from the tradition are as interesting as his indebtedness to it. He presents neither tempter nor victim in black and white terms. The Green Knight is, perhaps, a devil, but he is unlike the devil of tradition. Granted, he has some diabolic traits, if we may judge these from folklore: he wears green and seems to live in the north, he is supernaturally large, he can change his

form or exist without his head. When Gawain sees the
Green Chapel he thinks that here the devil might tell
his matins (2188), and says that it must have been the
fiend who imposed this meeting on him (2193). Devils
were often thought to be in league with witches and
sorceresses, and there was nothing to prohibit a fiend
from teaching men good lessons by tempting them.[31]
Doubtless the medieval audience would have suspected
him and his lady of being fiends, as Hamlet suspects his
father's ghost. We are not told whether they are fiends,
and in the last analysis we are probably not supposed to
know. If the Green Knight is a fiend, he is a very amiable
and comic one, and he ends by proffering most unfiend-
like congratulations on Gawain's virtue. Perhaps it is
devilish of him to mitigate the seriousness of the hero's
fault, but the rest of the court joins in the laughter, and
the reader with them. Short of arguing that the *Gawain*
poet, like Milton, was of the devil's party without
knowing it, one has to conclude that the Green Knight
and his lady, if fiends at all, were not very frightening
ones.

*

The hero's "fall" is played down in the same way.
Adam succumbed to temptation and Christ did not;
Gawain, on the other hand, is ambiguously tempted into
a wrong which shames him but amuses everyone else.
Until the third temptation Gawain has avoided the
lady's attempt "to haf wonnen hym to woȝe." When he
returns the lord's second gift with the two kisses he has
received, the lord remarks wryly, "Ȝe ben ryche in a
whyle, / Such chaffer and ȝe drowe" (1646-1647), but
he adds the warning that the third trial will not fail and
enjoins him to be merry before sorrow overtakes him.

[31] See Dale B. J. Randall, "Was the Green Knight a Fiend?" *SP*,
LVII (1960), 479-491.

The author, as we have seen, includes several aspects of "pride of life" in the third temptation in order to make it clear which one touches Gawain's weak spot. Outside, the hunter chases a crafty fox, which almost escapes; inside, Gawain is caught by the crafty temptress. She appears with breast bared, and Gawain wakes with the thought "How þat destiné schulde þat day dele hym his wyrde" (1752), the very fear by which she conquers him. She asks of him a token, but he says he has none worthy of her; she proceeds to offer one to him, a ring of great value, which he declines. Next she offers him the girdle, finely wrought and beautiful, but he refuses gold and treasure. He has, then, avoided avarice and vainglory—the desire for wealth, honors, rich apparel, and the like. Only then does the lady succeed in tempting him with the promise that he who wears the girdle "myȝt not be slayn for slyȝt vpon erþe":

> Þen kest þe knyȝt, and hit come to his hert,
> Hit were a juel for þe jopardé þat hym iugged
>   were,
> When he acheued to þe chapel his chek for to fech;
> Myȝt he haf slypped to be vnslayn, þe sleȝt were
>   noble. (1854-1858)

This is one of the few places in the poem where we are allowed to know the hero's thoughts. And what is he thinking? he is imagining *how nice it would be*. The thought "come to his hert," the girdle would be a "juel," the "sleȝt were noble"—the language is emotional and intense, for the idea entices him. What we are witnessing is *delectatio*, the state in which one responds with "delight" to a suggestion: his own wish to stay alive has been stimulated by the temptress' offer, but as yet he has consented to do nothing except, perhaps, let himself think an evil thought. The poet is very indirect about it: Gawain allowed the lady to speak, he says, "And ho bere on hym þe belt and bede hit hym swyþe— / And he granted—and hym gafe with a goud wylle" (1860-1861). We do not hear the words they say, do not see him decide. We watch the girdle change hands, and then, quite suddenly, Gawain promises "to lelly layne fro hir lorde"—to conceal it *loyally*! It is the central moment in the poem, and it occurs before our eyes, but we are hardly more aware of what has happened than Gawain himself.

There follows a curious occurrence. Gawain goes to a church and confesser, asking the priest to "lyfte his lyf and lern hym better / How his sawle schulde be saued when he schuld seye heþen" (1878-1879). Although we do not learn what he has confessed, we are told that the priest "sette hym so clene / As domezday schulde haf ben dizt on þe morn" (1883-1884), and we observe that Gawain is merry when he leaves. When the lord returns from hunting, Gawain voluntarily offers his kisses (there are three this time) before the lord has had a chance to ask for them. "You're very fortunate in this exchange," says the lord. "Never mind about that," says Gawain, "I paid what I owe." It seems almost as if he had been confessed and absolved in huggermugger; for confession was not complete without satisfaction, and Gawain makes no satisfaction[32]—he is hardly out of the confessional before he breaks faith with the lord, and of course he retains the girdle; we do not know, for that

[32] See John Burrow, "The Two Confession Scenes in *Sir Gawain and the Green Knight*," MP, LVII (1959-1960), 73-76. The requirement of satisfaction is expressed in the following: "Cordis contritione moritur peccatum, oris confessione defertur ad tumulum, operis satisfactione tumulatur in perpetuum," *Old English Homilies . . .* , ed. Richard Morris, EETS, o.s. 29 (London, 1868), pp. 49, 51. See also *Piers Plowman*, B. XIV, 16 ff. and Skeat's note.

matter, that he even mentioned it in the confessional. When he goes forth, we are told that he wears the girdle not for its wealth nor for "pride of its pendants," but "for to sauen hymself, when suffer hym byhoued" (2040). The knight who leads him to the Green Chapel tempts him to escape, promising not to reveal the secret. Gawain resists this temptation—rather hypocritically, it seems, since he retains the girdle—and says "Ful wel con dryȝtyn schape / His seruaunteȝ for to saue" (2138-2139): *God* can save his servants!

After this somewhat furtive leave-taking, with its touches of nervous bluster, it is still more curious that Gawain puts no hope in the girdle. He approaches the Green Chapel saying "I wyl nauþer grete ne grone; / To Goddeȝ wylle I am ful bayn, / And to hym I haf me tone" (2157-2159). When he sees the horrid structure he begins to suspect that the devil made this agreement with him in order to destroy him (2191-2194), but he resigns himself:

'Let God worche! "We loo"—
Hit helppeȝ me not a mote.
My lif þaȝ I forgoo,
Drede dotȝ me no lote.' (2208-2211)

But while Gawain professes a willingness to die, he flinches under the ax. At the first stroke he twists in fear—it is no wonder he disliked it, says the author, since he had no hope of rescue (2307-2308). This seems to settle the question of his faith in the girdle: if all his avowals of resignation to God's will had been mere vacuous hypocrisies concealing his faith in it, he would not involuntarily betray his fear. True, if he did not fear death there would be little suspense in the last scene; but he could go on fearing death without keeping the girdle. In the last scene we *do* wonder whether the girdle will work its supposed charm. Perhaps, in a quite unexpected way, it does.

The girdle, as we have said, is a symbol of Gawain's failing and appears to stand for a wrong way of accommodating worldly means to knightly ends. It does not suggest any active pride which revolts against God; Gawain takes it simply to preserve his life. This "pride of life" he owes to the weakness of the flesh, which makes it possible for him to be tempted. Still, temptation is not sin. Gawain experienced suggestion and delectation, but he could be said to have sinned only if he gave consent. On this point the poem is exceedingly ambiguous, and we shall best settle the question of Gawain's sinfulness if we review each transgression by itself: (1) Foremost, Sir Gawain loved his own life;[33] the Green Knight says this, and Gawain admits it. He does, however, excuse it by claiming that Adam, Samson, and others were also tempted by women through the weakness of the flesh. (2) He permits himself to think of the girdle with *delectatio* and fails to exercise rational control over the thought—which could be called a sin of omission. (3) He accepts the girdle; when the poet says "he granted," this must constitute a sin of commission. Yet, having taken it, he seems to put little faith in it. (4) He apparently makes a false confession, since he does not restore the girdle. (5) He breaks faith with the lord, as he promised the lady. (6) He "schranke a lytel" under the stroke of the ax, though he had proclaimed his faith in God and his willingness to die. (7) He is discourteous to the Green Knight when his fault is revealed, though only for a moment.[34]

[33] See J. F. Kiteley, "The Knight Who Cared for His Life," *Anglia*, LXXIX (1962), 131-137.

[34] It is difficult not to note here that there are seven transgressions. One remembers the proverb *Septies in die cadit justus* (based on

This list, if at the cost of some repetition, has convinced me at any rate that every one of Gawain's transgressions has about it some qualification. It is as though the poet meant to tantalize us with the possibility that Gawain committed only an indiscretion, not a sin. The reader with an eye for such subtleties could argue, for example, that Gawain did not really do wrong in taking the girdle because he never put any active faith in it; perhaps therefore he did not confess to having it. Or, if the priest in the confessional had dissuaded him from believing in it at all, Gawain would not have needed to return it. If he did not need to return it, he did not make a false confession. As for his breaking faith with the lord and his moments of cowardice and discourtesy, they are chiefly transgressions against the chivalric code; as sins, they are venial. This much equivocation would leave only two important sins: his love of life and his permitting himself an evil thought. Love of life, taken as self-preservation, could be excused as a phase of natural law. Hence his only sin is the evil thought. And it is true, the poem ends with the motto *Hony soyt qui mal pence*.

Yet I do not really think Gawain's failings can be mitigated in this way; they are rather mitigated by the laughter at the end, by the comic tone throughout. The point is that the tiniest peccadillo, however insignificant it may seem by itself, leads to others. A perfectly natural weakness of the flesh leads Gawain into a perfectly

---

Prov. 24:16). The number seven had symbolic significance to medieval men and was proverbially associated with the Seven Deadly Sins. I should not want to say that these seven transgressions are schematized or distinct in the poem or that Gawain has failed in seven and precisely seven ways. Undoubtedly others would total up his failings differently. On the other hand it is possible that the poet vaguely had the sum of seven in mind as he demonstrated how one failing of Gawain's led to others.

understandable wish to stay alive; this leads him to permit himself the *thought* of taking the girdle, and in that moment of weakness he allows the girdle to be thrust upon him. Girdle in hand, he promises not to admit that he has it. And so he is confronted with a conflict between his loyalty to the lady, the lord, and the Church. Immediately he makes what seems a questionable confession and breaks faith with the lord. Having once disturbed the fine balance of *indifference* to his own existence, the whole structure of his existence, as formulated by the chivalric ideal, falls frighteningly apart, and those chivalric virtues which govern worldly action become in part unattainable. The active life of the knight *requires* that initial instinct of self-preservation; but just because of it, the best of knights falls short of perfection. The only other way—and this the author does not even hint at—would be to renounce the order of chivalry altogether and seek perfection in a higher state of life. Rather than that, the author accepts the dilemma of the hero, and the dilemma of chivalry itself, in a spirit of comic irony.

3. THE WORLD OF *SIR GAWAIN*: THE SINNER AS COMIC HERO

We have been speaking all along as though Gawain's temptation and his moral failure were serious matters; and taken by themselves, they are. The poet treats his story with so much humor, however, that it is difficult to fancy him a hardshell moralist. If the chivalric ideal, the weakness of the flesh, and the mutability of the World were not sources of anxiety to him, neither were they objects of ridicule. The problem is that in some slight degree they were both. As with all high comedy— that of Chaucer, for example, or Shakespeare, or Pope— there is something profoundly serious at the heart of it.

The world of *Sir Gawain* is many-faceted and marvelous, and a little frightening; but it is also unreal and, just for that reason, reassuring. Things are set to rights at the end, and if the world of the poem is the World of Christianity, filled with the lust of the flesh, the lust of the eyes, and pride of life, we are expected not to turn from it with contempt but to detach ourselves from it with a wise and philosophical humor.[35]

This effect, which is a matter of style, is attained chiefly through the tone—the attitude of the author toward his subject and his audience. In part this tone derives from the humorous exaggeration and extravagance of the description; as in *Gulliver*, the story begins with the kind of detail conventional to the genre, leads the reader slowly to the threshold of credulity, and then pushes him beyond it. We are with Arthur's court, among "alle þe wele of þe worlde," the "most kyd knyȝteȝ," the "louelokkest ladies," and the "comlokest kyng" (50-59). They are in their first age, the most fortunate under heaven, at a high feast dining on fresh meat, with twelve dishes for every two, and both beer and wine. But the king, by custom, will not eat until some adventure is undertaken. So far all is familiar—we are in the world of romance with its splendors and superlatives. The feast, it may be, is suspiciously the Feast of Fools,[36] when

---

[35] Despite its predominant humor, very little has been written of the comic aspects of *Sir Gawain*. There are some pertinent remarks by Elizabeth M. Wright, *"Sir Gawain and the Green Knight," JEGP*, XXXIV (1935), esp. 157-163; and see R. H. Bowers, *"Gawain and the Green Knight* as Entertainment," *MLQ*, XXIV (1963), 333-341. Bloomfield, pp. 15-16, mentions an unpublished paper by John Conley, which I have not seen. I am indebted to Mr. Robert Hall for showing me an unpublished paper which examines the "game" element of the poem.

[36] See Henry L. Savage, "The Feast of Fools in *Sir Gawain and the Green Knight*," *JEGP*, LI (1952), 537-544.

the lower clergy were allowed to parody the rites of the Church (later, the poem itself will in a way poke fun at some churchly opinions). And we note ever so slight a touch of skepticism on the author's part toward Arthur's boast: Arthur is "sumquat childgered" (86), he says—a little boyish. But on the whole it is no surprising start; nor is it a surprise that a challenging knight enters the feast—it would be a surprise if one did not, and if he were not large and wondrous to behold. This knight, however, is something more. He is one of the tallest on earth—half giant, thinks the author, though really a man—good looking, strong, small waisted, and (we get the detail only at the last) overall a bright green!

The three stanzas which follow (151-231) are an elaborate description of the knight, in which all his gear and clothing are catalogued in the traditional manner.[37] But the passage becomes a droll burlesque through constant reminders that everything is green: a green mantle, green hose, and green clothing—with embroidery of gold, gold spurs, and *fil d'or* knotted into the horse's mane, to be sure—but the rest green including his hair and his horse. Last, we are told that he had no shield or armor and no weapon but a green holly branch and a dreadful battle-ax, the latter carved in green and hung with green tassels. The whole company falls into a dead silence, "as if all had fallen asleep"; and, the author adds, "I think not *all* for fear, but some for courtesy."

The spirit of the whole passage is festive and game-like—it is, the Green Knight says, a Christmas game.[38] And, as the Green Knight plays a game with the court, the author plays games with the reader. He goes on hinting that it is all a joke and implying that the reader

[37] With the satire of this convention one should compare Chaucer's, in *Sir Thopas*, VII, 857-887.
[38] Line 283. Cf. lines 365, 683.

knows some things which Arthur and his court do not. In part this is so: it is all preposterous, and we know perfectly well there is a catch to it somewhere. At the same time the author withholds from us just what it is and keeps us guessing. In the beheading scene that follows, this balance is somewhat upset. Gawain takes the ax, strokes off the head, and the company watches it roll improbably away, kicking it as it goes; the knight retrieves it, holds it up by the hair so the mouth can talk, tells who he is, and is off with a fierce roar. The scene is so outlandish that no one could have guessed it: the reader has been pushed into the realm of the grotesque and the marvelous, and here no surmises are possible. But just at the moment when the reader begins to take part in the astonishment of the court, the author lets the court relax into the amused incredulity which he had before permitted the reader. Who was he? they ask each other, and the king and Gawain laugh and grin:

> To quat kyth he becom knwe non þere,
> Neuer more þen þay wyste fram queþen he watȝ
>   wonnen.
>   What þenne?
> Þe kyng and Gawen þare
> At þat grene þay laȝe and grenne,
> ȝet breued watȝ hit ful bare
> A meruayl among þo menne. (460-466)

Then the king sits down to eat—"I haf sen a selly, I may not forsake"—and bids Gawain hang up his ax, "þat hatȝ innogh hewen."

This effect of amused suspense, turning at last into surprise amid the laughter of the court, is repeated at the end of the poem. The repetition is like others—the two beheading scenes, the two New Year's days, the two passages on the arming of the knight. Everything in the poem seems paired or matched; and this symmetrical design in part produces its gamelike, ironic tone.[39] The principle of balance and symmetry is of course most noticeable in the first scene at the castle. Here a great dinner is set with many dishes and fine sauces, which Gawain calls a feast; it is a fish dinner, though, since Christmas eve is a fast day, and he is drolly reminded that these culinary splendors are a penance—"Þis penaunce now ȝe take, / And eft hit schal amende" (897-898). After dinner the company hears evensong, and in the chapel Gawain sees for the first time the beautiful young lady with her ugly, aged companion.[40] On the next day, after a true Christmas feast, Gawain learns that the Green Chapel is nearby and agrees that while waiting to leave he will exchange what he wins in the castle for what the lord wins hunting. Throughout there is a fine balance of contraries: the revolution of the seasons, the warlike shield and its religious emblem, the unpleasant journey and the agreeable life in the castle, fasting and feasting, youth and age, beauty and ugliness, and at last the agreement to give what each has gained.[41]

I have shown elsewhere[42] how the second, third, and

---

[39] A number of such contrastive elements are pointed out by Charles Moorman, "Myth and Mediaeval Literature: *Sir Gawain and the Green Knight*," *MS*, XVIII (1956), 164-172. Moorman remarks that the slaughtering of the animals suggests the beheading which is to come, and he shows how the court of Arthur is compared with the court of Bercilak. In each of the major scenes, at the court, the castle, and the chapel, there is an ironic taunt against Arthur's court and Gawain's virtue.

[40] For the principle of description by contrast in this passage, see Derek A. Pearsall, "Rhetorical 'Descriptio' in *Sir Gawain and the Green Knight*," *MLR*, L (1955), 129-134.

[41] Berry, *The Age of Chaucer*, pp. 152-155, compares this element of contrast in the poem with that of *Wynnere and Wastour*.

[42] Donald R. Howard, "Structure and Symmetry in *Sir Gawain*," *Speculum*, XXXIX (1964), 425-433.

fourth divisions of the poem are constructed on the principle of an elaborate balance between the events at the castle and those at the Green Chapel. This is best shown in diagram:

(1)	arming of the knight and description of the shield (536-669)	arming of the knight and description of the girdle (1998-2041)
(2)	journey to the castle (670-762)	journey to the Green Chapel (2069-2159)
(3)	description of castle (763-810)	description of Green Chapel (2160-2211)
(4)	three temptations (1126-1869)	three strokes of the ax (2212-2330)
(5)	confession to priest (1876-1884)	confession to Green Knight (2378-2438)

This structural parallel helps, through symmetry and contrast, to give the beheading scene at the end its air of suppressed mirth and its atmosphere of wonder: we feel that we have been through it all before, yet all is new and strange. When Gawain leaves the castle for the Green Chapel, his shield is not mentioned: the passage ends with a description of the girdle and a reminder that Gawain is wearing it not for avarice or vainglory, but to save his life. The mist which hovers about the chapel and the streams flowing through it create an atmosphere of eerie uncertainty, very different from the explicit perils of the earlier passage: here, the perils are to come at the *end* of the journey. Again, unlike the lord's castle, so new, so idealized that it seems almost illusory,[43] the Green Chapel is ancient and gnarled, in part

---

[43] On the castle, see Tolkein and Gordon, pp. 94-95; and Robert W. Ackerman, " 'Pared out of Paper': *Gawain* 802 and *Purity* 1408," *JEGP*, LVI (1957), 410-417. Ackerman shows that the line refers to a custom of serving food on festive occasions covered or

subterranean—such a place as the devil at midnight would say his matins in—like a cave or the crevice of an old crag, overgrown with grass. It is at the fork of a roaring stream, and the air is split with the ominous, and comic, whirring of a grindstone. Finally, the three strokes of the ax are short and suspenseful, wholly different from the elaborate ritual of temptation with its accompanying hunts and kisses. We know something is going to happen; we hear a noise *as if* someone were grinding a scythe! But when Gawain gets under the ax, we are completely in the dark. Even when his neck is nicked on the third stroke and he bounds up in self-defense, we are puzzled. When he had accepted the girdle, we knew exactly what had happened; here we are more confused than ever. We know the facts, but they make no sense.

The explanation of course follows at once. As soon as Gawain's fault is revealed to him he flares up at the knight, flinging the girdle at him. Then he confesses. This confession parallels his confession to the priest after he took the girdle. That earlier confession was presumably invalid, but (as in life) we are left to guess what passed in the confessional. In the second confession (though made to the Green Knight) Gawain is genuinely contrite, he makes an honest confession (2379-2386), he promises to do better (2387-2388), and of course he does public penance by wearing the girdle. The court's judgment of his sin, however, is far less severe than his own—in an excess of humility he twice confesses covetousness, although this is specifically denied in the poem. He wears the girdle as a sign of the weakness of the flesh, and the rest of the court join him in wearing a

---

crowned with paper decorations in such shapes as that of a castle. Cf. Chaucer, Parson's Tale, x, 444.

green band across their chests. The king, agreeing to do so, comforts him, and the rest laugh.

This elaborate parallelism, with its multiple contrasts of mood and tone, has the effect of restoring a norm which was set askew by the knight's curious adventure. The ritual balance of the incidents comes in the end to do what comedy always does: it restores the status quo, it purges extremes of conduct and experience and returns the reader to a comfortable equanimity. We are in the realm where we find ourselves at the close of *The Tempest*, *The Rape of the Lock*, or the Nun's Priest's Tale. Gawain's journey itself is a figure of this comic balance. Unlike any *tragic* hero, Gawain returns to the starting place and, however chastened, is greeted with laughter which dispels his sobriety. The mysterious and marvelous, which in tragedy remain ultimately incomprehensible, are here rationally explained away. Things have been set to rights; and we are asked, as always in comedy, not to *feel* the hero's experience but to *think* of it, to understand.

The author very carefully jumps in and out of the scene in order to prepare us for this ending. Throughout the temptation scenes he has titillated the reader by giving and withholding information, allowing the reader to join in his own amusement at the hero's plight, as if sharing a private joke. At the Green Chapel, however, we are in a sense left alone with the hero. When the third blow falls but only grazes Gawain, the reader is puzzled—and, as the startling explanation comes out, amazed. But now the author has disappeared from the picture; he neither comments nor shows amusement. Instead, Sir Gawain makes a rather stuffy speech about how often men have been beguiled by women and how on that account he ought to be excused.[44] Then he returns to the court and tells his story in great mortification, showing his wound and girdle, and blushing with shame. All of this is mildly sobering, for of course the weakness of the flesh is a serious matter. But just as the reader's amazement in the first division was dispelled by the king's good cheer, his serious thoughts are dispersed here when the king comforts Gawain and the court laughs. The comic balance of the ending restores the world of the poem to its original order—not without showing us something important about it, but without upsetting the even-tempered attitude with which we are to view it. The "pride of life" is less serious in *Sir Gawain* because it is shown to be inescapable. For the aristocracy that is the way of the world, and all of Gawain's fearful journey has not changed it a jot.

Hence the symmetrical world of the poem is at once unreal and substantial—far in the past and idealized and yet plainly the world of real human conduct, of uncertainty and self-deception. It is too neatly balanced to be like the chaos of history itself, yet it is an unpredictable world full of surprises; and, from the long view, it is known to be ordered and right. Like the Christian life itself, it is a journey of uncertain destination whose joys are fleeting. But it is festive, at least on the surface. The poem begins with a feast, interrupted by the challenge and then resumed; and it ends, at Arthur's court, in laughter and good cheer. The knight is feasted twice when he arrives at the castle, and there is feasting each day when the lord returns from hunting. All the major

[44] After this speech, he learns that the Green Knight is under the power of Morgan le Fay, and (the knight reminds him) she is his aunt, Arthur's half-sister, so that her blood flows in his veins as Arthur's does. See Larry D. Benson, "The Source of the Beheading Episode in *Sir Gawain and the Green Knight*," MP, LIX (1961), 9.

actions, except the scene at the Green Chapel, take place in an atmosphere of good cheer, with pleasant company, the finest dishes, fresh meat, wine and beer, warmth, amusement, comfortable clothing, and plenty of sleep. But each of these actions is interspersed with a journey—the first to the castle (670-762), the second to the Green Chapel (1952-2188), and the third back to the court (2479-2488). These journeys are bleak, dangerous, foreboding, and Gawain endures at least the first of them without company and with little food, sleeping in his armor in cold and wilderness. In contrast to the feasting scenes, they produce an atmosphere as suggestive, and as medieval, as the famous allegory about the sparrow in the Venerable Bede: like it, they evoke the image of human life as an indeterminate passage through dark and cold, with only temporary warmth and cheer.

This sense of the transitoriness of specific events is reflected in the treatment of time. The beginning and ending place the story in the stream of history—"Siþen the sege and þe assaut watʒ sesed at Troye"—and this adventure which happened in early Britain is drawn from and restored to that historical sequence.[45] The poet describes the revolution of the seasons as a part of the irreversible motion of the worldly order, in which "wynter wyndeʒ aʒayn, as þe worlde askeʒ" (530); so, when Gawain returns to the court, the passage begins "Wylde wayeʒ in þe worlde Wowen now rydeʒ" (2479). This linear time, as it stretches backward to the Creation and forward to the Last Judgment, embraces the worldly order, the *saeculum*. But in so far as the poet selects Gawain, singles out *his* temptation, *his* weakness, *his* pardon, he employs an inward psychological time which telescopes historical succession of events by

[45] See Bloomfield, pp. 18-19.

memory and sense perception. At the beginning he presents himself as having the power to select a span of time from recorded history. In the temptation scenes he allows us to see simultaneously, through his own sweeping eye, the hunting outside and the dalliance within. The hunting is interrupted and suspended while we return to Gawain's chamber; and even then the conversation is interrupted while we observe the hero's thoughts—he debates for a moment whether he should go on pretending to sleep ("þen he wakenede," the poet adds!) or, later, whether he should accept the girdle.[46] His voyages to the castle and back to the court are likewise foreshortened, as if they were sequences of events existing all at once in the memory of the poet—or the hero—from which selections can be made at will. But in so far as Gawain is discovered to share with all human souls the inherent weakness of the flesh, the omnipresence of external temptation, and the possibility of Grace, he takes part not merely in the flux of events but in the fundamental Christian meaning of history.

Through this relationship of individual event to the working of Providence in history, the specific events in Sir Gawain's life are presented in some measure as metaphors of the life of man, and specific spans of time as metaphors of the entire temporal World. His fall is the fall of man, his weakness the weakness of the flesh. The three temptations which he undergoes are like those of Adam and Christ, and of all men. The girdle suggests pride of life, the love of one's own existence; even the tiny nick on his neck may suggest the wounds of Christ and thus the Redemption (the poem ends, in fact, with a reference to the Crown of Thorns). So the emblem which appears at the end of the manuscript, *Hony soyt qui mal pence*, is applicable specifically to Gawain and

[46] See lines 1195-1199, 1855-1858.

generally to all who read his story:[47] Gawain failed by first permitting himself to think an evil thought; but since all are subject to the weakness of the flesh, we should not think ill of him for his failure. To say that the religious dimension of the poem is inconsistent with its status as a literary work and (in Markman's phrase) "more suited to the pulpit" is to miss the point: the religious implications, far from being the shadowy subtleties of a recherché intellectualism, were what the age considered universal truth. And yet, however richly the work suggests fundamental Christian doctrine, the poet betrays at the center of everything a concern rather for the World itself, as he betrays a delight in his story per se. *Sir Gawain* is, one might say, not a Christian poem but a poem of knighthood written in, and therefore embodying, a Christian ideology.[48]

[47] The meaning of the phrase and its consistency with the theme of the poem does not contradict the possibility, however moot, that it is a reference to the Order of the Garter. On this, see Israel Gollancz, "Chivalry in English Poetry," in Prestage, pp. 177-178. After examining the manuscript I am convinced that the motto is in a different hand from that of the text. The writing is larger, the ink seems a different color, and several letters are different: the *y* has a hook where the scribe's *y* is straight, the *s* extends below the line where the scribe's is flush, the *l* and *s* are evenly curved where the scribe's are angular, and the final *s* is differently formed. While all of this discourages the notion that the author himself may have supplied the motto, it does not rob it of its significance: it may represent the response of an early reader and be the first critical comment on the poem's theme.

[48] It can also be seen as an English poem which reflects an emerging English nationalism. The adventure is carried out for the glory of King Arthur's court, as Morgan le Fay's plot is designed for its humiliation; at beginning and end, the author reminds us how many events and adventures have happened in England since Troy fell and Brutus first came there. No doubt he was using King Arthur's court as a mythic prototype of the English nation and its past glories—see Bloomfield, pp. 18-19. There is national feeling also in his proud use

And knighthood is seen from a respectful and amused distance. Nothing in *Sir Gawain and the Green Knight* is presented more winningly than the conception of the ideal knight. When first introduced, coming forward to offer himself for the challenge, Gawain's humility and courage strike the note of idealism: he is the weakest and the feeblest of wit, he says, and the loss of his life would have the least importance (354-357). Later, through the pentangle shield, we are informed of his perfection in chivalry; and in all of his conduct, until the moment he takes the girdle, he performs to the letter all the intricate chivalric precepts. Even with girdle in hand, he continues to profess his faith in God and his duty to the court. His failure, which begins in a moment of worldliness and with a touch of "pride of life," is conceived in the end as a breach of the chivalric ideal: he makes his "true" confession to the Green Knight, and the Green Knight absolves him, as do Arthur and the court. To be sure, he has made a confession which seems questionable and has loved his own life; but he

---

of traditional material and native verse form: see lines 33-36, and cf. P. J. Frankis, *"Sir Gawain and the Green Knight*, line 35: with lel letteres loken," *N&Q*, CCVI (1961), 329-330. Still, Arthur is presented as a boyish and somewhat comic figure, his court is ebullient and festive, and the whole adventure is viewed whimsically as an outlandish Christmas game. Hans Schnyder, in "Aspects of Kingship in *Sir Gawain and the Green Knight*," *ES*, XL (1959), 289-294, argues that Arthur is immature and imprudent, sacrificing a knight against impossible odds to satisfy his pride—but this misses the comic spirit of the work. The English nationalism, however winning it may have been to men of the fourteenth century, and however moral it may seem to us, is treated with comic detachment. Arthur's court is far in the past, lovely and noble, of course, but a little unreal and in some ways absurd. It is idealized and "romantic," but in the end it is shown, like everything else, to be subject to shortcomings and failures.

has failed as a Christian only because Christianity helped shape the chivalric code—and even at that, he has remained chaste. Given the ideal of perfection and the relative degree in which one can attain it, Sir Gawain has transgressed less than anyone else. Chivalry, though good as an institution, is a thing of this World, and like all the things of this World it is flawed and uncertain. He who would follow it must preserve and therefore value his own life, must love himself enough to be brave; but because of this necessary self-esteem, he will be beset forever by temptations. Hence the comic balance with which the poet treats the chivalric ideal encompasses, almost miraculously, the saddest and most tragic facts about the World: that the flesh is weak and the World imperfect, that all our best ideals are impossible of fulfillment, and that, for everyone but the blessed martyrs, pride of life is a condition of life itself.

CHAPTER SIX

THE SEARCH FOR
THE WORLD

On the one hand I want to plunge into
the midst of created things and, mingling
with them, seize hold upon and disengage
from them all that they contain of life
eternal, down to the very last fragment,
so that nothing may be lost; and on the
other hand I want, by practising the counsels of perfection, to salvage through their
self-denials all the heavenly fire imprisoned
within the three-fold concupiscence of the
flesh, of avarice, of pride: in other words
to hallow, through chastity, poverty and
obedience, the power enclosed in love, in
gold, in independence.

That is why I have clothed my vows
and my priesthood . . . in a determination
to accept and to divinize the powers of
the earth.

—Pierre Teilhard de Chardin,
Hymn of the Universe
(London, 1965), pp. 128-129

HE PATTERNS of medieval thought treated in the foregoing chapters—the conception of the World and the conviction of its instability, the psychology of temptation, the three lusts by which men may be tempted—though not wholly foreign to modern times, are unfamiliar now, and largely forgotten. Freud —to single him out as a specimen and spokesman of the modern world—sounds for a moment quite medieval when, at the beginning of *Civilization and Its Discontents*, he says that everyone "seeks power, success, riches for himself and admires others who attain them, while undervaluing the truly precious things in life."[1] Freud even names as the sources of suffering "the world," "the body," and "our relations with other men"[2]—and the correspondence with "the World, the flesh, and the devil" is all the more evident since, later, he explains the devil as the aggressive and destructive tendencies of others.[3] Yet the style and content of his discourse is wholly modern. Turning from the traditional mind-body dualism of western thought, Freud explains religion as an illusion based on the child's feeling of helplessness and his longing for a father; and having removed soul, deity, and eschatology from the world picture, he concludes (here, at least) that the end of human life is happiness.[4] Again, Freud's topography of the mind resem-

---

[1] Sigmund Freud, *Civilization and Its Discontents*, trans. Joan Riviere (Anchor ed., Garden City, N.Y., 1958), p. 1.

[2] p. 17.   [3] p. 72.

[4] For the possible influence of Christian thought on Freud, through his reading of Flaubert, *Les tentations de Saint Antoine*, see Ernest Jones, *The Life and Work of Sigmund Freud* (3 vols., New York, 1953-1957), Vol. I, p. 175. Freud wrote to his wife that Flaubert's work "throws at one's head the whole trashy world." Freud might

bles the medieval one.[5] The id is comparable to the "suggestions" of medieval morality, the superego comparable to "reason"; perhaps even the ego, as a mediating function, is comparable to "will." To Freud, however, the authoritative superego with its guiding conscience is implanted by culture, not God. And its function of controlling impulses does not, as in medieval thought, necessarily have a healthy effect: it can bring about repression and guilt, which in turn bring mental disorders. Self-knowledge is salutary in both Christianity and psychoanalysis, but for wholly different reasons—in the one because it encourages repentance and a renewed vigilance against suggestions, in preparation for the afterlife; in the other because it mitigates repressed feelings of guilt, making one more able to avoid pain and know pleasure in this life. Freud refers to false standards and names "power, success, and riches" as their objects, yet his true standards are of this world; and one notes the absence from this triad of the lusts of the flesh, which he treats as id-impulses or as the "pleasure principle"—urges more fundamental than the wish for power or riches. Even in his idea of sublimation, which puts value on spirituality, Freud warns us that "temptations do but increase under

---

have read of the Three Temptations in Spinoza's *Tractatus de intellectus emendatione*. See Spinoza, *Opera*, ed. Carl Gebhardt (Heidelberg, 1925), Vol. II, p. 5. On Freud and Spinoza, see Stuart Hampshire, *Spinoza* (Harmondsworth, 1951), pp. 141-144; and Norman O. Brown, *Life against Death: The Psychoanalytical Meaning of History* (New York, 1959), pp. 46-49.

[5] Psychologists have lately been at pains to eradicate from psychoanalytic theory those elements inherited from western philosophical tradition, notably Freud's tripartite and individual-centered psychology. See, for example, Jurgen Ruesch and Gregory Bateson, *Communication: The Social Matrix of Psychiatry* (New York, 1951), p. 62.

constant privation, whereas they subside, at any rate temporarily, if they are sometimes gratified."[6]

Intellectual historians have often tried to show how religious and transcendent categories of medieval thought came to be transformed into secular and worldly standards in modern times, and no doubt Freud's use of western philosophical tradition to formulate psychoanalytic theory could be interpreted as a phase of this general movement in the history of western thought. Freud would have argued, however, that the aspects of human behavior which he described are observable facts which medieval men had grasped unconsciously and expressed in the language of myth and symbol. By and large, modern psychological thought would recognize in the medieval conception of temptation a fundamentally sound insight into human strivings for affection, property, and power. While this may help us grasp the essential humanity of medieval ideas and poems, however, it is no substitute for understanding them historically. We shall misunderstand medieval poems in the gravest way if we relax into the premise that beneath their religious trappings lie our own familiar notions. Reading fourteenth-century poetry requires knowing the very feeling of its thought, the dimensions of its mythic and symbolic world, the reality of its underlying threats and doubts—knowing, if we can, the styles of life and thought which medieval literary styles reflect. And we go to this trouble for the same reason that we do so with *Hamlet*, or any classic: not because we want to learn all the pedantic rules of revenge tragedy or because we care anything per se about the quaint and hollow conventions of the Elizabethan stage, but because everywhere in and behind those rules and conventions lies an

[6] Freud, p. 80.

act of human consciousness which still draws us to itself. Had western culture developed differently, we should instead be reading, perhaps, the tale of patient Griselda or the *De arte moriendi*. We read *Hamlet* or the *Troilus* because each has something to say not only to man about humanity but to western man about western civilization. We attempt, that is, to recapture the feeling of historical styles in their fullest complexity not to escape into the past but to understand it in its relation to the present.

In what follows I am going to describe some stylistic traits which the *Troilus*, *Piers Plowman*, and *Sir Gawain and the Green Knight* have in common. These make up a basic style,[7] or elements of a basic style, which may be observed in the three poems. I shall not propose that this style corresponds to any style of painting, music, or architecture, or to the "Gothic" or other styles—though I do not mean to reject such a possibility. While every element of this style can probably be found in other periods, the way these elements are combined, and the ideas they reflect, are characteristic of the fourteenth century in England. The three poems, though widely different, show certain traits in common which, taken as a basic style, help us single out what is individual and unique in each. In some other poems one could find other basic styles of the fourteenth century; it would be interesting to compare such styles, to seek out their common characteristics, and to compare them to the styles of other periods or other cultures, or to the styles of other art forms. But that would be another book.

I. TIME AND SPACE

The writer's conception of time is a central element in

[7] On the concept of basic style and its use, see Roy Harvey Pearce, *The Continuity of American Poetry* (Princeton, 1961), pp. 9-16.

any literary style because it governs his ordering of events and his treatment of their place in history. In the Middle Ages the World—as the *saeculum*, the "age" of worldly things—was identified with time, being the state prior to eternity. Yet the things of this World, imperfect and transitory as they may be, had their highest significance as types of eternal truths. In all three poems time is linear—a stream of years from which single events may be selected out of recorded history. The *Troilus* chooses a period of three years preceding the fall of Troy; but it refers back to a former, legendary age of Thebes and looks forward to an age when the West was founded, when a Christian poet in England could take up his "olde book" and retell the Trojan story. *Sir Gawain* chooses an episode from the time of Arthur, but the beginning and end of the poem look back to the time when the "sege and þe assaut watȝ sesed at Troye" and forward to the present when the story is retold "With lel letteres loken, / In londe so hatȝ ben longe." *Piers Plowman* recounts a series of dreams in which selected incidents of redemptive history are recalled in the mind of a dreamer who exists in the present.

But this linear time, from which unique events may be selected for present examination, has the power to suggest not merely the future which followed it but the timeless truth which it reenacts.[8] The love of Troilus and Criseyde takes place before the age of Christianity; but it illustrates the Christian lesson that earthly loves, being transitory—being bound by time—are not satisfying and are therefore not a worthy object of human endeavor in comparison with the "pleyn felicite / That is in hevene above." Piers Plowman is at first glance a simple agrar-

[8] On time in medieval literature, see esp. Georges Poulet, *Studies in Human Time*, trans. Elliott Coleman (Baltimore, 1956), pp. 3-13.

ian figure who might be found laboring in any English countryside; but he becomes the leader of an earthly "body politic," the historical succession of the apostolic priesthood, and even Christ Himself, who, incarnate in the stream of linear time in an earthly body, is beyond and above time. Sir Gawain's quest takes place in a given length of time, and his failure, a violation of the chivalric ethos, is finally forgiven by the court; but his temptation is remarkably similar to the temptation of Adam and of all men, so that when he is chastened and forgiven his story suggests the timeless facts of man's weakness and God's mercy.

All literature, to be sure, sees the general and universal in the particular and the temporal; but this mode of presentation is peculiarly medieval because it sees in each unique event of the past not merely general truths, but specifically Christian truths for the individual, society, and the World. Two of the three poems, however, also embody a mode of presentation which is more "humanistic" than Christian, seeking not to generalize about past events but to commemorate them. The *Troilus* and *Sir Gawain* both tell the story of a human action and thus preserve the name and reputation of a man, not because of any higher or broader significance but because of the unique and essential worth of his historical deeds. Sir Gawain is to be remembered and his name preserved because he was the best of knights; and the memento which he and the court wear commemorates a fundamental and inevitable fault within the compass of the highest excellence—a fault which may be looked upon with humor because it accompanies a virtue of so much distinction. Troilus' story, too, is told not just because of his tragic love or because of the moral lesson which may be drawn from it, but because his deeds and virtues as a knight put him next only to Hector, because he died honorably in the crucial fall of Troy. In both poems the past, taken as a series of unique events in the stream of time, is preserved and recounted because of the worthy actions of individual men. The poet assumes the power to confer fame upon great men, as the poets of the Renaissance were to boast, by granting them a measure of immortality in the successive stream of human lives through the preservation of their actions, their stories— if you will, the very *style* of their lives.[9] It was the glory which Chaucer's Knight spoke of when he said,

> And certeinly a man hath moost honour
> To dyen in his excellence and flour,
> Whan he is siker of his goode name.
>
> (1, 3047-3049)

Perhaps, in fact, this phase of Renaissance humanism was directly inherited from the chivalric ethos and was so enthusiastically espoused by humanists because it gave them status in the eyes of an aristocratic society.

Time, then, is represented as a succession of passing years and of unique events moving from Creation to Doomsday, out of which noteworthy examples may be chosen because they deserve to be commemorated in story. Nevertheless the unique event illustrates and re-capitulates such Christian truths as the vanity of worldly things or the imperfection of man, which are demon-

[9] On fame as a Renaissance ideal, see Jacob Burckhardt, *The Civilization of the Renaissance in Italy*, trans. S. G. C. Middlemore, ed. Irene Gordon (Mentor ed., 1960), pp. 128-134; and Edwin B. Benjamin, "Fame, Poetry, and the Order of History in the Literature of the English Renaissance," *SR*, VI (1959), 64-84. On the idea of fame as an earthly immortality and its relation to the medieval con-cept of time, see Ernst H. Kantorowicz, *The King's Two Bodies: A Study in Mediaeval Political Theology* (Princeton, 1957), pp. 273-291.

strated by *all* the unique events of the World. Events of the past are preserved in story because they are distinguished and different from the mass of events, yet they have their profoundest significance because of what they share with all events through all of time. The poet treats events as being unique and having a specific duration, occurring over a certain number of days or years within the movement of time from Creation to Judgment; but time may be telescoped or ignored because the *meaning* of all unique events is reducible to a finite number of truths. The day-to-day succession of events may be interrupted and altered; simultaneous events may be depicted; time may be turned back through memory or story; and the future may be predicted through the author's hindsight or insight. In the *Troilus*, for example, the events happen in a period of three years; but their meaning is that of all passing loves, all fallen cities—and this truth is perceived by hero and narrator alike only at that point where the narrator retreats into the present and the hero is removed from time altogether. Again, *Sir Gawain* takes place during the succession of the four seasons; but the meaning of the events is made clear only when the year has passed and the New Year begins again, continuing the stream which stretches back to the fall of Troy, forward to the present, and beyond. So, in *Piers Plowman*, Will's dreams follow one another chronologically in stated days and years, but the dreams themselves recall the Christian past and foretell the future. This twofold meaning of time reflects the medieval idea, inherited from writers like Boethius and St. Augustine, that from man's view the World is a single duration of time, but from God's view an eternal present in a timeless and universal plan. From the one perspective linear time moves; from the other it stands still.

The Search for the World

All this is a familiar picture of time—familiar in medieval thought, familiar even in the thought of the present day. That time is linear, that (as opposed to eternity) it lasts only as long as the World itself, that it may be molded by the creative imagination—none of this can surprise us. But it is not often enough observed that in the later Middle Ages linear time, though irreversible, is simultaneously figured as a succession of "revolving" seasons and years and in that sense *does* repeat itself.[10] Each poem represents a single cycle or

[10] The cyclical view of time is the "natural" one, being based on observable revolutions of sun and moon, seasons, generations of men, day and night, bodily functions (notably the menstrual cycle), not to say of artificial revolutions in time like that of the seven-day week. Christianity imposed upon the cyclical view of time a linear concept of age or ages, beginning with Creation and ending with Judgment. See esp. Oscar Cullmann, *Christ and Time: The Primitive Christian Conception of Time and History*, trans. Floyd V. Filson (rev. ed., London, 1962). See also Helmuth Plessner, "On the Relation of Time to Death," in *Man and Time: Papers from the Eranos Yearbooks*, ed. Joseph Campbell, Bollingen Series xxx, 3 (New York, 1957), pp. 233-263; and Benjamin Lee Whorf, *Language, Thought, and Reality* (reprinted Cambridge, Mass., 1964), pp. 152-159.

To an extent the cyclical view of time was always present in medieval thought, but it seems to have received increased emphasis in the fourteenth century. It will not escape attention that the motif of Fortune's Wheel involves a cyclical view of events. D. W. Robertson, Jr., *A Preface to Chaucer* (Princeton, 1962), p. 301, points to the repetitive character of the unique event in medieval literature; and one should take note of his reference to Henri de Lubac, *Exégèse médiévale: Les quatre sens de l'Écriture* (2 vols., Paris, 1959-1964), Vol. I, pp. 558-571. Erich Auerbach, *Mimesis: The Representation of Reality in Western Literature*, trans. Willard Trask (Anchor ed., Garden City, N.Y., 1957), mentions this cyclical or repetitive quality in the treatment of events on pp. 137-140 and 169-170.

Robertson and Auerbach explain the phenomenon with reference to exegetical theory, but there were other influences, particularly on the reassertion of the idea in the fourteenth century. Kantorowicz,

revolution in which the end recapitulates the beginning.
Sir Gawain uses the turning of one year, beginning and
ending on New Year's Day; the main event of the poem,
the "beheading" which Gawain must face, is planned
from the outset to happen in precisely a year's time. The
Troilus suggests a year's passing through its imagery of
the seasons, so that events of an actual three years' duration seem to occur within a single revolution of the
seasons.[11] In *Piers Plowman* the same cyclical tendency
may be found in images which relate to the liturgical
year and to the three ages of man.[12] Thus each poem returns us to a starting point, suggests a new beginning and
an unpredictable future. We have passed across one
stretch of time to another, none of it ever to be retraced;
yet all of it is arranged in cycles which repeat a funda-

---

pp. 283-291, shows how a cyclical concept of time grew with the
practice of annual taxation; taxes, originally demanded for unique
specific necessities or emergencies, came to be demanded annually, in
the fourteenth century, on the grounds of *perpetua necessitas*. Moreover, the invention of mechanical clocks in the earlier fourteenth
century must have encouraged the feeling for the cyclical and
repetitive character of events. Lynn White, Jr., *Medieval Technology
and Social Change* (Oxford, 1962), p. 125, reports that Nicholas
Oresmus (d. 1382) was the first to use the metaphor of the universe
as a vast mechanical clock. White makes also this suggestive observation (p. 124): "Suddenly, towards the middle of the fourteenth
century, the mechanical clock seized the imagination of our ancestors.
Something of the civic pride which earlier had expended itself in
cathedral-building now was diverted to the construction of astro-
nomical clocks of astounding intricacy and elaboration. No European
community felt able to hold up its head unless in its midst the planets
wheeled in cycles and epicycles, while angels trumpeted, cocks crew,
and apostles, kings, and prophets marched and countermarched at
the booming of the hours."

[11] See Henry W. Sams, "The Dual Time-Scheme in Chaucer's
Troilus," *MLN*, LVI (1941), 94-100.

[12] See John F. Adams, "*Piers Plowman* and the Three Ages of
Man," *JEGP*, LXI (1962), 23-41.

mental and predisposed pattern. This dual nature of time, at once irreversible and cyclical, was reflected in the very idea of the calendar: a unique event of Christian history like the Resurrection, which occurred only once for all time, was repeated annually at Easter, weekly on Sunday, even daily in the mass. The liturgical year itself reenacted Christian history. Indeed the pattern is fundamental to the medieval idea of human life itself, which found events like the Fall recapitulated daily in the lives of men.

This repetitive or cyclical character, inherent in the nature of all single events and durations, is further represented at the end of each poem by a recapitulation of events or states described at its beginning. It is this cyclical quality in the nature of events, more perhaps than anything else, which capsulates the essential spirit of each poem. In *Sir Gawain* the second "beheading," recalling the first, repeats the drollery, the surprise and wonder, the final amused release of the earlier scene. The arming of the hero, his journey to the Green Chapel, and the three strokes he receives match point for point his earlier progress to the Green Castle and his three temptations. The reader has, at the end, the curious sense of a *déjà vu*: strange and wonderful as it is, it all seems vaguely familiar. And this effect helps to create the comic resolution at the end. When the explanation is finally out, things seem less ominous; Sir Gawain returns to Arthur's court, where there is feasting and merriment as there had been at the beginning; and the poet draws us back into the sweep of time away from the court, as he had drawn us toward it in the opening lines. *Piers Plowman*, too, ends with a recapitulation. Conscience is to become a pilgrim, renewing the search for Piers that had begun early in the poem. We know that the search has been partially a success. But the poet never releases us from our sense of striving and incomprehensibility:

when Conscience becomes a pilgrim again, the repetition expresses the circuitous, yearning quality of the poem in its confident presentation of the World as enigma and quest. Again, the *Troilus* ends with an ironic recapitulation of past events. We hear Diomede declare "he that naught n'asaieth, naught n'acheveth" (v, 784), the very argument with which Pandarus had won over Criseyde. We hear Criseyde declare "I mene wel" (1004), the very protestation Troilus had made to *her*, and watch her offer Diomede the brooch Troilus had given her. The narrator, seeing it all, repeats the line "And thus he drieth forth his aventure" (1540), with which he had ended Book 1. Once more we see Criseyde unconsciously stumble through doubts and decide on love; and we see Troilus brought into the other part of his "double sorrow" by the same lady and the same kind of decision which brought him out of the first. All of this creates the sense of brevity and vanity which the ending states from the view of a higher wisdom. Troilus, standing on the eighth sphere looking down at this little spot of earth, can laugh again—not as before at the folly of lovers, but at the World. In each poem the events in time are irreversibly finished at the end of the poem, and time continues irreversibly. Yet in each poem it is implied that succeeding events on earth will repeat the conditions of life and reveal again the central truths enacted in the work itself.

*

This tendency to break down the tangible, sequential reality of time in order to suggest truths which are timeless is a pattern also seen in the treatment of space and movement. In the earlier Middle Ages the wandering and homelessness of monks and hermits was viewed as a particular kind of holiness, since it removed one from the distractions of family life and from the affairs of the *polis*.[18] The desert fathers wandered aimlessly into a wilderness not for the mere pleasure of ascetic discomfort but to free themselves from the World. In early monasticism the *gyrovagi* or *circumcelliones* wandered from one monastic community to another, and early missionaries, notably the Irish, wandered afar partly to convert the heathen, partly to have the solitude of the eremitic life. The pilgrimage, an institution of the Latin Church, differed from this eastern tradition of ascetical homelessness in one significant aspect: the pilgrim had a *destination*, and usually an intention to return home. The crusades had a rather ambiguous meaning, therefore, since it was uncertain whether the crusader would die at his destination or return to the starting place, and of course some crusaders remained in the East out of preference. Expeditions, whether for exploration, conquest, or the conversion of the heathen, might be one- or two-way voyages. The one-way voyage had traditionally a spiritual goal and was undertaken solely for the sake of it; the returned pilgrim was the more "worldly" because he had new knowledge which he could disseminate or a special grace which might permit him to be an example, or curiosity, to others. After the fourteenth century the idea of wandering comes to be conflated with the search for the new world; even the one-way journey then loses its particular spiritual quality, becoming rather a search for a better place to live or, at most, an escape from persecution. But until the fourteenth century the one-way voyage retained its prestige as a form of worldly

---

[18] On the general subject of homelessness in the Middle Ages, see Hans Frhr. von Campenhausen, *Die asketische Heimatlosigkeit im altkirchlichen und frühmittelalterlichen Mönchtum*, Sammlung gemeinverständlicher Vorträge und Schriften aus dem Gebiet der Theologie und Religionsgeschichte, No. 149 (Tübingen, 1930).

recklessness and spiritual searching; and the two-way pilgrimage had lost repute on account of the usually sportive intentions of pilgrims and the large number of abuses to which the institution lent itself. It is interesting to speculate whether Chaucer did not intend, at least in some unconscious way, that the Canterbury pilgrimage end at its destination; for the ambiguity about voyaging preserves itself in Chaucer's desire to make the pilgrimage to Canterbury a figure of earthly life, a voyage from which there is no return:

> . . . the wey, in this viage,
> Of thilke parfit glorious pilgrymage
> That highte Jerusalem celestial. (x, 49-51)

In the *Troilus* one does not find this motif of voyage or wandering. The action takes place in and about various palaces of the city Troy. Criseyde goes off to the Greeks with the intention of returning, but she is not in search of anything, and of course she does not come back. Only at the end of the poem, after the death of the hero, does a voyage of any significance occur. And only at that point does space become a meaningful element in the poem. Time, which put an end to their first night, has meant delay and longing and indecision; but it is physical distance which brings their love to an end. Finally physical and temporal distance merge in the image of Troilus on the eighth sphere. Troilus is sent on a one-way journey "Ther as Mercurye sorted hym to dwelle"—spatial relationships, like temporal ones, are dissolved, and he sees earth and World in their true smallness.

In *Sir Gawain* the hero's journey is the central episode of the poem, but it is ambiguous whether he is to return or not. Even with the magic girdle in hand, he does not seem to entertain much hope of surviving the adventure.

Yet he does gain from his voyage more spiritual enlightenment than he had bargained for, and he does return
to the court appropriately chastened. The sense of space
which the poet creates is far greater on the voyage away
from the court, especially between the court and the
Green Castle, than on the return. On his way to the
Green Castle, where Gawain will be tempted, the journey is long and arduous; there is a sense of the passage
of great time. From the castle to the Green Chapel,
though the trip is unpleasant and the site grim, the
distance is short. And space is altogether telescoped when
he returns to the court:

> Wylde wayeȝ in þe worlde Wowen now rydeȝ
>
> . . . .
>
> Ofte he herbered in house and ofte al þeroute,
> And mony aventure in vale, and venquyst ofte,
> Þat I ne tyȝt at þis tyme in tale to remene.
>
> (2479-2483)

The lesson is already known and there is no point in
showing a quest or struggle. Yet the return voyage,
however hastily disposed of, has an effect of great importance. Gawain has traveled away from the world he
knows into an unworldly adventure; to leave him at the
Green Chapel would be to leave him detached from the
life of the court, against whose ideals he has sinned, in
confrontation with a higher truth. His quick return to
the court cancels out any suggestion that the chivalric
life should be renounced: rather, Gawain is chastened
and restored to the World.

In *Piers Plowman* the movement of the dreamer takes
the form of aimless wandering in the Malvern Hills.
There is no destination or progress. At one point the
dreamer returns home to his family, but at the end of
the poem he is wandering still, like the *gyrovagi* of early

Christianity.[14] Yet the return voyage, with its element
of purpose and destination, is concentrated in his dreams:
each dream is itself a return voyage into a separate
sphere of reality. Because each return to consciousness
leaves him with some reason to go back again into his
world of visions, there is a sense of circularity and futility in his wandering; but because he does gain truths
from his dreams and because these truths follow in a
developing progression, there is a sense of a final, if
unreachable, destination. Hence the poem creates an
ambivalent effect of futility and purpose, of circularity
and progress. At the end the dreamer is to continue
dreaming, and Conscience is to go off on a pilgrimage in
search of Piers Plowman. It does not seem as if the
quest will ever be complete, yet the dreamer has already
learned a great deal about Piers Plowman—Piers has
been alternately found and lost, each time with renewed
insight. In the same way the pilgrimage to St. Truth,
interrupted by the plowing of the half acre, never even
approaches its destination, yet *something* has been gained.
This ambiguity in the nature of the dreamer's voyage
reflects what the Middle Ages felt about the search for
truth—that it could be successful in this World through
the right use of human faculties and through revelation,
but that it could never approach that perfect truth which
is to be attained only in the life beyond.

2. THE IDEAL AND THE ACTUAL

In their treatment of time and space all three poems
evoke a sense of the transitoriness and imperfection of
worldly things. Each poet holds up an ideal, but his
purpose is to show that in this World the ideal, though

[14] See Morton W. Bloomfield, *Piers Plowman as a Fourteenth-
Century Apocalypse* (New Brunswick, 1961), pp. 70-71.

always to be sought, is never to be attained. The doctrine
of perfection was itself, as we have said earlier, a way
of taking into account the conflict between Christ's command to be perfect and the fact of human imperfection
which resulted from the Fall. Hence each poem presents concrete images of an ideal which lies beyond man's
reach. And because perfection is thus a matter of degree,
each poet accepts in a tentative way the value of worldly
things and worldly pursuits. If the highest perfection
lies in a wholly ascetic renunciation of this World, there
is still a perfection, if a lesser one, in those activities
which can improve the World. And if every worldly
activity is inferior to some higher activity, it is still
superior to some lower one. In the sensual love of the
pagan Troilus one can see all of the reasons why a
Christian knows that worldly loves "passeth soone as
floures faire." The love itself creates anxiety and sorrow;
it enslaves the lover and brings about a loss of his freedom; its highest pleasures must be curtailed by time and
the contiguous character of ordinary events; it is no
sooner enjoyed than the lover experiences an increase
of his desires; its object is fickle and subject to the turn-
ings of "remuable Fortune"; the ennobling effect upon
him diminishes when his happiness is gone, for he fights
the war doggedly in hope of vengeance and in search of
death. And yet despite all of this, or even because of it,
the love affair is presented with a lyrical and dramatic
intensity which no purely ascetic moralist would permit
himself. The *Troilus* is a poem in praise of love, in praise
of the human dignity of love; but the poet shows with
a regretful and sometimes comic irony that love is a
limited and partial joy, a beauty like that of "floures
faire" which may be enjoyed, though only for a time.

In *Piers Plowman* this sense of the value of earthly

pursuits despite the imperfection of the World is a recurring motif at the heart of the dreamer's "visions." Man cannot in this World escape the body, and so he must supply the body's needs; yet it is the body itself which tempts him to the lust of the flesh, the lust of the eyes, and pride of life. The social order, the body politic, is intended to supply through labor the needs of individuals, and the ideal of a Christian commonwealth is proposed as the right means of doing so. But just because the body politic is composed of individuals it is, like the body itself, susceptible to corruption. The Pardon, for example, presents an ideal of justice for this World but excludes mercy for the World's failings; the priest impugns it because it will not really succeed in providing for the World's needs. Piers' reaction, to renounce the World and care less about sustenance, was one possible solution for medieval man; but it was itself an imperfect solution—had not the needs of earthly life still to be supplied? So the dreamer turns from passive observation of the World's problems to an active search for "Do-wel." He examines the active life and the ideal of a Christian commonwealth as solutions to the problem of the World and finds that neither can be brought off by fallen men. Yet there is always hope that in some limited way these possibilities can be fulfilled, and at the end the search for Piers Plowman patiently continues.

In *Sir Gawain* the perfect knight, who evinces in the face of a wholly unequal trial the exemplary virtues of chivalry depicted on his shield, must fail in one small respect by loving his own life; and that failure leads him into a tangle of other failures. But his quest, though marred by this imperfection, is considered worthwhile—in part because the knight learns from it the important lesson of humility, in part because he has maintained his perfection to such a great extent. While he wears the girdle as a reminder of his failing, the court wears the baldric to commemorate his success. The relativity of perfection is dramatized in that ambiguous moment at the end when Gawain returns to the court in shame for his "couardise and couetyse" while the court laugh and celebrate his high "renoun." For knighthood itself is seen to have a fundamental worth and therefore justly to deserve worldly glory, in spite of its inescapably worldly character.

Each poet agrees that the quest for perfection, the pursuit of ideals, ought to go on, ought never to be given up. But each finds, in the relative and hierarchical character of earthly perfection, a tension between the demands of the quest and the incompleteness of its success. All three poets adopt something like the position which Petrarch states at the end of the *Secretum*, that "it is in the true order that mortal men should first care for mortal things; and that to things transitory things eternal should succeed." Against this notion, however, Petrarch makes St. Augustine retort with a characteristic *de casibus* sentiment, teaching contempt of the World:

O man, little in yourself, and of little wisdom! Do you, then, dream that you shall enjoy every pleasure in heaven and earth, and everything will turn out fortunate and prosperous for you always and everywhere? But that delusion has betrayed thousands of men thousands of times, and has sunk into hell a countless host of souls. Thinking to have one foot on earth and one in heaven, they could neither stand here below nor mount on high. Therefore they fell miserably, and the moving breeze swept them suddenly away, some in the flower of their age, and some when they were in midst of their years and all their business.[15]

[15] *Petrarch's Secret* . . . , trans. William H. Draper (London, 1911), pp. 176-177.

The warning was important, and the Middle Ages always took it seriously. But it was occasioned by Petrarch's frank statement that mortals should care first for mortal things. Such warnings would not have been repeated so often if the secular and "humanistic" feeling had not been so strong.

The difficulty in understanding this secular or humanistic strain in late medieval thought is not that of grasping the idea, which is clear enough, but of grasping precisely the style in which it was expressed, the emotional tone with which it was held. Men like Petrarch looked upon the World and found in it a positive, human value, though limited and imperfect. They also looked away from the World toward the highest possible life—but that was only in Heaven and not a choice they could make for the present. Perfection was to be desired, but the most perfect of men, the saints, the virgins, the martyrs, were especially called to their high state, and such a calling was not for all. There was therefore a sadness about worldly things because they are limited, and because the life eternal lies beyond those limitations. But there was joy in the hope of that perfection to be found in the life beyond, and joy, though qualified, in the limited perfection of the here and now.

This partial and tentative acceptance of worldly pursuits within the compass of an ascetic viewpoint, this uneasy tension between the inferior secular pursuit which is at hand and the superior heavenly one which is beyond reach, springs from the opposition in each poem between the actual and the ideal, between the image of a perfect life and the circumstantial details of everyday life as it is actually lived. Destiny, magic, and eschatology may hover over the characters, but they live their lives prodded and bound by the circumstantial, contiguous character of everyday events. Erich Auerbach has explored the origin of this "figural" and "creatural" realism as a stylistic trait of late medieval literature; but it is a mistake to suppose that this realism in style is an expression of a new secular feeling, a new interest in worldly affairs and things.[16] The details of everyday life are, rather, an encumbrance to man and illustrate the transitory and unsatisfactory character of his existence. In the *Troilus*, the elegant, aristocratic life of the principals, with its feasts and temples and glorious deeds of war, is darkened by the day-to-day, circumstantial necessities which impinge upon their lives. Calchas deserts to the Greeks, leaving Criseyde frightened and alone.

[16] Auerbach does not specifically state this, but seems to suggest it, e.g., on pp. 138-139, 176-177. On the other hand, he appears to believe, as I do, that realistic detail in late medieval literature often enhances the ascetic and otherworldly aspects of late medieval Christianity—see, e.g., pp. 217-219, 227-229. Part of the difficulty in getting at Auerbach's position, I suspect, is that he makes no clear and explicit distinction between "figural" and "creatural" realism. Beyond this, he has little to say about the *secular* ideals of the late Middle Ages. In treating *Yvain* he concludes that "courtly culture was decidedly unfavorable to the development of a literary art which should apprehend reality in its full breadth and depth" (p. 124). In this he ignores the very considerable element of "realism" in Chrétien's work—its emphasis on the anxieties of individuals (as of widows or unmarried knights) and on the practical choices they needed to make; on conflicts among cultural attitudes (as between the chivalric or feudal atmosphere of the tournament and the courtly or domestic atmosphere of the castle); on the examination of motives and on the need of maintaining *mesure* (without which the hero collapses into madness). As Auerbach overlooks this realistic element in *Yvain*, he disregards elsewhere the fact that the idealism of courtly culture reflected and molded behavior, that it was chiefly secular in character, and that such secular ideals were quite probably the precursor of Renaissance humanistic ideals. What I say here and elsewhere on these points does not so much dispute as, I hope, extend Auerbach's exploration in specific texts of late medieval thought and feeling.

Troilus in the temple of Pallas sees her by chance and is struck down by love. The difficulty of bringing that love to fruition occurs in an aura of practical, quotidian detail—the exchange of letters, the arrangement of places, the smoky rain, the secret door, the ladies asleep outside the room, the lantern, the dawn. So the tragic circumstance is a matter of practical necessity—an exchange of prisoners, a meeting of parliament, a matter of discretion. Troilus in a famous speech runs through all the reasons why, as a prince and lover, he cannot carry her off or ask his father for her (iv, 541-574). And of course once out of Troy, Criseyde's return is the more unlikely for the facts of distance, walls, and opposing armies. It is the events of the everyday, all of them in the hand of Fortune, that make earthly felicity so small "To respect of the pleyn felicite / That is in hevene above." Although Fortune is the handmaid of the great destinal forces which destroy cities and topple heroes, her power is over the tangible, specific things of this World, her realm that of day-to-day existence.

In *Sir Gawain*, too, quotidian domestic realism is a phase of the imperfection of human life. The details pile up in abundance to create a stark contrast between the fleeting comforts of court life and the terrors and homelessness of the knight's quest. The poem begins and ends in an atmosphere of feasting and merriment, of warmth, sleep, food, and drink; and the temptations themselves are carried out in the same setting of elegance and comfort. The journeys from court to castle and from castle to Green Chapel, on the other hand, are bleak and foreboding; we are made to suffer the coldness of armor in winter, to see icicles, to hear the forest silence, to feel hungry and alone. Hence Gawain's temptation to love his own life comes not simply from the lure of the lady or the comforts of the castle, but from the bleakness and hideousness of wandering, of being removed from civilized comfort and community, of facing the unpredictable. The Green Chapel itself, with its fog and crags, and its grindstone, is symbolic of the terror and unpredictability in any solitary undertaking, for any man who faces a test of his virtue, and death, by himself. Because it is grotesque and exaggerated, unreal, and therefore comic, we are made to anticipate the comfortable return to court, the everyday life upon which the unpredictable does not *seem* to impinge. Part of the delight of the ending is the reassurance which it gives us to see Gawain's world pushed back into history, where the future is no longer unpredictable. And part of the delight is the homely pleasure of getting back from a trip or coming in out of the cold. Yet the fact about everyday life which lurks in the background is that at any moment its predictability may be disturbed; the whole episode began, after all, when the outlandish knight appeared, unexpected, on New Year's Day. And even when it is all explained away by the Green Knight, we are reminded that Morgan le Fay lies in wait at any feast, in any castle, behind all polite forms, inside all promises.

In *Piers Plowman* everyday life appears at the core of every dream. The very first vision fastens upon the hard fact of a social order in which men must labor to provide the necessities of life. This simple, domestic necessity—that of providing sustenance and creating a world which stands between man and nature—raises the central concerns of the poem: how can we sustain and endure life and yet not fall in love with the World, at the peril of our souls? And the answer, the ideal of a just social order, a Christian commonwealth, is shown to fail because, when men act as they do in ordinary life, they forget about duty and ideals. Satisfy hunger and you get greed and sloth; yet it is hunger itself which creates the need for a social order. All those passages which have provided historians with realistic details of fourteenth-century social life are emblematic of the pressure of *worldly* life in its day-to-day insistency: Glutton, trooping off to confession, waylaid in the tavern and returning home drunk; the pilgrims plowing the half acre, snoozing and grousing, and "wasting"; Hawkyn with his soiled coat, wailing like a gargoyle for his sins; the friars, corrupted, betrayers of their high calling, underfoot everywhere. All this in the course of everyday life puts the poet in search of ideals and solutions and at the same time makes ideals and solutions impossible.

The element of secular concern in these poems comes, therefore, *not* from their representation of everyday reality but *from their expression of secular ideals*. Each poet turns to an ideal which goes back to the twelfth century. These ideals are all products of the twelfth-century "renaissance" and reflect the rise of secular feeling; yet each has the dignity and weight of tradition behind it, and is ostensibly Christian and even ascetical. Chaucer, in the *Troilus*, turns to courtly traditions of the earlier French school, depicting an adulterous and pagan love; and he concludes with a Christian rejection of worldly loves which echoes twelfth- and thirteenth-century writings *de contemptu mundi*. Yet it is consistent with both traditions for Chaucer to conclude, with regrets, that worldly loves are transitory and unsatisfying and to suggest, with reservations, that they have a positive, if limited, worth. In *Piers Plowman* the ideal of a Christian commonwealth harkens back to the early twelfth century, before the development of that rift between church and state which by Langland's time had become dichotomous. Yet it is an ideal for this World, by which the worldly needs of men are to be supplied and their lot in the World improved. Piers' anger when he tears the Pardon is chiefly frustration that the World will not put into practice what is best for it. Just for this reason human life must continue to be an unfulfilled but not entirely hopeless search for perfection, individual and social. In *Sir Gawain* the hero is depicted according to the earlier tradition in which he was the perfect knight; and the chivalric ideals of the poem are the traditional high-minded ones, with a strong religious overtone. His virtues are both knightly and Christian, and his failure is a violation of both chivalric and Christian standards. Yet the seriousness of his failure, though seen from the Christian viewpoint as a sin, is ambiguous; and he is finally forgiven by the court, not by the Church. The imperfection of human actions, which is an object of regret in the *Troilus* and *Piers Plowman*, becomes the object of amusement in *Sir Gawain*. The knight has succeeded in the eyes of the court, despite his flaw, and the glory of his deeds is to be celebrated and preserved. The very fact of human imperfection, the very unattainability of *all* ideals, makes these secular ideals immanent as a possibility. Man must make a beginning with what he has at hand. For that matter, Christianity had always attempted to make peace with things secular if for no other reason than to establish the Church as an institution in the World. The secular elements of the late medieval ideology are not so much explicit ideas as feelings and emotions expressed in tone and style. Courtly love, the Christian commonwealth, the chivalric ideal—all involve a secular temper within the compass of a Christian ideology. The major change in the growth of secular thought involves, therefore, a diminished feeling of guilt over secular concerns and a growth of emotional attitudes which tend to rationalize that guilt or to excuse those lures.

3. IRONY

To speak of the "rise of secular feeling" is, then, to speak in a kind of shorthand. There had always been secular feeling in the sense that men had always salivated at a beefsteak or turned their eyes to a trim ankle. All the talk during the Middle Ages about the lust of the flesh, the lust of the eyes, and pride of life makes this clear if common sense does not. And there had always been ideas about legitimate secular activities at least to the extent that medieval men were willing to use the foolish things of the World to confound the wise. What happens beginning with the twelfth century is not that secular feelings come into existence, but that they come more often to be acknowledged, expressed, rationalized, and in some instances espoused. To remove prohibitions of this ideological kind or (worse) to suggest reasons for favoring what a culture prohibits is always a matter of the utmost delicacy; think how much in our own time people have wrangled about homosexual or premarital relations, or even drinking or card-playing. It is, of course, just such conflicts and changes in the values of a culture which become the concerns of a literary work; and it is just such concerns, charged as they are with emotion and doubt, that prompt the literary artist to put himself at a remove from his subject matter.

That is why each author has found a way to maintain a distance from his material, to shield himself from its implications. Each writer is present in his work, to be sure, and his attitudes are a part of its style. Yet in no case have critics been able to agree about these authors' opinions, for in each poem those opinions are masked and ambiguous. Each poet represents himself, so to speak, as an outsider observing a game. We watch the game develop play by play, we see processes of winning and losing take shape. As with all games there is an element of chance and haphazardness, of unpredictability; at the same time there is an element of ritual and a certain body of rules by which the game is played.[17] But the poet, like us, is an observer, not a player. Moreover, two of the poets, as if in place of themselves, have created within the world of the poem a figure who oversees and manipulates events. While we know that the "maker," the poet, is finally the plotter of his story with the power to select and alter the material of his sources, we are made to believe that he is a passive recipient and recorder of events, observing with us the machinations of this other plotter in the story. Thus Chaucer poses as a bookish devotee of love with no practical experience of it. His own attitude ranges from eager approval and envy to regret and renunciation. He lets us see him omit and summarize material, or hear him comment on it, but he would have us believe that all of it is a body of fact preserved in "old books." The "real" manipulator of events is Pandarus; it is he (much more than Pandaro in the *Filostrato*) who plans and oversees the love affair, persuades the lovers to enter into it, arranges their meeting, and engineers the consummation. In some degree he is a reverse image of the narrator—like him, unsuccessful in love, taking a vicarious pleasure in the affair; yet he sees it all from the pagan values of their world, while the narrator stands at a distance from those values and finally disavows them. Those values are chiefly the rules of the game of love, the familiar body of convention observed in the conduct of an adulterous courtly affair espoused on a "pagan" principle of *carpe diem*. Pandarus, the adherent of that principle, actually

---

[17] I am here indebted, of course, to Johan Huizinga, *Homo Ludens: A Study of the Play Element in Culture* (Beacon ed., Boston, 1955).

says, at the moment when Troilus first blushes before revealing the name of his lady, "A ha! . . . here bygynneth game" (I, 868). Later he declares guiltily that he has begun "a gamen pleye, / Which that I nevere do shal eft for other" (III, 250-251), that he has become a procurer "Bitwixen game and ernest" (254). Troilus, too, refers to the affair as a "game" (1084); when he vows fidelity, he begins "The game, ywys, so forferth now is gon" (1494); and at the end he declares that he has "lost the cause of al my game" (v, 420). It is a game of chance—Fortune, indeed, is really the power of chance events. And at its outcome the poet can only say,

> Swich is this world, whoso it kan byholde:
> In ech estat is litel hertes reste.
> God leve us for to take it for the beste!
>
> (v, 1748-1750)

This gamelike quality is still more evident in *Sir Gawain and the Green Knight*. The Green Knight himself describes his outlandish request as a Christmas game (273, 283), and the author echoes his words (365, 495), though Gawain himself does not think it so (692). The author, always amused and detached, watches over the story as it progresses; Gawain obeys the one simple rule of the "beheading game" by appearing at the Green Chapel to receive the knight's stroke, and along the way he obeys the far more elaborate rules of Bercilak's game in the castle. The central event occurs when, though only once, he is led to cheat. Even the ritual three strokes of the Green Knight have a contrived, gamelike quality; and the return to court, with its festive air and its commemoration of Gawain's quest through the wearing of the baldric make, in effect, a game of the whole incident and its outcome. The word "game" in Middle English, with its connotation of festiveness and fun, precisely

indicates the spirit of the poem. There is less a feeling
of chance than of contrived sport; and like many a
knightly game—the joust, or the quest itself—its purpose is to test the hero. The author stands outside the
test, as witty and good-humored as the Green Knight
himself. In the Green Knight he has created a plotter
or manipulator who, like Pandarus, plans the events
and amusingly brings them to a conclusion. Like Pandarus, too, the Green Knight is a comic figure, a joker
and ironist, amused at the events as he plots and watches.
And, just as Pandarus is the representative of an inimical
philosophy, so the Green Knight is the representative of
the inimical tempter Morgan le Fay. But Pandarus becomes powerless at the outcome, while Chaucer retreats
into the consolation of Christianity and disavows the
pagan world he has described; the Green Knight, on
the other hand, explains to the hero what his fault was,
while the author keeps counsel and, presumably, agrees.

Piers Plowman deals rather with dreams than with
any kind of game: but dreams and games have in common their removal from everyday practical affairs, their
"unreality," and their element of unpredictability. The
dreamer's wandering itself has the random, unreal,
repetitive character of game; and in his dreams, though
there is nothing like rules, there is a curious logic and
a sense of almost ritualistic progression. Langland, like
the other poets, is outside of the events, a passive observer rather than a participant. But in the other poems
the events occur at a selected point in the past and are
objectively distant in the realm of history: in *Piers Plowman* they occur in the present, "inside" the dreamer,
where they are permitted to sweep across *all* of redemptive history from the Creation to Doomsday. Unlike
Chaucer or the *Gawain* poet, Langland does not claim to
be recording a story passed down to him by an authority;

he is recounting his own visions as they have come to him, and he is indebted to no tradition or authority, only to the *vis imaginativa* and to God. There is no plotter or manipulator, either in or out of the story. Will speaks directly of himself and suggests that he is a figure in his own dreams, although he has little more than the role of observer. On the other hand the figures in his dreams are like himself and can be understood as fragmented aspects of himself. Hawkyn, the active man and penitent, and Conscience, the seeker, are probably projections of the author-dreamer's own states of mind. Piers, associated at first with the common man, is, like the dreamer, a wanderer, searcher, and pilgrim. Yet he becomes the *object* of Conscience's search as he is associated with the apostolic priesthood, the episcopacy, and with Christ Himself. In this respect the poem seems to represent God and man actively in search of each other; and the poet, though involved in this search, is able to observe it, in his dreams, at a distance.

This removal of the poet from the subject and action of his poem accounts for the irony in each work. Irony, in a general sense, depends on the disparity between the actual and the ideal, between what is observed and what is hoped or expected. In each poem the ideal is disappointed by events which the poet must, as an observer, report. Were the authors to state explicitly that men are weak or men's ideals unrealistic, the ironic effect would be lost; by maintaining a distance, they succeed in saying both. We know that the love of Troilus and Criseyde shows the transience and vanity of earthly loves; but we also know that ideal love can never exist in this World as it exists in the life beyond. We know that the figures in *Piers Plowman*—Mede, Waster, Hawkyn, and for that matter Will himself—are sinners; but we also know that a Christianized *mundus* is not for this World. We

know that Sir Gawain erred in loving his own life; but
we also know that without that flaw few knights could
survive.

All of this, which is the irony of life itself, accounts
for the verbal irony which comes to be part of the texture
and style of each poem. Its purpose is to remind us of
the disparity between the ideal and the actual. In *Piers
Plowman*, Langland shows, for example, how some of
the Seven Sins will be led to go on sinning after shrift—
"I am sory," says Envy, repenting, "I am but selde
oþere, / And þat makiþ me so mat for I ne may me
venge" (A. v, 105-106). Or, again, when Hunger comes,
the dreamer wryly tells how "Blynde & bedrede were
botind a þousand / Þat leyʒe blereyed and brokelegged
by þe hye waye" (A. vii, 177-178). In such passages he
reminds us of the futility of schemes for an improved
World even as he delineates them. Again, in *Sir Gawain*
the author remarks in the opening scene that not *all* the
knights were silent out of fear: "I deme hit not al for
doute, / Bot sum for cortaysye" (246-247); and in the
temptation scene he lets Gawain swear to the lady that
he will *loyally* keep his agreement with her—"to lelly
layne fro hir lorde" (1863). In the one passage he points
to the fear, and in the other to the equivocation, which
is going to bring Gawain's fall. Chaucer, throughout the
love affair of Troilus and Criseyde, keeps reminding us
of the non-Christian character of their love and of the
fleshly core which pulsates under the idealized courtly
superstructure. Pandarus, at the end of his long interview with Criseyde, hints at a time "Whan ye ben his
al hool, as he is youre" (ii, 587), and Criseyde answers
hastily "Nay, therof spak I nought, ha, ha!" "O, mercy,
dere nece," answers Pandarus, "What so I spak, I mente
naught but wel." Yet it is part of the power of the work
that it suggests everywhere the disparity between utter-

ance and reality, between what is spoken and what is "meant."

All three poets, in adopting this ironic manner, put Christian ideals at the center of things while recognizing that the center of things is intensely human and frail. To the medieval mind human conduct is inevitably other than what it should be. Of any work that we have mentioned, perhaps this irony is closest to the tone of the *De amore*. For Andreas, if I read him aright, did not in any sense intend to endanger or discredit Christianity by teaching the gentlemanly art of loving; at the same time he was not merely using courtly love to illustrate sensuality and urge the love of God. He saw love, rather, as an amusing game, agreeable in itself and of some limited value to men, pleasant and quite worth a thought in this transitory World—but worth nothing in comparison with eternal life. This last did not prohibit him from taking an interest in love, and his irony permitted him to do so while still counseling "rejection" in the end. Accuse him of heresy against the God of Love, or against the Christian God, and he can show you where he avows his faith in the one and the other. Such an equipoise would be cynical, perhaps, if one did not feel that in general courtly love was carried on exactly with this ironic tone, as Christianity most assuredly was not. It would be hypocritical, too, if Christianity did not always come off first. Still, it was this very tone of irony, taken as an element in the style of late medieval literature, which permitted men in some measure to decrease their expectations of ideal conduct in the World.

This tone is sustained in each of the three poems until its end. If the irony were meant only as a device for teaching charity, there might well be a final Christian utterance in which the ploy was exposed. But, while there *is* a final Christian utterance in each poem, there

is no disruption of the author's detachment, no change
of his tone. Hence there is no strong sense of finality at
the end. A common mode of medieval narrative (I am
thinking of the *Gesta Romanorum*, exempla, and the
like) concluded with an explicit moral which gave the
story, sometimes gratuitously, a religious meaning. But
by the fourteenth century the story has already inherent
in it a religious and moral meaning, and the final statement is not merely redundant; on the other hand, because of this very consistency in tone the final statement
may be the less explicit, and perhaps the less moral. The
great lines at the end of the *Troilus* are of course the
sincerest Christian profession; but this does not mean
that every word of the epilogue must be taken as equally
serious. Chaucer's hope that his poem will be accurately
preserved and his dedication to Gower and Strode have
an intimate and familiar tone which contrasts with the
high sentiments of the closing stanza. His address to
"yonge, fresshe folkes" is moving and rhetorically
powerful; but in the lines that follow "Lo here, of
payens corsed olde rites" (v, 1849), with its reference
to "swich rascaille" as Jove, Apollo, and Mars (1853),
he strikes a tone of slight exaggeration which, at least
for a moment, casts some doubt on the firmness of his
position in the epilogue; moreover he concludes the
stanza, in perfectly parallel form, with "Lo here, the
forme of olde clerkis speche / In poetrie" (1854-1855),
even though he has scarcely finished praising Vergil,
Ovid, Homer, Lucan and Statius. He seems hardly less
elusive here than in the poem itself; his balance between
involvement and detachment, seriousness and irony, the
high and the familiar styles—all is consistent with the
tone and manner of the poem. *Piers Plowman* sustains
its ambiguous balance, too, in its closing lines. After the
great idealistic and apocalyptic visions of the *Vita de*

Do-best we are prepared for a final scene in which the Christian commonwealth is established on this earth. Instead, the World remains the same: a brewer protests that he will cheat the people; a priest rants against cardinals; a lord argues that he can take from the produce of his lands what he wants; the friars swarm about, full of avarice and intemperance, enchanting the people. And Conscience becomes a pilgrim again, in search of Piers Plowman. *Sir Gawain* ends with the knight's return to court, where he is hailed as successful and virtuous even while he himself continues his shame over his failure and vice. The audience is ambiguously caught between the knight's shame at his fault and the court's cheer at his "perfection." The story does not properly end but loses itself in the sweep of history.

In all three works the ending leaves us with a series of events which are concluded but not quite resolved, which have come to a close in fact but not in meaning. The game which the poet depicts and watches is the life of his culture, its players and rules being the men and ideas of his time. The gamelike quality in each poem, with the author at a remove in his role as ironic kibitzer, produces at the end of each work the dubious finality of all games: when the players are done and their eyes meet, winner to loser, they know they will play again.

4. THE SEARCH FOR THE WORLD

The concern of each poem grew out of social and cultural changes, and these, at a given moment in history, appear in the guise of conflicts, of polarities. Irony, as a formal literary effect, is in most cases a reflection of these contrarieties: for the irony of events, the irony of life itself—except when it is truly "cosmic"—is most often produced by the feeling of uneasiness with which men acknowledge the gap between past and future—between the heritage of a culture which is familiar, and that part of the future which, as it takes shape, threatens us with its strangeness. Beneath the irony of fourteenth-century literature lies the great drift toward a secular spirit beginning in the twelfth century—the rise of cities, the separation of church and state, the emergence of secular ideals—which initiates a search for a common world. In the fourteenth century and after, the World of medieval thought, traditionally unstable and transitory, came to be conceived as a realm in which the very evanescence of life itself conferred a pseudo-immortality through historic processes operating in the successive stream of human lives.[18] Earthly "glory," which will continue on earth after one's death, became a legitimate reward for great deeds. Hence the activities which medieval moralists had belittled became allowable and praiseworthy. The lust of the flesh could now be called love, a high-minded emotion expressed by aristocratic behavioral conventions, itself the source of virtue. The lust of the eyes could be represented as activity necessary to sustain the body, activity best carried out by a society in which ruler and ruled cooperated to protect and control property and production. The pride of life could be condoned because honor and reputation were a legitimate reward for earthly accomplishments—the "glory" or fame of knights and humanists—which, because it was bestowed on the "great," became the concomitant of power. And, since fame was conferred by writers, learning became a necessity in the courts of princes: "True glory," says Castiglione, "is entrusted to the sacred treasury of letters."

It is emblematic of these changes that Petrarch, de-

[18] See Hannah Arendt, *Between Past and Future* (New York, 1961), pp. 63-75, and *The Human Condition* (Chicago, 1958), esp. pp. 248-320.

bating with St. Augustine in the *Secretum* about the adequacy of his spiritual life, related lust of the flesh with his love of Laura, lust of the eyes with his love of learning, and pride of life with his desire for glory and fame. Yet these Renaissance enthusiasms—the notion of courtly or "platonic" love, the new fervor for classical and scientific learning, and the humanistic emphasis on the immortality of fame as a reward for individual worldly achievements—were never espoused without some feeling of hesitancy. Petrarch himself, we are always reminded, was a "transitional figure" who took up the new learning, the new love, and the new immortality with an unregenerate feeling that in the end earthly things are vanity. This he did in the terms of typical medieval hierarchies. Perhaps in the last analysis Petrarch's great originality as a thinker lies in the frankness with which he stated his own secular interests and his reasons for indulging them, even while conceding their inferiority to things eternal. The polarity between the ascetic and humanistic estimates of the World, a legacy from the hierarchical cast of medieval thought, was never resolved or synthesized. When the Middle Ages despised the World as something transitory and disappointing, it did so with regret and private attraction; when the Renaissance espoused the world as something brave and new, it did so with doubt and guilt.

This polarity in western thought originated in the Middle Ages and is implicit even in writings on contempt of the World. These writings, for all their zeal and harshness, conceal a fundamental worldliness. They are a phase of the rise of secular feeling. We find little that is like them before the twelfth century, yet they remain in vogue throughout the Renaissance. They are avowedly concerned with the World and with worldly things. Their sad descriptions of the misery of life and the mutability of earthly joys betray an appetite, or at least a taste, for mundane pleasures. Their argument that all worldly pursuits are disappointing suggests the premise that disappointing things are to be eschewed just because they fail to please; indeed such writings often name the alternative to life's discomforts not as a heavenly reward but as an earthly one, comparable to the *vita solitaria* of the humanists—peace of mind and freedom from fear. The satiric aspect of these writings, moreover, posits the desirability of moral and social corrections in the here and now. And their tendency to rhetorical flourish suggests that their authors were, in Dr. Johnson's phrase, able "to receive some solace of the miseries of life, from consciousness of the delicacy with which they felt, and the eloquence with which they bewailed them." Perhaps, like Rasselas, they "longed to see the miseries of the world, since the sight of them is necessary to happiness."

Now of course the Church always had found certain sanctions for worldly pursuits. St. Anselm of Canterbury in his *Carmen de contemptu mundi* and Hugo of St. Victor in his *De vanitate mundi* both allow that there is something of grace in created nature; both even admit that there is some good in marriage. But by far the more usual procedure among writers on contempt of the World was to set to one side these sound arguments for an allowable worldliness and condemn *all* worldly activities *en bloc*. They made, in other words, a one-sided and exaggerated statement of the case. They expressed the uneasiness which men must have felt over an increasing secular spirit, while at the same time they betrayed an ambivalence about the worth of mundane things. And perhaps most important, in stressing only one side of the argument they invited statements for the other.

The kind of relationship which exists between the

religious and secular elements in medieval thought does not, I believe, change during the Renaissance. I am not sure that it has changed even in modern times. Probably most people think of a smaller, and chiefly French, proto-renaissance in the twelfth century and then a great Italian one in the late fourteenth, with an increase of secular feeling everywhere moving steadily along, and with a steady decline in asceticism. But if this is the case, how are we to account for the continuing and even increasing emphasis upon contempt of the World? It seems more likely that what occurred was an increase in the intensity with which the two attitudes opposed each other—an increase of emphasis on *both* the dignity of man *and* the contempt of the World, with an increased awareness of their opposition and an increased discomfort (sometimes expressed in humor and irony) over the unsteady balance struck between the two. At the same time a specific change did occur between the twelfth and seventeenth centuries: contempt of the World, with all its attention to what is transitory and vain in human life, did call forth clearly delineated ideas about the proportionableness of man's body, the soundness of his reason, his place in the scale of being, and his hope of attaining an earthly immortality through his own works. And these notions became explicit just when we would expect it—in Italy in the early fifteenth century and in England with the Reformation;[19] but then the Reformation stressed grace and deprecated works, when we would least expect it. It is simply a mistake to argue that the events in Italy which Jacob Burckhardt described did not happen, but it is as much a mistake to argue that ascetical and antihumanistic notions were not current

[19] On treatises *de dignitate hominis*, see Charles Edward Trinkaus, Jr., *Adversity's Noblemen: The Italian Humanists on Happiness*, CUSHEPL, No. 475 (New York, 1940).

during the high Renaissance. The change which brings the Middle Ages to a close is in the end a shift in emphasis and emotive force among preexisting elements.[20]

If the Renaissance of the Burckhardt tradition is not strictly a dividing line or watershed of European history, it becomes increasingly difficult to interpret the fourteenth century in England as the first tremor of its sixteenth-century Renaissance. *Piers Plowman*, in fact, looks back to an ideal of a Christian commonwealth characteristic of the twelfth century, which was outmoded and unfeasible by Langland's time; and of course it uses the older, native tradition of alliterative verse. *Sir Gawain*, also a poem of the alliterative "revival," presents a story which, the author informs us, "In londe so hatȝ ben longe," a story from the old tradition, that of Gawain the perfect knight. Chaucer was, it is true, influenced by Dante, Boccaccio, and probably Petrarch, but this did not make him, as used to be thought, an *inglese italianato*, much less a humanist. Indeed, in the *Troilus* he took the Renaissance work of Boccaccio and medievalized it, enduing it with Christian philosophical "doctrine" and with the courtly mode of the French tradition. Yet there is nothing like it in English before Chaucer's time, nothing which combines the worldly and the ascetical or exalts and scrutinizes love with such artistic richness. Nor is there anything in the alliterative tradition comparable with *Piers Plowman* and *Sir Gawain*. All this is not a looking-back but a late coming. Since the twelfth century England had been in the possession of Normandy—its aristocracy was French, whatever was fashionable, even in sport and dress, was French. But how in literature? The language itself had

[20] In support of this point, see esp. Beryl Smalley, *English Friars and Antiquity in the Early Fourteenth Century* (Oxford, 1960).

been in flux, and literary taste had faltered upon the importation of French works and French forms. It was only now, when England had regained a national culture and a native language, that Englishmen could put what they had learned from the French and Italian poets to effective use in English. And yet, just because this renaissance comes so much later in England than in France, it is the more advanced. It brings secular and ascetical themes into a sharper conflict than had been allowed before; it gives the secular a more prominent and lustrous role; and it poses the search for the world as a more legitimate and pressing concern. To be sure, periodization in history, being always an act of imagination, is always somewhat arbitrary. Yet it is a curious fact, and one perhaps which should be allowed to influence our attempts at periodization, that the French renaissance of the twelfth century comes to fruition in England in the age of Chaucer almost exactly as much later as the Italian Renaissance of the fourteenth century was to bear fruit in the age of Shakespeare.

The journeys of exploration which began in the fifteenth century can be understood as an embodiment, made possible by technology, of the fundamental search for a worldly realm of actions and "things" which are not merely sources of temptation but legitimate objects of human striving.[21] This geographical search was never

---

[21] An aspect of this search which deserves further study is that poets, after the close of the Middle Ages, continued a search for the world through the examination of language itself, including rhetorical conventions and traditional symbolic associations which language transmits. Poets examined, in their poetry, the implications of language itself as a phase of reality, a special key to the meaning which underlies experience. On this, see various essays of Sigurd Burckhardt, notably "The King's Language: Shakespeare's Drama as Social Discovery," *AR*, XXI (1961), 369-387. In this attempt—because of the inextricable relatedness of language and experience—poets were

wholly a success, since men bring old attitudes and conflicts with them into new places. A far more promising tendency, of which we have a beginning in the three poems examined above, was to look within man at these attitudes and conflicts. Yet it was only in the nineteenth century, when the entire terrestrial world was close to being known, only when migration and exploration lost their tinge of strangeness and wonder, that western man began to look systematically within himself at his own psychological processes. Today, even armed with the discovery of the unconscious, and with the chance of finding in ourselves the true value of worldly life, we continue to seek other worlds beyond our own—in outer space; nor do we yet know how much the exploration of outer space is a continuation of this older search for the world or how much it is hatred of the world and a wish to escape it.

In the nineteenth century, European culture actually "found" the world in the sense that it could espouse a realm of common experience which exists independent of a Creator; but the discovery does not seem to have

---

inevitably frustrated: a common world could not be known *except* through language, so that their search was circuitous. Until the eighteenth century the pun, the conceit, the quibble therefore continued to be notable stylistic traits in literature; and beginning with the eighteenth century, men attempted to normalize and "improve" language. Swift's picture of men carrying bundles of objects for a language is a picture of hopelessness. Until mathematics became the "language of physics" and other symbolic languages (as that of symbolic logic or of computers) were invented, ordinary or "natural" language remained the medium of all intellectual pursuits, the central vehicle of culture; until then, linguistic and literary study and the art of prose composition retained the central role in education. If it is true that there has been a "loss" or "acculturation" of language in the twentieth century, this must be associated with the loss or acculturation of our notions about a common world.

occasioned much joy. The romantic poets were probably the loudest in their celebration of the natural and secular realms, but nearly all of them experienced a strong negative reaction to the world and nearly all espoused some kind of religious or transcendent beliefs.[22] Perhaps men always view worldly things with ambivalent emotions, yearning for sainthood here and eternity hereafter; but it is difficult not to conclude that in part the modern attitude toward the world, like so much of the language with which it is expressed, has been shaped by medieval and Renaissance estimates of the relationship between the religious and the secular. The world continues to seem alluring—perhaps in our less jaded moments even brave and new; in another mood we continue to find it temporal and unsatisfying. Still, if our feelings about the world have retained much from earlier times, our picture of the world itself has altered radically. For a while, perhaps, during the nineteenth century, "the world" was truly a realm of human activity and experience in the compass of a natural universe, where man, not God, was central. But ironically at this point in history the sense of a common world became obscured (so it is argued) by the growth of "mass" society and culture; men came to see themselves as powerless against sweeping historical processes which obscured their sense of individuality and of community—even the terrestrial orb becoming part of an infinite system. The "loss" of language as the central vehicle of culture, which is said to have occurred in the twentieth century, appears to coincide with, or follow from, this "loss" of the common world. In the twentieth century language itself begins

---

[22] See Morse Peckham, "Toward a Theory of Romanticism," *PMLA*, LXVI (1951), 5-23; and Robert Langbaum, *The Poetry of Experience: The Dramatic Monologue in Modern Literary Tradition* (Norton ed., New York, 1963), pp. 9-37.

to be seen as a mechanism evolving through its own internal processes; the private, idiolectal quality of language becomes available to the poet; and ambiguity becomes the darling of literary critics.

Because of this modern sense of world-alienation, the medieval image of the World, despite its differences from our own, is probably more cogent to us than it was to men of the eighteenth and nineteenth centuries. To the Middle Ages earthly things seemed unreal and unstable just because they were "of this World"—because they were part of a duration which was to end; to us they seem unstable because they are part of unending processes which pervade nature and history. To the Middle Ages it was the whole World together which was to be subsumed in eternity. In the eighteenth century, as Hannah Arendt has pointed out,[23] the numbering of years backward from the birth of Christ marked a new conception of time as going not merely forward into an infinite future but backward into an infinite past. This meant that just as immortality had been established as a process in the stream of human lives, eternity was established as a process in the natural order. Geography and cosmology, once realms of stability to be explored and charted, themselves came to be endued with what had previously been eschatological characteristics—with boundlessness of space and endlessness of time. And just because all things are a part of such endless processes, "things" came to be pictured as if in constant flux, permanent only in their relation to these processes; in our own time the possibility of altering and effecting natural processes through human action has made the mundane sphere seem so much the less stable.

On the other hand each of these fourteenth-century

[23] *Between Past and Future*, p. 67.

poems, in spite of its emphasis on Christianity in its ascetical and eschatological aspects, presents at its heart what seems a very modern image of man striving after tangible earthly goals. Troilus seeks love, Will seeks a solution to the economic problems of society, Sir Gawain seeks the glory due to knightly deeds. Each succeeds in part and fails in part; but each author suggests that, while the final ends of the Christian life are of such transcendent importance as to make all else seem vain, there is still an essential dignity in man's striving for these limited, earthly goals, an irreducible worth in man's efforts on his own behalf. Few today would disagree; yet in various ways we continue to turn from worldly things with the cry that all is vanity, that "the world can no longer offer anything to the man filled with anguish."[24] In pursuit of pleasure, property, and reputation we cast about for a vocabulary of negation similar to the old religious one—we talk of *Angst*, nothingness, the absurd. Modern literature, the theater and cinema, a vast body of psychological commentary from Freud to Norman O. Brown, continue to remind us of our *ennui* and dissatisfaction, as if we were to learn again the medieval lesson that fleshly desires cannot be satisfied. In the economic sphere we can, with an improved technology, produce goods on the assumption that they are after all what supply human needs and wishes; but the world we have thus created is the more unstable and transient because mass production requires obsolescence. Even the goals of fame and honor, once called the last infirmity of noble mind, come to seem less real as we discover how in mass society opinions and beliefs can be manipulated by technological means; in place of reputa-

[24] Attributed to Heidegger by Albert Camus, *The Myth of Sisyphus*, trans. Justin O'Brien (New York, 1955), p. 18; source not cited.

tion we speak of "public images" which can be made and unmade by human effort. The conditions of mass society, the lonely crowd, the darkling plain—all of it seems to create anew the medieval image of a world which is transitory, disappointing, vain. Whether this image is an idea or cultural state inherited from the Middle Ages, or a condition of life itself, we have yet to learn.

INDEX

Abelard and Heloise, 29

abstinence, 53

Ackerman, Robert W., 226n23, 246-47n

Acquoy, J. G. R., 71n73

active life, 174, 185-88, 201, 209, 222, 241

Adam, 43, 49, 52, 235, 239; temptation of, 44, 47f; and Eve, 48, 57-61

Adams, John F., 184n28, 266n12

adultery, 82, 89, 102

Aimeric de Peguilhan, 105

Alain de Lille, 74

Alcuin, 47n10

allegory, 13-31, 33, 36-40, 84, 213, 261-64; dream, 204-205; levels of, 17-18; personification, 212-14; in *Piers Plowman*, 169, 172, 195-99; in *Sir Gawain and the Green Knight*, 227n25, 250-53

almsgiving, remedy for avarice, 53

Alulfus, 45n5

Ambrose, St., 52n18, 53, 53n22, 58, 91n20

anagogical, *see* allegory

Anastasius Sinaita, 48n11

ancient world in Chaucer, 136f

Ancrene Riwle, 92n

Andreas Capellanus, 18, 38, 86-88, 93-97, 101, 101n34, 106, 109, 111, 155n, 288

Angelom of Luxeuil, 51n, 59n39

Anselm of Canterbury, St., 69, 293

Anselm of Laon, 51, 52n17, 54n26

antifeminism, 84, 96, 122, 150, 248f

anti-utopianism, 33

apocalyptic ideas, 166, 185

apostolic succession, identified with Piers, 189

Aquinas, Thomas, St., 51n, 63, 136n, 220, 225

Arendt, Hannah, 27n34, 75n, 291n, 299

aristocracy, attitudes of, 101; *see* courtly love; chivalry; knighthood

Aristotle, 47n9, 136n

Arthurian legend, 13

asceticism, 8, 69, 97, 104, 192, 201, 269, 276, 292, 294, 296

Athanasian Creed, 176-77

Auerbach, Erich, 140n92, 265n, 277

Augustine, St., 3, 37, 45f, 46n8, 48, 49, 50n16, 51n, 52n19, 56, 58, 59, 67-68, 68n62, 91, 123n72, 126, 180f, 183n22, 264, 275, 292

author, self-projection of, 283-87

avarice, 43, 45, 47-50, 53, 57, 163, 166, 170, 191; almsgiving as remedy for, 53; in *Piers Plowman*, 168-69; *see* lust of the eyes

Averroës, 86, 88, 92, 95

Avicenna, 85

Baldwin, Charles Sears, 23n25

Baldwin, Ralph, 14n1

Bateson, Gregory, 258n5

Baugh, A. C., 92n

Bede, 51n, 52n20, 53, 53n24-25, 59, 250

Index

Index

Meech, Sanford B., 80n3, 111n51, 112n53, 116n60, 118n, 120n, 126n78, 153n104, 155n

mens, associated with Adam, 58

Mensendieck, Otto, 184n26

Meroney, Howard, 167n5, 185n33

Meyer, Paul, 62n48

Middle Ages, idealized view of, 27, 30; style of life, 6; as opposed to "modern," *see* modern

Milton, John, 3

ministeriales, 97f

Mitchell, A. G., 171n

Mithraism, 46

"modern" (as opposed to "medieval"), 7, 75, 259; attitude to world, 27f, 299-301

Moller, Herbert, 97, 100n32, 101n34, 102n35, 106n40

monastery, as earthly paradise, 66

monastic writers, 7

monasticism, 69, 89, 190; comparable to knighthood, 221; literature of, 40; monastic rule (vows), 55f, 69, 72

money, *see* avarice

Montaigne, 158

Moorman, Charles, 245n39

Morris, Richard, 237n

Moses, temptations of, 53

Mougel, D. A., 71n72

movement (in literature), *see* space

mundus, *see* "World"

Muscatine, Charles, 111n51, 112n52, 114n, 134n83, 142n, 147, 149n100, 152-53, 153n-105, 155n

mutability, 159-60; in *Sir Ga-* *wain and the Green Knight*, 231-32

Myrick, Arthur Beckwith, 80n3, 106n41, 123n73, 153n106

mystical body of Christ, 4, 193

natural law, 110, 201, 225, 240

nature, 51, 73-74, 107-108, 109, 160; in *Sir Gawain and the Green Knight*, 231-32

Neilson, William Allen, 96n

Nemetz, Anthony, 16n8

Neoplatonism, and courtly love, 85

Nilus, St., 56n31

Nitze, William Albert, 106n42, 231n

"nucleus," 19, 36, 38f

number symbolism, 16, 19, 46n8

obscene, in medieval literature, 28-29

O'Gorman, Edmundo, 46n8, 66n58

oppositions, 28, 275-81, 290; in literature, 211; *see* conflict, hierarchy, dichotomies

Oresmus, Nicholas, 266n10

original sin, 43; *see* Adam

Osgood, Charles G., 24n29, 37n51

Ovid, 24, 115

Ovide moralisé, 22

Owen, Charles A., Jr., 127n, 152n102

Paget, Violet (Vernon Lee, pseudonym), 99f

Painter, Sidney, 96n, 98n29, 99, 220n6, 220n9, 220n10, 225n-20, 226n21

Panofsky, Erwin, 35

Pascal, 74n

Index